Bodmin Moor
An archaeological survey

Volume 1:
The human landscape to *c* 1800

English ⌗ Heritage

Archaeological Report no 24

RCHM
ENGLAND

Supplementary Series no 11

BODMIN MOOR
An archaeological survey

Volume 1:
The human landscape to *c* 1800

by Nicholas Johnson and Peter Rose

with contributions by
Ann Carter, John Hampton, Peter Herring, Rob Iles,
Jacqueline Nowakowski, the late R W Smith, and Cyril Wardale

Editor: Desmond Bonney

Cornwall Archaeological Unit
Historic Buildings & Monuments Commission for England
Royal Commission on the Historical Monuments of England
1994

First published 1994 by English Heritage and the Royal Commission on the Historical Monuments of England

This publication has been funded by the Royal Commission on the Historical Monuments of England

Text: typeset by Ann Buchan Typesetting
General maps: reprographics by Cosmographics, printing by Victoria Litho
Printed and bound by Derry & Sons Ltd., Nottingham

A catalogue record for this volume is available from the British Library

English Heritage, Keysign House, 429 Oxford Street, London WIR 2HD

Royal Commission on the Historical Monuments of England, Fortress House, 23 Savile Row, London WIX 2JQ

Cornwall Archaeological Unit, Old County Hall, Station Road, Truro, Cornwall, TR1 3EX

ISSN 0953–3796
ISBN 1–85074–3819

Contents

List of illustrations

List of tables

List of abbreviations

CAU   Cornwall Archaeological Unit
CCRA   Cornwall Committee for Rescue Archaeology
DoE   Department of the Environment
NAR   National Archaeological Record
NMR   National Monuments Record
OD   Ordnance Datum
OS   Ordnance Survey
PRO   Public Record Office
RCHME   Royal Commission on the Historical Monuments of England
SMR   Sites and Monuments Record

Preface

During the 1970s the climate of rescue archaeology in Britain began to change. In towns and cities newly formed urban excavation units were coming to grips with the problems posed by the demolition of early townscapes by modern development; and in most rural areas a county archaeological team or, in some cases, a regional unit was available to respond when destruction threatened important sites. Even so, it was clear that there was no hope of dealing adequately with large-scale threats posed by agricultural expansion or by other extensive processes of destruction which were putting whole landscapes, not merely individual sites, at risk. Not least among the problems facing archaeologists was the disconcerting fact that although many of these threatened landscapes were known to be archaeologically important, it was frequently impossible to present the evidence in convincing detail. Because so little detailed survey had ever been undertaken in these areas the basic knowledge of what they might contain was not available, and without it there was often little more to be done in the field than to watch and record as destruction proceeded.

In Cornwall, matters came to a head in 1975 with the proposal to construct the Colliford Reservoir on Bodmin Moor. This development, perhaps more than any other, served to drive home the point that, without essential survey data, it is difficult to assess the true magnitude of threat within a landscape and almost impossible to organise an adequate rescue response. Such circumstances also pose the question of whether destruction is inevitable, or whether the most important features of an ancient landscape might be preserved by modifying the development proposals. Again, without basic survey data the archaeologist has little hope of identifying the sites and complexes most deserving of attention and thereby of establishing priorities for rescue or preservation.

It was against this background and with pressures at national level to map archaeological evidence provided by air photographs that the Directorate of Ancient Monuments and Historic Buildings (then of the Department of the Environment, now English Heritage) agreed to finance a survey of the archaeology of Bodmin Moor. If a threat comparable to Colliford Reservoir should occur in the future, we would be ready to meet it.

The nature of the monuments together with the extent and physical topography of Bodmin Moor suggested that a combination of air and ground survey techniques could be used to advantage. A partnership developed between the Cornwall Committee for Rescue Archaeology (CCRA) – now the Cornwall Archaeological Unit (CAU), a section of the Planning Department of Cornwall County Council – with their wide knowledge of the county and extensive experience of moorland survey; the Royal Commission on the Historical Monuments of England (RCHME), with its capacity to undertake both large-scale photogrammetric survey and extensive fieldwork; and the Directorate of Ancient Monuments and Historic Buildings (later English Heritage), with its responsibilities for monument management. The three organisations readily accepted the challenge and cooperated to ensure that resources were made available.

Since 1979, when the project got under way, aims and approaches have been regularly scrutinised and, where necessary, revised under the stimuli of innovations in method and changing perceptions of how the data should ultimately be used. One outcome of the project has been a feeling, common to all those involved in it, that however important the archaeological discoveries the conceptual and methodological advances are of equal significance. This publication reflects that belief: it is hoped that this example of the results of modern high-standard archaeological survey will direct the reader's attention towards the fundamentals of fieldwork practice, data analysis, preservation strategies and landscape management.

It should be noted here that this volume does not attempt to address the industrial archaeology of Bodmin Moor and its attendant problems. Originally it was intended to do so but as work proceeded it rapidly became clear that the extent and very specific nature of the industrial remains required separate treatment. This material will now be the subject of a companion publication.

Only time will tell how successful the Bodmin Moor project has been, but its completion is itself evidence of successful collaboration between three major British archaeological organisations. We hope that the practical lessons learnt on Bodmin Moor and the collaborative spirit which carried the project through will find a ready application elsewhere. If that proves to be the case this publication will have achieved its purpose.

G J Wainwright
Chief Archaeologist,
English Heritage

T G Hassall
Secretary,
Royal Commission on
the Historical Monuments
of England

C G Griffin
County Planning Officer,
Cornwall County Council

Acknowledgements

In the first place, thanks are due to the two national organisations who have funded the project. The Historic Buildings and Monuments Commission for England (now English Heritage) paid for part of the air survey, and for all but a small part of the Cornwall Archaeological Unit contribution. The Royal Commission on the Historical Monuments of England paid for part of the air survey, for the whole of the 1:2500 field survey, and for the publication of the volume. The Cornwall Archaeological Unit would like to acknowledge their foresight and forbearance in seeing the project through to its publication.

Many people are involved in any large project, though the core staff may be few. The Cornwall Archaeological Unit would like to single out certain individuals who gave freely of their time, expertise, and unpublished information to make the survey a success.

For excavation data, the Unit would like to thank Daphne Harris, Sandra Hooper, and Peter Trudgian (Stannon Down cairns); Frances Griffith, and David Austin and M Walker (their respective excavations at Colliford); Sandy Gerrard (Stuffle); Paddy Christie (for information about C K Croft Andrew's excavations at Davidstow).

For field survey and other data, the Unit would like to thank Peter Herring (Brown Willy survey and much other medieval information; also the surveys of Codda and of Fernacre cairns); Jacqueline Nowakowski (post-medieval settlement); Sandy Gerrard (Penkestle Downs), Helen Buxton (Brown Gelly); J Gask (Bearah Tor chambered long cairns); Peter Trudgian (air photographs of the Roughtor area).

In addition to the assistance acknowledged above, there are of course the very many landowners who, without exception, allowed access to their land. The Unit would like to mention in particular Peter and Piers Throssel who allowed unrestricted access to Garrow, Fernacre, and Butterstor – and to Brown Willy for Peter Herring's survey – as well as allowing the use of the farmhouse at Garrow as a survey base; English China Clays International Ltd, for access to their holdings, and the Duchy of Cornwall for access to the Rillaton Estate; Mr J Vickery for access to Carneglos; and Mr A C Fairman of South Penquite Farm for much local information.

English Heritage would like to acknowledge information and advice during the preparations for publication from Kate Owen, Stephanie Taylor, and Robin Taylor of the RCHME.

At CAU, Nick Johnson and Peter Rose answered with infinite patience and care many requests for information from English Heritage, as did Desmond Bonney at a very busy time after his retirement from the RCHME. Veronica Smith's painstaking labours of coordination at the RCHME's office in Salisbury were much appreciated at English Heritage.

The following members of staff and consultants for the three organisations involved contributed as indicated below to the survey and its publication:

From the RCHME, John Hampton acted as Air Photo Coordinator. In the preparation of the 1:25 000 maps, the successful achievement of the skilled tasks of air photo interpretation and plotting was largely due to Ann Carter. Technical support and guidance in this component of survey was provided by the Department of Photogrammetry and Surveying at University College, London. The Field Coordinator was Cyril Wardale, and the Surveyors were Norman Quinnell and Martin Fletcher.

From CAU, the Coordinator was Nicholas Johnson, and the Surveyors were Peter Rose, Nicholas Johnson, Roger Radcliffe, Ann Preston-Jones, Adam Sharpe, and Sandy Gerrard. The draft of the 1:10 000 map (North-west Bodmin Moor) was prepared by Nicholas Johnson.

Illustrations were drawn by Adam Sharpe at CAU, and by Peter Spencer at the RCHME

The text editors for English Heritage were Sue Martin (as consultant) and Margaret Wood. Final preparation for press of the artwork within the volume was by Karen Guffogg. The cover was designed by Andrew McLaren, who also undertook final preparation of the general maps. Liaison during the printing of the general maps was by John Clark (as cartographic consultant).

The French translation of the Summary was by Annie Pritchard, the German translation by Katrin Aberg.

Typesetting was by Ann Buchan Typesetters.

Summary

Bodmin Moor is not very large, compared with many other upland areas. It is not particularly rugged or bleak, but it is exceptionally rich in archaeological remains. From a coherent block of moorland of c 230 sq km in the early nineteenth century, the Moor has been reduced today to less than 95sq km, broken up into many discrete blocks.

Whilst the archaeology of the Moor was well known it was not well recorded, and was increasingly under threat. This survey is an attempt to redress this imbalance, using aerial photography, photogrammetry, and field survey. The work was undertaken by the Royal Commission on Historical Monuments for England and the Cornwall Archaeological Unit and sponsored by the former and by English Heritage. Remains within 193 one-kilometre squares, including all of the area of moorland now surviving, were plotted photogrammetrically from aerial photographs at a scale of 1:2500, and 175 of the one-kilometre squares were checked in the field at that scale. Over 15 square kilometres were checked and surveyed in the field at a scale of 1:1000. Very many monuments and sites were surveyed in detail at larger scales. Detailed site descriptions, plans and photographs have now been entered into the National Archaeological Record and the Cornwall Sites and Monuments Record.

The photogrammetric survey included plotting of all features not shown on the Ordnance Survey maps of the area, but visible on the air photographs. The field and additional information was confined broadly to prehistoric and medieval remains. Industrial remains were investigated by a subsequent survey and will be published in a companion volume (in preparation).

The method of survey using air photographic transcription followed by field survey was used here in an upland context for the first time. It proved to be very effective in an area where the existing map base provided only minimal fixed points on the ground. All the remains mapped have been fully described and are shown on distribution maps (in the end pocket) showing the prehistoric and medieval landscapes.

The results have been spectacular, including the identification of many prehistoric monuments, settlements, and defended sites, and a large number of medieval settlements and field systems. Among the prehistoric monuments were 4 long cairns, 354 round cairns, 16 stone circles, 8 stone rows, and 16 standing stones. There were 211 prehistoric settlements, including 1600 round houses. Seventeen prehistoric defended sites were identified. Medieval sites were represented by 37 deserted shrunken medieval settlements including 65 longhouses, 62 herders' huts, 227 medieval field systems, and a variety of ecclesiastical sites. Over 544 kilometres of previously unrecorded prehistoric and medieval boundaries were mapped.

Several classes of site, particularly long cairns, stone rows, and transhumance huts were previously unknown on the Moor, and the survey has brought to light considerable numbers of other classes of sites. Of the greatest importance, however, is the ability, achieved by the survey, to view in their entirety both prehistoric and medieval landscapes with all their constituent parts. The articulation between sacred, burial and farming areas, and the use to which the intervening spaces were put are of vital importance in understanding how cultural change has moulded the landscape we see today as well as hinting at what we might expect to find in more lowland areas.

This comprehensive survey will form the basis for a programme of statutory protection and conservation management. It will bring to a wider public the meaning and importance of this cultural inheritance.

Résumé

Comparée à beaucoup d'autres régions de hautes terres, la lande de Bodmin, Bodmin Moor, n'est pas très étendue. Elle n'est pas non plus particulièrement accidentée, ni exposée au vent, mais elle est d'une richesse exceptionnelle en matière de trouvailles archéologiques. Consistant au début du dix-neuvième siècle en une étendue de lande d'une superficie d'environ 230 km^2 d'un seul tenant, elle ne représente plus aujourd'hui qu'une surface de moins de 95 km^2, divisée en de nombreuses parcelles séparées.

Bien qu'on ait été tout à fait au courant de la richesse archéologique de la lande, on ne l'avait pas soigneusement répertoriée et elle était de plus en plus menacée. Cette étude a pour but de remédier à cette lacune grâce à la photographie aérienne, la photogrammétrie et le levé de terrain. Les travaux ont été entrepris par la Commission Royale pour les Monuments Historiques d'Angleterre et la Section Archéologique de Cornouailles, une aide financière a été apportée par cette première et par English Heritage. Les vestiges, à l'intérieur des 193 carrés d'un kilomètre de côté qui couvrent, entre autres, toute la lande qui reste à ce jour, ont été soumis à des relevés photogrammétriques à partir de photographies aériennes à l'échelle de 1/2500, et 175 des carrés ont été levés sur le terrain à la même échelle. Plus de 15 km^2 ont été examinés et levés sur le terrain à une échelle de 1/1000. On a établi des relevés détaillés sur de plus grandes échelles pour de très nombreux monuments et sites. Des descriptions précises des sites, des plans et des photographies se trouvent maintenant répertoriés dans le Fichier Archéologique National et celui des Sites et Monuments de Cornouailles.

Le relevé photogrammétrique s'est accompagné du repérage de tous les éléments qui ne figuraient pas sur les cartes d'état-major de la région mais étaient visibles sur les photographies aériennes. D'une façon générale on a confiné le champ des recherches et les renseignements supplémentaires aux vestiges préhistoriques et médiévaux. Les vestiges industriels ont fait l'objet d'une étude ultérieure dont les résultats seront publiés dans un ouvrage (actuellement en préparation) qui fera pendant à celui-ci.

C'était la première fois que l'on utilisait dans un contexte de hautes terres une méthode de travail qui consistait à utiliser une transcription de photographies aériennes suivie d'un levé de terrain. Ce procédé s'est révélé extrèmement efficace dans une région où la cartographie existante ne fournissait qu'un minimum de points fixes au sol. Tous les vestiges relevés ont été minutieusement décrits et figurent sur des cartes de répartition (dans la pochette de couverture dos) qui mettent en évidence les paysages préhistoriques et médiévaux.

Les résultats ont été spectaculaires, on a pu identifier de nombreux monuments préhistoriques, des sites d'occupations et des ouvrages de défense, ainsi qu'un grand nombre d'occupations médiévales et de systèmes de rotations de cultures. Parmi les monuments préhistoriques, on a découvert 4 cairns longs, 354 cairns ronds, 16 cercles de pierres, 8 alignements de pierres et 16 pierres dressées. Il y avait 211 sites d'occupations préhistoriques comprenant 1600 maisons rondes. On a également identifié 17 sites préhistoriques avec fortifications. Les sites médiévaux étaient représentés par 37 occupations qui avaient été réduites et désertées et comprenaient 65 maisons allongées, 62 huttes de pâtre, 227 systèmes de rotations de cultures et une variété de sites religieux. On a dressé la carte de plus de 544 kilomètres de limites préhistoriques et médiévales jusqu'alors non répertoriées.

On ne soupçonnait pas l'existence sur la lande de certaines catégories de sites, les cairns longs, les alignements de pierres et les huttes de transhumance en particulier étaient totalement inconnus jusque là; les recherches ont également mis en lumière un nombre considérable d'autres types de sites. D'une importance primordiale, toutefois, est le fait que grâce à cette étude, on peut voir, en même temps, et dans leur intégrité, à la fois le paysage préhistorique et le paysage médiéval, chacun avec toutes ses parties constituantes. Les liens entre les lieux sacrés, funéraires et agricoles et l'usage que l'on faisait de l'espace restant sont d'une importance vitale car ils nous aident à comprendre comment les changements culturels ont modelé le paysage que nous voyons aujourd'hui et nous donnent quelques indices sur ce que pouvons nous attendre à trouver dans les régions de basses terres.

Cette étude exhaustive servira de base à un programme de protection légale et de gestion de la sauvegarde des monuments. Elle permettra à un plus vaste public de comprendre la signification et l'importance de cet héritage culturel.

Zusammenfassung

Im Vergleich zu anderen Hochlandgebieten ist das Bodmin Moor nicht sehr ausgedehnt. Es ist außerdem weder besonders zerklüftet oder rauh; es birgt dafür jedoch einen außerordentlichen Reichtum an archäologischen Relikten. Von einem einheitlichen Heidelandgebiet von ungefähr 230 km² zu Beginn des 19.Jahrhunderts ausgehend ist das Moor heute auf ein Areal von weniger als 95 km² zusammengeschrumpft, das außerdem in viele vereinzelte Blöcke aufgeteilt ist.

Obwohl der archäologische Befund auf dem Moor gut bekannt ist, ist er bisher jedoch nicht gut aufgezeichnet worden und ist außerdem in letzter Zeit in zunehmendem Maße gefährdet. Die vorliegende Landesaufnahme ist daher ein Versuch hier ein Gleichgewicht herzustellen, wobei Luftaufnahmen, Photogrammetrie und Geländevermessungen herangezogen wurden. Die Arbeiten sind von der Royal Commission on Historical Monuments (England) und der Cornwall Archaeological Unit durchgeführt worden und wurden von der RCHM (England) und English Heritage gefördert. Auf 193 einen Quadratkilometer großen Arealen, die das gesamte noch erhaltene Heideland umfassen, wurden archäologische Relikte photogrammetrisch von Luftaufnahmen in Maßstab 1:2500 übertragen und auf 175 der einen Quadratkilometer großen Areale wurden sie dann durch Geländebegehungen in diesem Maßstab überprüft. Über 15 km² wurden im Gelände untersucht und im Maßstab 1:1000 vermessen. Eine große Anzahl der Denkmäler und Fundstellen wurden in ihren Einzelheiten in einem noch größeren Maßstab vermessen. Eingehende Beschreibungen der Fundstellen, Pläne und Photographien sind jetzt in der National Archaeological Record und der Cornwall Sites and Monuments Record eingetragen.

Im Rahmen der photogrammetrischen Aufnahme wurden alle Befunde übertragen, die auf den Karten der Ordnance Survey für dieses Gebiet bisher nicht eingetragen aber auf den Luftaufnahmen sichtbar waren. Die im Gelände gewonnenen sowie die zusätzlich erarbeiteten Informationen beschränkten sich hauptsächlich auf die vorgeschichtlichen und mittelalterlichen Befunde. Relikte industrieller Tätigkeit wurden in einer anschließenden Landesaufnahme untersucht und sie werden in einem Parallelband (in Vorbereitung) veröffentlicht.

Diese Art der Landesaufnahme, wobei sich eine Geländevermessung an die Luftaufnahmenübertragung anschließt, ist hier zum ersten Mal für ein Hochlandgebiet eingesetzt worden. Sie erwies sich als sehr erfolgreich für ein Gebiet, wo die bestehende Kartenbasis nur ein Minimum an festen Bodenpunkten liefern konnte. Alle kartographierten Relikte wurden ausführlich beschrieben und sind jeweils auf den Verbreitungskarten für die vorgeschichtlichen und mittelalterlichen Landschaften (im Rückdeckel) eingetragen.

Die Ergebnisse sind erstaunlich. Es wurden eine große Anzahl von vorgeschichtlichen Denkmälern, Siedlungen und Verteidigungsanlagen sowie zahlreiche mittelalterliche Siedlungen und Ackersysteme festgestellt. Zu den vorgeschichtlichen Denkmälern gehören vier langgestreckte Cairns, 354 runde Cairns, sechzehn Steinkreise, acht Steinalleen und sechzehn Menhire. Es fanden sich weiterhin 211 vorgeschichtliche Siedlungen mit zusammen 1600 Rundhäusern. Weiterhin wurden siebzehn vorgeschichtliche Verteidigungsanlagen festgestellt. Mittelalterliche Fundstellen sind mit 37 Wüstungen einschließlich 65 Wohnstallhäusern, 62 Hirtenhütten,

227 mittelalterlichen Ackersystemen und einer Vielfalt von geistlichen Fundstellen vertreten. Über 544 km von bisher nicht festgelegten vorgeschichtlichen und mittelalterlichen Eingrenzungen wurden kartographisch aufgenommen.

Mehrere Kategorien von Fundstätten, ins besondere die langgestreckten Cairns, die Steinalleen und die im Zusammenhang mit Transhumanz stehenden Hütten waren bisher auf dem Moor nicht erkannt worden. Außerdem erbrachte die Landesaufnahme eine beträchtliche Anzahl zusätzlicher Fundstättenkategorien. Die überwiegende Bedeutung der Landesaufnahme liegt jedoch darin, daß sie es möglich machte, die vorgeschichtliche wie auch die mittelalterliche Landschaft als eine Einheit zusammen mit ihren Bestandteilen zu betrachten. Die Beziehung zwischen Sakral-, Begräbnis- und Ackerbaugebieten und die Nutzung der zwischen ihnen gelegenen Areale sind von grundlegender Bedeutung, wenn man verstehen will, in welcher Weise Kulturwandel die Landschaft geformt hat, die wir heute vor uns sehen. Gleichzeitig wird hierbei angedeutet, was man in tiefer liegenden Gebieten finden könnte.

Diese umfassende Landesaufnahme wird als Grundlage für ein Programm mit Bezug auf den gesetztlichen Denkmalsschutz und die Denkmalspflege dienen. Sie wird außerdem die breite Öffentlichkeit mit der Bedeutung und dem Wert diese Kulturerbes bekannt machen.

Note on general maps

Map 1, 'Bodmin Moor: the prehistoric landscape', is used in conjunction with Chapter 4, with Map 2 acting as a reference to the relationship between the prehistoric landscape and later development. Map 2, 'Bodmin Moor: the medieval and later landscape to c 1808', and Map 3, 'North-west Bodmin Moor', are the main reference plans for Chapter 5.

Map 2 has been compiled from three main sources, as follows.

Cartographic sources

Information shown in black has been taken from the 1808 Ordnance Survey manuscript sheets and selectively from the Tithe Maps. The OS surveyors' sheets of 1808, at a scale of 2″ to 1 mile, provided the base for the first edition of the OS 1″ map of 1813. They show settlements and give some indication of land use, including enclosed areas and also individual fields, the latter usually only schematically. The detail of the fields has been taken from the Tithe Maps, but in most cases only for those areas shown as enclosed on the 1808 version. The 1808 information is used in preference to the more detailed maps of c 1840 because although most of the field pattern is the same on both sets of maps there are also changes; by 1840 a large number of new holdings appear in areas that had previously been open moorland, typically single farms with blocks of rectangular, straight-sided fields.

Another example will illustrate the composite nature of the map. In the Fowey valley the settlements at Carkeet, Hill and Ninestones (area centred SX 219735) are shown as ruins in 1808 and 1840. The field boundaries are shown on the Tithe Map as ruined or disused and these are indicated in red. Each of these settlements was subsequently reoccupied, and in the case of Karkeet the fields were completely reorganised as large rectangular enclosures. Similarly, the settlement at Stuffle (SX 180721) is shown on neither the OS 1″ map (first edition) nor the Tithe Map, but it is on the Lanhydrock Atlas (1696) and also on the OS 6″ map (first edition 1881). In this reuse after a lengthy abandonment, the early form of the fields appears to have been retained to some extent, and this has been shown on Map 2, although neither settlement nor fields were in use in 1800.

Archaeological sources

Results from the air and ground survey are shown in red on Map 2. The achievement of the air survey has been under-emphasised here because boundaries have been recorded from the air which are not on the modern OS maps: these do appear on the Tithe Maps, and have therefore been shown in black, not red on Map 2.

Three main classes of remains have been recorded: settlements, relict cultivation, and industrial activity. The industrial archaeology is to be given separate treatment elsewhere and is not shown on Map 2, but its relevance to this period must not be forgotten. The selection of features for inclusion on Map 2 is the result of a series of decisions, principally in disentangling the prehistoric from the post-prehistoric. In many cases interpretation is simple because boundaries and relict cultivation are associated with settlements of recognisable medieval form; in others the remains clearly integrate with the post-medieval field patterns and can be broadly dated by association, as these patterns generally incorporate and fossilise elements of medieval field systems. (This will be apparent from description in Chapter 5, and from examination of Map 2.) This still leaves many instances where prehistoric and medieval remains seem inextricably enmeshed. Normally the extent of medieval use (or reuse) is fairly clear; what is far from clear, for example at Trewortha Marsh (SX 226760), is whether the field system is entirely, partly, or not at all prehistoric in origin.

Documentary sources

An index of place-names in Cornwall, part of the Cornish Place-Names Survey undertaken by Oliver Padel as Place-Names Fellow of the Institute of Cornish Studies (University of Exeter), has been made available for use as a digest of historical data to establish the medieval 'credentials' of each settlement – that is, whether or not it is mentioned in medieval documents. The index is organised alphabetically by parish, and the early forms of each name are listed with the date of their occurrence. On Map 2 each settlement name is accompanied by the date of its earliest reference. This cannot be equated with the date of origin of a settlement, which may well have been long before the earliest surviving written record of it. In a few cases it is also not clear whether early references relate to a settlement name or to an area name: for example Menniridden, St Neot (SX 171724, north-west of Stuffle), is recorded in 1401, but it does not appear to have existed as a settlement before c 1840 and has not been shown on Map 2. However, we have already seen in the case of Stuffle that settlements may be reused after a period of abandonment; Menniridden might be another example.

Many of the abandoned settlements can be linked to recorded medieval place-names (see Map 2 and Table 8) and thereby to documentary information about them. This is simplest for the more recent desertions: Garrow continued in use as a farm to the present century; Carwether appears as a field name on the 1840 Tithe Apportionment, having survived long enough to be shown but not named on the first edition of the OS 1″ map. The names of other settlements can be deduced because they derive from topographic names that have continued in use to the present day. Louden is one example, referred to only once as a settlement, in 1288 (Maclean 1873, 355); Lamlavery is another, probably taking its name from a prominent rock and recorded as a tenement in 1440 and 1489. The case of Rowden is a little different; the existing settlement of Rowden (SX 112790) is called West Rowden on the Tithe Map and is first so recorded in 1334. The 'East Rowden' thereby implied is likely to be the single longhouse at SX 11517931. Similarly the deserted settlement on the west side of Bray Down (SX 18298194) may possibly be the 'Little Bowithick' recorded in 1302 and 1454 and implied in 1427 by 'Muchel [*Great*] Bodhedek'.

Topographical place-names, both Cornish and English, are by far the most common type. The impression is that every hill had its name and any newly established settlement took its name from that hill. This is so often the case that even where a deserted settlement does not have documentation a reasonable guess can be made at its name: for example, the small settlement on Redhill Downs (SX 20577057) may well have been called 'Redhill'.

On Map 2, as in Table 8, names which are uncertain or no more than reasonable guesses are in quotation marks. Names in brackets indicate the locality only, not the place-name of the settlement.

1 Introduction

by Nicholas Johnson

1 Setting and location

(*see Fig 1; Map 1*)

In popular mythology Cornwall is a place of holidays remembered, an endless strip of coast with rugged cliffs and sandy beaches, cream teas, pasties, saffron cake, John Betjeman and King Arthur. The locals wear sou'-westers, fish for pilchards and fearlessly launch lifeboats into impossible seas; the 'hard-rock men' romantically dig for tin below picturesque engine houses. At night they smuggle, lure ships onto the rocks and sing 'Trelawney', and in the morning go to chapel to make amends. For many Cornwall *is* the sea and the coast is Cornwall's attraction.

One can be forgiven for not realising that there is an 'inland'. It is not only the area of irritating traffic jams which have to be negotiated on the way to somewhere else but is, in fact, where most people live. To early writers much of the area was moorland waste, and for those who did not travel along the coast Bodmin Moor must have been as inhospitable as Daphne du Maurier describes it in *Jamaica Inn*.

In its widest context Bodmin Moor comprises the 13 parishes surrounding the village of Temple (SX 146733): Advent, Altarnun, Blisland, Cardinham, Davidstow, Linkinhorne, North Hill, St Cleer, St Clether, St Breward, St Ive, St Neot and Warleggan (Temple is no longer a parish) – an area of some 400sq km. These parishes all have parts of the Moor within their boundaries and the farms around the moorland edge have rights of common pasture on it. The area of the present survey comprises some 193sq km, confined to the main moorland blocks.

Like much of the moorland in the South-West, Bodmin Moor was extensively occupied in the past. Although what is left is bleak and rugged, the area for centuries known as Fowey Moor (changed to Bodmin Moor by nineteenth-century mapmakers) has never been what can be termed wilderness; and many remains of settlement lie undisturbed to demonstrate this. Whilst the area may not be a precise fossilised image of past activity in lowland Cornwall, its preserved landscapes are an impressive reserve of prehistoric, medieval and post-medieval industrial

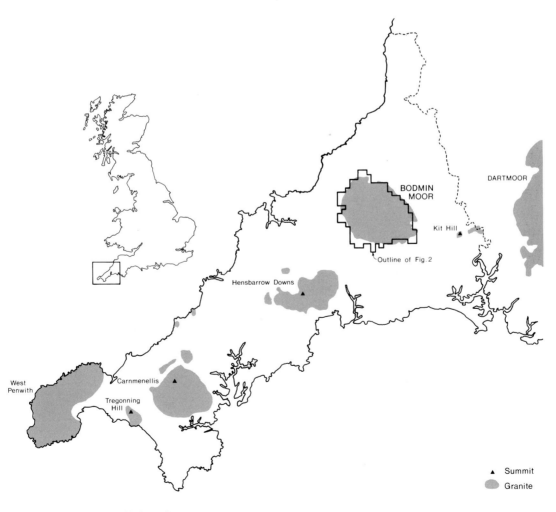

Fig 1 Bodmin Moor, Cornwall: location

remains, all relatively undisturbed. The historic landscape survives, though precariously, only because the area is not used intensively today. Unlike lowland Cornwall, subsequent activity has not swept away most of what has gone before.

Around the edges of Bodmin Moor and along its river valleys, settlement patterns have not changed for a millennium except where moorland has been enclosed. The remains give us an inkling of the mechanisms and form of settlement in the lowlands now buried beneath and absorbed into the modern landscape. They also show us the variety of those features peculiar to marginal zones. The remains are not just stone versions of more widespread wooden forms, but include some probably found only in the uplands.

Bodmin Moor is not very large, compared to many other upland areas. It is not particularly rugged or bleak, but it is exceptionally rich in archaeological remains and it is disappearing at a rate of between 20 and 40ha every year. This survey seeks to identify its archaeological diversity and richness, and will form the basis for selective landscape protection and conservation management. To most people the country-side is 'natural' and its destruction removes 'natural habitats'. This survey will label much of it 'man-made' – an important though grossly undervalued concept in countryside conservation.

These upland archaeological reserves are precious and irreplaceable; they cannot regenerate and are slowly disappearing. One of the main objectives of this survey has been to find how best, both technically and economically, to record upland landscapes. The methods used and the results produced are discussed below.

2   Topography and climate

[Much of what follows is drawn from two recent reviews by Brewster (1975) and Caseldine (1980).]

Geology and geomorphology

Bodmin Moor is one of the six granite masses of the South-West (Dartmoor, Kit Hill, Bodmin Moor, Hensbarrow Downs, Carnmenellis, Penwith), intruded through the Devonian and Carboniferous sediments during the Armorican folding, approximately 275 million years ago. Gradual denudation has removed the slatey cover, giving rise to the rounded profiles we see today. The high tors such as Brown Willy (495m OD) and Kilmar (396m OD) were formed from areas of more solid and less jointed, coarse-grained granite which was less readily eroded. During the cooling of the granite a series of fissures was intruded, giving rise to veins of other igneous material and mineralisation. During the final period of cooling, three major structural altera-tions took place, one of which, kaolinisation, pro-duced china clay. (It is hoped to discuss the significance of these geological processes at greater length in a second volume of the survey, covering the industrial landscape.)

Periglacial weathering shaped the final character-

istic tor formation so familiar on Dartmoor, Bodmin Moor, and the other granite uplands. Extensive areas of tumbled stone known locally as 'clitter' (scree) occur around the tors and often form long linear bands of stone down the hillsides. Loose stone is easily available for building in these areas.

The drainage pattern follows lines of weakness in the granite and the rivers radiate out from the centre, although the majority run to the south. The rivers (De Lank and others) in the north-west drain into the Camel estuary and out to sea at Padstow; the south-ern and central rivers – Warleggan, Loveny (St Neot), Cardinham Water – drain into the Fowey, and the rivers in the east – Inny, Lynher, Penpont Water, and Witheybrook – drain into Plymouth Sound. Dozmary Pool (259m OD), Cornwall's only natural inland lake, lies in the centre of the Moor; Brown (1977) suggests that it has been a sheet of continuously open water since the late glacial period.

Soils

Little direct evidence for soil character prior to 3000 BC exists, and a general picture can only be gained through inference from vegetation types indicated by pollen samples. In the earlier Flandrian (8000–3000 BC), the broad range would have included podzols of varying character on the heath-ery and grassy upland hills, with some areas of impeded drainage; brown-earth types on the slopes under scrub and woodland; and developing valley bog in the valley bottoms with carr vegetation or grasses (Caseldine 1980). After 3000 BC the podzoli-sation and gleying of soils continued in the upland exposed areas and expanded with the shrinkage of woodland. The stagnopodzol is the most widespread soil on the Moor and may have developed from brown earths, perhaps largely after 3000 BC; they cover much of the area occupied by remains of prehistoric settlement on the gentler hillslopes.

Since the prehistoric period, many areas of the Moor have been almost continuously used for agri-culture and pasture and the soil status maintained. On the 'killas' (slate) surrounding the granite uplands the soils are generally well-drained, brown podzolic soils (Brewster 1975). Apart from the tors, granite is rarely found on the moorland surface *in situ*. Most of the Moor is covered with a mantle of weathered, locally derived, granitic gravel known locally as 'rab' or 'growan'. This generally supports a gritty, stony yellow-brown loam which may contain large boulders. Podzols, gleys, and peat all develop on the growan. The commonest, the stagnopodzol, is found on the gentler hillslopes and supports *Molinia-Agrostis* grasslands. Stagnohumic gleys occur to a limited extent below 200m and on higher steeper slopes and support *Agrostis-Fescue* grassland and bracken. The gleys occur on the hilltops such as High Moor, and support *Molinia* moor grasses and heather, some rushes and sedges, and also edge the valley peats. There are areas of blanket peat, although a great deal had been removed through extensive peat cutting in the past for the tin-smelting industry, as well as for domestic use, up until the Second World War. Some areas still survive on High

Moor and until recently on Smallacoombe Downs. Valley peats have often been disturbed by extensive mineral working and the three large reservoirs on the Moor have submerged others. From surface examination there are apparently a few areas of undisturbed bog in valleys below Garrow Tor, on Menacrin Downs, Cardinham Moor, and several other places. The recent discovery of pre-Roman tin-streaming works below a cover of peat at Colliford (Austin *et al* 1989) warns against the assumption of undisturbed peat deposits. The peat industry will be examined in more detail in the second volume of the survey.

Climate

Cornwall has a maritime climate, characterised by warm wet winters and cool summers, with precipitation continuing throughout the year. Anticyclonic conditions, bringing warm, dry, calm days, often with cloudless skies and unbroken sunshine, are most common in March, April, and September. Bodmin Moor, in common with other upland areas, experiences lower than average temperatures, increased cloud cover and rainfall. The northern central area of the Moor, rising above 300m OD, has an average annual rainfall of 1,778mm (70in) compared to 950mm (37.5in) at the north coast, only 10km to the north. The bulk of the remaining area above 250m OD has 1524mm (60in), with the periphery of the Moor receiving 1397mm (55in). April, May and June are the driest months. On average, snow and sleet fall on only seven days in the year. The relative humidity of Cornwall is high (86%) due to its proximity to the sea and to the prevailing moist westerly winds. Bodmin Moor has the greatest range of humidity in the county: low cloud and hill fog cover the Moor for long periods. The warmest months are July and August and throughout the year the prevailing westerlies are moist and heavily laden with salt. Gales are a common and unremarked feature of Cornwall and the stunting and wind-blown effect caused to trees all along the coast and in the uplands is an indicator of the power of the westerly winds. The entrances of the majority of the prehistoric round huts on the Moor face in a generally southerly direction, but many of those facing towards the west show evidence of protective porches.

The low winter light, the possibility of a light dusting of snow in March, and the optimum period of low vegetation cover in April, make these two months the best time for ground and air survey on the Moor.

3 Vegetational history

Caseldine (1980) suggests that in the Earlier Flandrian period (*c* 8000–*c* 3000 BC), there may well have been birch woodland in less exposed parts of the Moor: however, a pollen core at Hawks Tor (Brown, 1977) may indicate the dominance of juniper scrub and *Empetrum* (crowberry) heath with no woodland development. Caseldine confirms that tree and shrub pollen never reached more than 50–70% of the total pollen counted, and that wind exposure suppressed

woodland in all but the more sheltered valleys. Towards 5000 BC birch, hazel, and finally oak woodland may have been present in some areas (it is unfortunate that pollen cores may not be close to areas of early woodland anyway), but the Moor would have been dominated by grassland and heath. Recent work at Redhill Marsh (SX 168721) has confirmed the presence of birch twigs and bark of Mesolithic date (8655 ± 85 BP and 9250 ± 85 BP: GU–1739), thus emphasising the presence of woodland along the valleys and also indicating woodland utilisation at this date. Before this period the area supported 'birch and hazel wood and scrub with scattered stands of oak and perhaps also a limited occurrence of elm and pine in sheltered localities' (Walker and Austin 1985).

After 3000 BC there was a decline in woodland cover and by the early first millennium BC Brown found evidence of cultivation followed by increased invasion by *Pteridium* (bracken) and *Ulex* (gorse), perhaps denoting abandonment of fields and increased pastoral activity. Excavations under four cairns at Colliford (Griffith 1984; Caseldine 1980; Maltby 1980) provided evidence for only limited woodland by 1500 BC, restricted to the lower valley sides, and an open grassland environment. The results suggest a high degree of variability over the Moor, perhaps due to human activity, and that at this location at least deterioration only began at the time of occupation, immediately preceding barrow construction (Caseldine 1980, 13).

The two hilltop enclosures of Stowe's Pound (SX 258726) and Roughtor (SX 147808) both have many hut platforms, including some where stone has been pushed to one side. The assumption is that such cleared areas were for wooden houses and that wood must have been freely available at that time. In the absence of other dating evidence, this extensive use of wood may point to an Early Bronze Age or even earlier date.

In the wake of Bronze Age activity the area gradually developed into open moorland under a cover of *Molinia, Calluna, Erica* and *Ulex*. The main changes were the increased growth of peat, the (most recent) decline of heather moorland, and an increase in acid grassland. There is great scope for further palynological and pedological studies on the Moor now that the remains of past activity have been located (see Chapters 4–6).

4 Vegetation and land use change

An examination of place-name evidence, maps of all periods, and air photos (since 1946) gives a general picture of the decline in the extent of moorland in the face of agricultural improvement, afforestation, reservoir construction, and extractive industries.

The change in plant types on the Moor, in particular heather, has already been noted. In 1543 John Leland described Bodmin Moor as '8 miles by Morish and Hilly Ground and a great scarsite of Wod, in so much that the Counterey therebout brennith Firres [gorse] and Hethe' (Brewster 1975, 158). By the middle of the nineteenth century, overgrazing and repeated burning had reduced the areas of heather, and by 1936 Malim could say: 'The surface of the Bodmin Moors is of long coarse grass with both dwarf and ordinary gorse, a little heather spread about the hillsides and the usual bracken amongst the scattered granite rocks' (Malim 1936).

This is the picture today, but for how long? In the prehistoric and medieval periods large areas were grazed, and in the latter period substantial areas were also cultivated. There followed a period of contraction which was reversed, most notably in the nineteenth century, when large areas around Bolventor were enclosed. Farm creation continued until the early years of this century, and more recently areas of former moorland have been improved as a grassland supplement for existing farms. Moorland improvement has taken place largely outside the areas of common land. The figures below give a dramatic impression of the loss of moorland over the last 150 years.

1827 Greenwood's map	22,900 ha of unenclosed moorland
1938 *Land Utilisation Survey* (LD Stamp)	23,000 ha of enclosed and unenclosed moorland
1946 RAF air photographs	12,200 ha of enclosed and unenclosed moorland
1984 Air photographs; fieldwork and *Second Land Utilisation Survey* (Coleman and Maggs (1968)	9,500 ha of enclosed and unenclosed moorland

Between 1935 and 1946, 188ha of forest were planted, particularly at Halvana, and during the Second World War 350ha of common land were requisitioned, ploughed, and brought under more intensive cultivation (26ha on Fore Downs, St Cleer; 27ha at Napps Moor, St Clether; 297ha in Cardinham parish including Race Course, Cardinham, Tawna, and Long Downs) (Brewster 1975, 211). An airfield was constructed on Davidstow Moor, part of which was subsequently planted with conifers.

Since 1946, 2700ha of moorland have been lost: 1448ha to farming improvement; 714ha to forestry planting; 415ha to reservoir construction; and approximately 124ha to china clay expansion. Nearly 2000ha have gone since 1960, over 16% of the 1946 total. It is not clear how reliable the 1938 *Land Utilisation Survey* figure is; large areas enclosed and selectively grazed in the nineteenth century may have reverted to moorland vegetation by the 1930s, and the figure may therefore be artificially high. Furthermore, many areas of moorland are secondary moorland, in the sense that in the medieval period at least they were cultivated and have subsequently reverted. Greenwood's map broadly agrees with the Tithe Award Surveys of the late 1830s and early 1840s and the first edition of the Ordnance Survey 1" map of 1808. The figure of c 23,000ha of moorland in c 1800 appears to be reliable.

Between 1800 and 1946 Bodmin Moor shrank by nearly 50%, and since then it has shrunk still further;

it is now a mere 41% of the 1800 total (Johnson 1983, 9, fig 4). Since 1960, moorland has been ploughed, planted, dug away, buried, and submerged at an average rate of 80ha per year. Permission for nearly 200ha of afforestation has been refused over the last few years and a move to establish an army training area has been shelved; yet farming improvement carries on apace outside the 7500ha of common land. These changes, drastic as they are, occur piecemeal and are not always readily appreciated by the public. However, the more the blocks are nibbled at, the greater the length of improvable moorland edge. It was in the face of this scale of landscape change that the survey project developed.

5 Past archaeological work

by Peter Rose

The main elements of past work have been summarised chronologically in Appendix 1. It should be stressed that much of this research over the last 100 years has been underpinned by the work of the Archaeology Division of the Ordnance Survey, including major revisions in the 1970s.

Bodmin Moor failed to attract the high degree of early antiquarian interest that is found in West Penwith. Norden's description (1584) of King Arthur's Hall and the Hurlers stands in isolation until the second half of the nineteenth century, when the emphasis is almost entirely on the survey or description of stone circles, with the occasional but rare report of the opening of a cairn. An exception is Baring-Gould's work at Trewortha Marsh (1891; 1892), one of the earliest excavations on a deserted medieval settlement in Britain. This pattern continued largely unaltered in the first half of the twentieth century, with excavations at the Stripple Stones (Gray 1908) and the Hurlers (Radford 1935; 1938), and on barrows on Davidstow Moor (Croft Andrew 1942) – in this case in advance of destruction by military installations.

Curwen (1927) and Hencken (1932) had drawn attention to the importance of the hut circle settlements and their associated fields and enclosures, but no campaign of excavation was attempted until the 1950s, when Dorothy Dudley's investigations of settlements in West Penwith were paralleled by her work at Garrow. This extended to the excavation of medieval buildings at Garrow Farm (Dudley and Minter 1962–3). Further excavations on hut circle settlements were undertaken in the 1960s, at Smallacoombe in response to forestry proposals (Dudley 1963) and at Stannon in advance of china clay dumping (Mercer 1970). These have remained the only excavations of prehistoric settlement sites.

The sporadic activity of the 1960s and early 1970s gave way to an upsurge of interest in the Moor in the late 1970s, probably as a result of the growth of rescue archaeology and of interest in archaeology generally, and also because of a greater emphasis on 'landscape archaeology' and the recognition of the importance of Bodmin Moor in this context. The present survey can be seen as part of this trend.

2 Survey logistics

by Nicholas Johnson

1 Background

The County Archaeological Unit was established in 1975 as the Cornwall Committee for Rescue Archaeology (CCRA) – now Cornwall Archaeological Unit (CAU). It soon became clear, with the development of the Sites and Monuments Record (SMR), that whilst much was already known of the archaeological remains on Bodmin Moor, very little had been surveyed at a scale above 1:2500. Without precise information about such remains, control of development can never get beyond reactive programmes of work.

A series of proposals – to move Army training areas to the Moor, to build a new reservoir, and to extend forestry and china clay extraction – focused attention on Bodmin Moor. The SMR was inadequate for assessing the archaeological impact of future developments and whilst the Royal Commission on the Historical Monuments of England (RCHME) held information on a large number of sites, some of which were already scheduled Ancient Monuments, it was clear from the oblique photographs taken in 1976 by the Air Photography Unit of the RCHME that many more monuments, particularly field systems, lay unrecorded. Work on Dartmoor by Andrew Fleming and John Collis of Sheffield University had had a profound effect on upland studies in the South-West (Fleming and Collis 1973, Fleming 1978, 1983), not least in raising the possibility that large reave-like field systems may have gone unnoticed in Cornwall. It was clear that whilst other areas may not have had such extensive coaxial field systems, archaeological remains in upland areas could no longer be viewed as a series of isolated phenomena, but rather as components of coherent landscapes. A survey was needed.

Three organisations required information and those interests happily all coincided:

a The Cornwall Archaeological Unit
The SMR is used as the basis for development control, strategic planning and academic research. A survey of Bodmin Moor would improve the quality of the existing database and provide information for all three purposes.

b The Inspectorate of Ancient Monuments
(now English Heritage – the Historic Buildings and Monuments Commission for England)
The Inspectorate, in addition to supporting the development of the SMR, also required a reassessment of the Moor for the purposes of scheduling.

c The Royal Commission on the Historical Monuments of England
Although air photographs had been used for the purposes of identification and sketch plotting in upland areas, no large-scale photogrammetric plotting of archaeological remains in such areas had been

carried out. Bodmin Moor presented the Royal Commission with the opportunity of testing the efficacy of such work and, subsequently, of enhancing it by ground survey; in particular, much of the area lacked adequate ground control and thus required more than simple transcription.

2 Aims

a To update the existing record of the upstanding remains on the Moor for entry into the County SMR and the National Archaeological Record.

b To test the efficacy of various survey methods and survey scales.

c To enable reassessment of the protection afforded to the archaeological sites and of their future management needs.

d To provide an academic reassessment of the archaeological development of the Moor and a framework for future research designs.

e To provide the archaeological input to local and county strategic plans for development control and landscape management.

It was recognised that the survey would also provide information for guidebooks, leaflets, and trail guides.

3 Type and scale of survey

a The archaeology of the Moor, essentially the unenclosed, unimproved part of it, to be photogrammetrically transcribed at 1:2500 scale, using the 1km grid square as the basic unit. This is the smallest scale at which various details such as hut walls, entrances, and clearance cairns can be plotted to size.

b A proportion (c 10%) of the transcriptions to be enlarged to 1:1000 scale and used as a base for surveys of a range of complex archaeological remains.

c The remaining 90% of the transcriptions to be checked and enhanced in the field at 1:2500 scale as resources permitted.

d Selected individual monuments throughout the Moor to be surveyed at scales larger than 1:1000 to provide detailed examples of the monument types.

e The industrial remains (excluding peat-drying platforms) to be reserved for subsequent treatment in the field and for future publication, in the second part of this survey.

4   Study area
(*Fig 2, end pocket*)

The 400sq km comprising the full extent of Bodmin Moor includes much enclosed land, and it would appear that little can be added by aerial photography to what is already known of the latter. The survey has been restricted, therefore, to the unenclosed moorland and its immediate fringe, in all some 193sq km.

5   Organisation

The vertical photographs were taken by Cambridge University Air Photography Unit. Over 2000 oblique black and white photographs, together with a few in natural colour and false-colour infra-red, were taken by RCHME to supplement the vertical cover. The air photograph transcription was carried out by the RCHME (see Chapter 3).

The field checking of the transcription was originally to have been carried out by CAU, and it was hoped at first to check all detail at 1:1000. This proved altogether too ambitious and in the event the work was divided between CAU and RCHME, the latter working from a newly established local office in Exeter. CAU undertook the detailed survey at 1:1000 scale of some 15sq km, mainly in the northwest of the Moor, in the area of the complex remains at Garrow Tor, Louden Hill, Stannon Down, Roughtor, and Brown Willy. RCHME checked and revised the remaining 178sq km, mainly at the transcription scale of 1:2500; but some complexes, such as the settlements at Leskernick Hill (Fig 3) and Brockabarrow (Fig 8) were surveyed at 1:1000 scale and a number of individual monuments at larger scales.

At times during the course of the project both survey teams were diverted to other work on the Moor, in particular the recording of threatened sites.

In addition to the work of CAU and RCHME on the Moor, four other surveys took place. All four surveyors kindly allowed CAU full access to their work.

a   Peter Herring surveyed medieval remains on the Moor, concentrating in particular on Brown Willy (see Chapter 5), which formed part of the main CAU area. The results were incorporated in the survey, the work being methodologically compatible. Other detailed surveys included those of most of the longhouses on the Moor, the cairn cemetery at Fernacre (SX 152806), the cairns and settlement at Codda (SX 179793), the long cairn at Catshole Tor (Herring 1983), and the stone row and second stone circle at Leskernick.

b   Jacqueline Nowakowski surveyed the post-medieval settlement of the Moor, including the remains on Brown Willy (see Chapter 5). It was, therefore, felt unnecessary for the project to include detailed surveys of post-medieval settlements.

c   Sandy Gerrard surveyed the medieval tin industry of the Moor, in detail in St Neot parish. This work will form a major component of the second part of this survey, *The Industrial Landscape*. Part of his survey covered the medieval fields on Penkestle Moor (SX 177703), the results of which have been incorporated into the project.

d   Helen Buxton studied the prehistoric and medieval settlements of Brown Gelly (SX 201728), surveying the huts and longhouses at a large scale.

All these surveys at 1:1000 and larger, together with the large-scale surveys by CAU and RCHME, comprise a substantial sample of the Moor.

6   Summary of remains surveyed
(*air photograph survey and field survey*)

a   *Natural features*: rivers, streams, bog-edge, tors, prominent rocks, and clitter where this would be helpful in the field.

b   *Modern detail*: hedges, fences, farms, and other features delineating the moorland edge.

c   *Prehistoric remains*: settlements, fields and enclosures, ritual and burial monuments, clearance mounds, defensive enclosures, and trackways.

d   *Medieval and post-medieval remains*: settlements, fields, and enclosures; cultivation ridges, trackways, crosses, chapels, and wells.

e   *Industrial remains of many periods*: peat cuttings and peat stack platforms; mineral prospecting, working, and processing sites; china clay working and processing sites; granite quarries and stone-splitting sites; semi-processed stones (millstones etc); tramways, railways, and associated works and buildings. These remains, with the exception of the peat stack platforms, will be published in the second volume of the survey.

7   Survey statistics

Tables 1 and 2 attempt to give an idea not only of what has been gained through the detailed survey of the Moor but also of what this has involved in the field. The OS Archaeology Division surveys in the early and mid-1970s identified almost all of the prehistoric settlements on the Moor, although many additional hut circles have since been found. The majority of field systems, of whatever date, were also known but very few surveyed. The present survey has increased our knowledge of these very substantially, while for such features as stone rows and long cairns it has revolutionised our picture of the Moor. Tables 1 and 2 give an indication of the quantitative increase achieved by the present survey for certain of the commoner remains on Bodmin Moor.

Table 1   Numbers of huts, cairns, and clearance cairns surveyed together with areas of fields and cultivation remains

	Hut circles	Cairns	Clearance cairns	Prehistoric fields	Ridge & furrow
Pre-survey					
(1:2500 area)	714	170	25		
(1:1000 area)	367	70	18		
Total	1,081	240	43	28ha	3ha
Added by present survey					
(1:2500 area)	314	60	260		
(1:1000 area)	206	54	1,820		
Total	520	114	2,080	950ha	704ha
Overall total	1,601	354	2,123	978ha	707ha

Table 2   Length of field boundaries mapped (all periods)

Pre-survey total	8.2km	
From air photograph survey		
(1:2500 area)	370.1km	
(1:1000 area)	64.2km	
Added by field survey to air survey		
(1:2500 area)	81.8km	(22.1%)
(1:1000 area)	27.9km	(43.5%)
Total added by field survey to air survey	109.7km	(25.3%)
Total of air and ground survey	544.0km	

NB   The 1:1000 area (Garrow Tor, Louden Hill, Roughtor, Brown Willy, Stannon Down, Butterstor) contained the largest concentration of boundaries, and the relatively high increase through field survey compared to the 1:2500 area is due to the many strip fields on Garrow and Brown Willy

The statistics can best be summarised as follows: nearly 4200 structures of prehistoric and later date (including clearance mounds but excluding industrial remains) have been surveyed, nearly 2000 at 1:1000 scale and nearly 200 at 1:200 or larger. In addition, over 500km of field boundaries have been accurately surveyed, of which 452km are at 1:2500 and 92km are at 1:1000 scale. Over 700ha of cultivation ridges have been identified, more than 50ha of which have been accurately plotted at 1:2500 scale from air photographs.

3 Survey methodology

by John Hampton

1 Introduction

At the outset of the project, it was envisaged that an aerial photographic interpretation and transcription of all visible archaeological remains in the unenclosed area of Bodmin Moor should provide the foundation for a subsequent programme of detailed analytical field survey. Transcription was to be carried out by the Air Photography Unit of RCHME at a scale of 1:2500 and to a standard of accuracy that would allow it to be used by CAU as a basis for field survey at 1:1000.

As work proceeded, it quickly became clear that field recording at such a large scale was too ambitious for the resources available; progress was very slow, even when using the air photographic transcription, successfully enlarged to 1:1000, as a reliable survey base. Accordingly, during the latter half of 1983 it was agreed that the task of field recording should thereafter be divided between CAU and the archaeological staff of RCHME's recently opened office in Exeter. As a result of this new arrangement, CAU was eventually able to complete a 1:1000 survey of 15sq km of the 193sq km of Bodmin Moor that had been planned from air photographs, while a team of two RCHME field recorders was able systematically to revise and enhance transcription for the remaining 178sq km at the basic survey scale of 1:2500. In addition, the latter team carried out isolated larger-scale surveys of a representative selection of the area's most important and typical monuments.

2 Air survey

by Ann Carter

For the RCHME Air Photography Unit, the Bodmin Moor project presented a unique opportunity and challenge. For the first time in Britain, the antiquities of a substantial area of countryside were to be comprehensively mapped from air photographs at a scale sufficiently large to allow the realistic portrayal of each individual monument. Such air photographic transcriptions would need to be of sufficient accuracy for them to be used as a reliable basis for subsequent field-recording at 1:2500 and 1:1000 scales. This would require, in addition to the necessary experience of archaeological photo-interpretation, the use of an appropriate photogrammetric plotting instrument. In the event the results were plotted with the technical support and guidance of the Department of Photogrammetry and Surveying, University College, London.

From the beginning it was recognised that an air photographic survey of Bodmin Moor would present two major problems familiar to anyone involved with archaeological survey in highland and moorland environments: a lack of readily identifiable control points and considerable variations in ground height. In view of these twin constraints, it was apparent that full photogrammetric survey from stereoscopic vertical photographs was the only method that would allow the required levels of accuracy. For this purpose, new photographic cover of the whole of Bodmin Moor was specially commissioned from the Cambridge University Committee for Aerial Photography. Taken with the aid of a Wild RC8 air survey camera, this coverage was in the form of 17 linear runs of 9in × 9in photographs with 60% overlap between adjacent frames and 20% overlap between adjacent runs. To allow maximum resolution and to ensure that archaeological features were recorded before the onset of bracken growth, a total of 458 overlapping photographs was taken in May 1977 at a nominal scale of 1:7800.

When the project began, RCHME possessed no suitable equipment of its own, but was very fortunate in being offered the use of a Thompson Watts Mk II stereo plotting instrument housed within the Department of Photogrammetry and Surveying at University College, London. Designed in the 1960s, the Thompson Watts is an optical-mechanical device which removes the effects of camera tilt and height differences on the ground by recreating the position and orientation of the camera to the ground at the precise moment that each separate photograph was taken. Its use is limited to vertical air photography taken with metric air survey cameras with a focal length of approximately 6in or 150mm, whereas more modern computer-aided analytical stereo-plotters have the flexibility to work with a wider variety of source photography.

The instrument accomodates two overlapping vertical air photographs and enables the operator to recreate a stereoscopic scale model of the ground surface that is to be mapped. From this model, precise coordinates in three dimensions (X eastings, Y northings, and Z height) can be measured and automatically drawn out by the instrument to any chosen scale (for a more detailed account see Burnside 1979). Ideally, the control points that are used to provide a framework for establishing the orientation of each model are marked out as accurately surveyed and easily visible ground targets in advance of the taking of the aerial photographs. Alternatively, and in the case of the present survey, a perfectly satisfactory and more cost-effective framework of control can often be established through the use of specific geographical features (such as the corner angles of buildings or the intersections of field walls) identifiable both on the photograph and on an accurately surveyed Ordnance Survey map.

To bring the stereoscopic model to a defined scale requires an absolute minimum of two plan control points and three height control points, which should be well distributed about the model, and identifiable both on the ground and on the aerial photographs. It is recommended, however, that three plan points and four or more height points be used whenever possible to ensure a better check on the reliability of the survey. For the purpose of the Bodmin Moor survey, plan control points were provided by scaling the coordinates of points from published Ordnance Survey 1:2500 plans. Height control points were provided by spot heights and bench-mark values, also derived from published 1:2500 plans, and by contour measurements taken from OS 1:10 560 maps.

In practice, the derivation of plan control from Ordnance Survey maps proved more difficult than expected. In particular, it was discovered that modern OS 1:2500 plans of Bodmin Moor were not as accurate as would have been wished. These are directly derived from nineteenth-century survey of the area, and as a result of recasting from the original Cassini projection to the national Transverse Mercator projection adopted after the Second World War, significant but inevitable errors were created, especially in open rural areas where mapped detail is sparse (Seymour 1972). An additional problem was that for about half the total area of the Moor published maps provided insufficient height information. To increase the amount of both height and plan control it was necessary to apply a technique known as aerial triangulation, a procedure that enables the extra points required in each model to be computed from a relatively sparse distribution of known ground control points. For reasons of economy this was done only in those areas where it was absolutely necessary. As a result, it was not possible to perform the block adjustment that would normally be used to provide a best mean fit between adjacent runs of photographs as well as between adjacent frames within a run. Standard errors in fitting to the control (ie a measurement of the accuracy with which the computed coordinates compare with the true positions of the known ground control points) were nevertheless within acceptable limits as follows:

eastings ± 1.62m;
northings ± 1.47m;
height ± 0.59m.

Transcription was completed first of all in those areas where control had been provided by aerial triangulation. In the remaining areas, the models were fitted as accurately as possible between detail that had already been transcribed from adjacent strips of photographs. On a few occasions where it was not possible to carry over detail, a best mean fit had to be made to features shown on existing Ordnance Survey maps.

It was initially intended that transcription would be confined to archaeological features not already depicted on published OS 1:2500 plans. However, it soon became obvious that much of the existing mapped information bore only a limited resemblance to what was visible on the air photographs and that it would therefore be necessary to transcribe systematically all archaeological structures, regardless of earlier survey. Furthermore, if transcriptions were to be of maximum benefit to those responsible for field revision, it was essential that they should also depict important natural and modern man-made landmarks in their correct relationship to the archaeological detail so that the new archaeological survey could, if necessary, be carried out independently of existing Ordnance Survey plans.

For the purposes of field revision and subsequent archival storage, photogrammetric transcriptions were produced in the form of translucent overlays to standard 1 × 1km OS 1:2500 map sheets. Altogether, photo-interpretation and transcription for the 192sq km of Bodmin Moor took approximately 200 working weeks to complete, detailed archaeological photo-interpretation accounting for the bulk of this time.

Although photogrammetric transcription was made directly from a specially commissioned sequence of vertical photographs, numerous other photographs from RCHME's own collection were used to assist with the identification and detailed interpretation of archaeological features. In all cases, this was oblique photography taken in overlapping runs and thus suitable for stereoscopic viewing. The majority of this material took the form of black-and-white prints, but some false-colour infra-red and natural colour photographs were also available. The change of perspective and scale offered by this supporting low-altitude photography proved most helpful. Although almost all the archaeological features thus recorded could subsequently be recognised on corresponding vertical images, these were often more easily seen and understood on the larger-scale oblique photographs.

The greatest single obstacle to photo-interpretation and the confident recovery of archaeological information was posed by the natural vegetation of Bodmin Moor. Some parts, for example East Moor and Davidstow Moor, are characterised by open grassland within which upstanding archaeological features can be recognised easily and reliably from air photographs. Leskernick Hill (Figs 3 [end pocket], 4) is a similarly open, unshrouded area whose air photographic transcription required the addition of very little detail during field checking. Despite this, two important new discoveries were made during field survey – a stone circle (Fig 21, 3) and a stone row – demonstrating that even in the most favourable of conditions certain classes of monument remain extremely difficult to detect from the air.

In other parts of the Moor where the ground is covered, sometimes quite densely, with scrub, gorse, and natural scatters of large boulders, the identification of archaeological features from air photographs proved much more difficult. For example, the west side of Garrow Tor (Fig 5, end pocket), by contrast with the rest of the hillside, is well covered by gorse with scatters of boulders on the higher slopes. As a consequence, comparatively more detail was added during field survey in this western area than elsewhere. Although many of Garrow Tor's hut circles could be identified from the air photographs on account of their substantial construction, associated field boundaries were much slighter in form and often quite obscured by the gorse growing on and

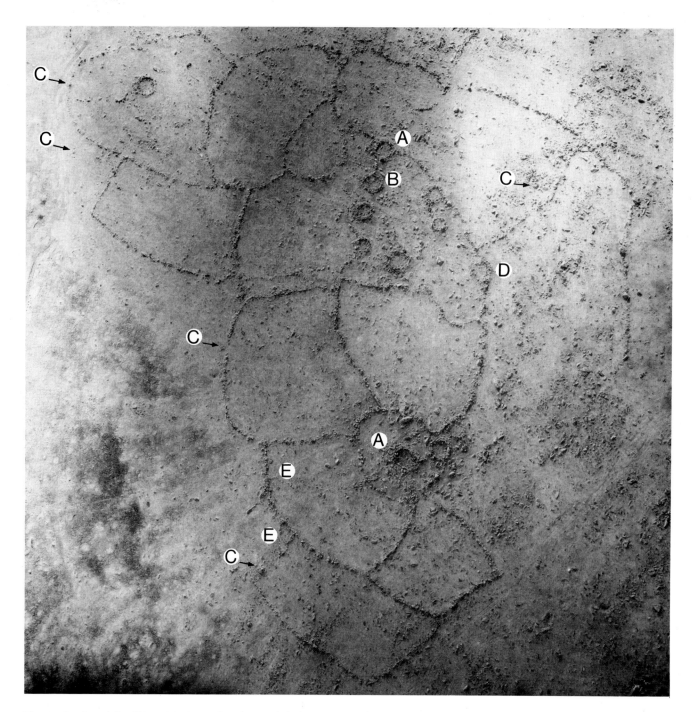

Fig 4 Leskernick, SX 183800, settlement and field system, north and upslope at right: A, huts with 'porches'; B, subdivided hut; C, small cairns; D, hut robbed for enclosure wall; E, structures/huts attached to field walls. Print shows eastern area of survey plan, Figs 3 and 28. (Photo NMR SX 1879/2/197, 28 February 1979; Crown Copyright Reserved)

around them. Indeed, some boundary features could be detected on the photographs only through variations in the height and texture of the covering vegetation. In some parts of the Moor, tree cover could also present problems. The earthwork of Allabury on the north-eastern edge of the Moor was already known and its approximate position was obvious on the photographs, but its detailed planning nevertheless had to be carried out entirely in the field because the site is completely ringed and obscured by trees.

Just occasionally, it was found that archaeological features were more obvious on aerial photographs than on the ground. At Stowe's Pound (Fig 6, *end pocket*) a series of 'hut platforms' appear as roughly circular patches of cleared ground outlined by arrangements of stones and sometimes terraced. Although these features are quite easily recognised from the air, especially when recorded on false-colour infra-red oblique photographs, they were found to be more difficult to identify on the ground.

3 Field survey, RCHME

by Cyril Wardale

1 Background

During the latter half of 1983, when the programme of air photo transcription was well advanced and fieldwork by CAU already in hand, RCHME was able, contrary to original expectations, to allocate field staff to the project. There was already an agreement that all fieldwork should be finished by April 1985 and this left, therefore, little more than 18 months for the field checking. In the event this had to be further reduced to accommodate other RCHME commitments in the South-West, especially map revision work for the Ordnance Survey, leaving as a result no more than 140 man-weeks for the work.

Given these limitations, it was clear that it would be far more useful to check the transcribed information for the whole of the remainder of the study area rather than supplement the CAU field programme with further intensive work on a small area. An extensive survey, though inevitably limited in detail, was felt to be essential to the overall view necessary to informed decisions on future conservation and management of the archaeological remains on the Moor. Thus in the autumn of 1983 two RCHME field recorders, N V Quinnell and M J Fletcher, under the direction of C F Wardale, took on the task of ground verification of the transcribed information for the large area of the Moor (c 90%) which up to that stage had had to be set aside for checking at some unspecified time in the future.

Within the twin constraints of time and manpower, a level of field recording was defined compatible, as far as possible, with the overall objectives of the project and designed to complement the fieldwork for which CAU had already assumed responsibility. To meet the timetable little search was made of documentary sources, few air photographs were consulted (other than those used for the transcriptions) and the number of large-scale plans made of individual sites was kept within strict limits. In addition, and by agreement with CAU, industrial remains were left aside for future consideration.

2 Aims

RCHME fieldwork on Bodmin Moor had three main aims:

a to check the 1:2500 air photograph transcription, making amendments and additions as necessary, thus bringing the survey to a uniform standard and scale for the whole of the study area. Limited resources and a tight timetable required, however, that areas of cultivation remains, additional to those transcribed, be noted but not surveyed in detail.

b to provide descriptive reports, supplemented where necessary by measured surveys at a scale larger than 1:2500, of the field monuments within the study area, whether previously recorded or not.

c to furnish the Ordnance Survey with plans of all antiquities, together with their names or descriptive terms, for depiction on the relevant large-scale OS maps, for this area 1:2500.

3 Planning and programming

Planning of the work had to take into account a number of constraints, of which the four most important were:

a *manpower* No more than two field recorders with supervisory support and back-up were available.

b *travelling time* Working from Exeter, some 50 miles from the nearest access point to Bodmin Moor, meant that work stations nearer to it had to be used. The Moor was divided into four quadrants and the work carried out from temporary bases in Camelford, Launceston, Liskeard, and Bodmin.

c *weather* The uncertainty of the weather on Bodmin Moor had by far the greatest influence on the work rate. The very dry summer of 1984 was quickly counterbalanced by the extremely wet autumn and winter of 1984/85, during which work schedules had frequently to be revised.

d *vegetation cover* Because of its relatively low altitude large tracts of Bodmin Moor are covered in bracken, which obscures archaeological information both on air photographs and on the ground. At best it makes observation and survey difficult and at worst impossible. It was therefore necessary to ensure that remains in such areas were investigated during late winter and spring.

4 Sources

Throughout the project the basic range of source material used in the field was as follows:

a *the record cards and accompanying index maps* (at 1:10 000 or 1:10 560 scale) of the National Archaeological Record, the former since computerised and online. (Examples of a record card and map are shown in Figs 7 and 8.) The Bodmin Moor study area involved the major parts of eight maps and smaller parts of a further eleven.

b *the 1:2500 air photograph transcription* Monochrome copies of the transcribed information were supplied for field use on film, emulsion-coated on both sides. The photo image was printed on the obverse, thus allowing the final (inked) version of field additions and amendments to be clearly distinguished on the reverse. Each plan conformed to the National Grid and covered a 1km square. (For examples, see Figs 3, 5 and 9, end pocket.)

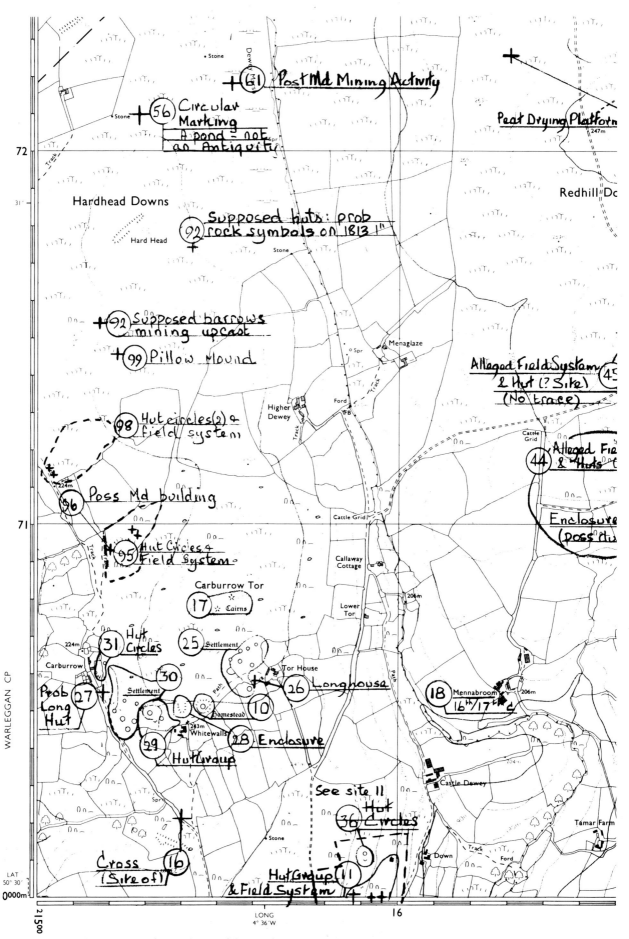

Fig 7   Example of NAR record map (part of SX 17 SE. Reproduced from the 1:10 000 map with the permission of the Controller of Her Majesty's Stationery Office, © Crown copyright.)

```
1:10 000 SHEET NO: SX 17 SE        NAR NO: 33.00   COUNTY(NEW): Cornwall      (OLD): Cornwall
NGR:    SX 16057477             NGR QUALIFIER: CE  DISTRICT: North Cornwall
DEFINITIVE RECORD & REF:                           PARISH: Blisland
TYPE:    Cairn          FORM: Other Structure      CONDITION: D               PERIOD: BA
DOE STATUS:-  GUARDIANSHIP NO:     0   SCHEDULED NO:    0    LISTED BUILDING GRADE:
OTHER STATUS
SITE NAME AND MAIN FEATURES:   "Brocka Barrow" : cairn circle - remains of a round cairn


RECOMMENDED OS PUBLICATION:   Cairn (NR)




DESCRIPTION


SX 16057477 : pecked circle 14.0 m in diameter.   Undescribed.    (1)

Cairn symbol shown and named "Brocka Barrow".      (2)

Ruined cairn 15.0m in diameter overall, situated on the summit of the ridge
called Brockabarrow Common.   Surveyed at 1:2500.       (3)

Listed.     (4)

On the broad summit ridge of Brockabarrow Common, at 306m OD, within an area of
rough moorland pasture where there as been much peat cutting in the past is the
remains of a round cairn.   It appears to have comprised a ring of parallel
orthostatic slabs set 1.0m apart and measuring about 15.0 m in diameter
overall. The majority of these have been removed leaving a band of small
earthfast stones suggesting the circle was in fact a wall.
Slightly N of centre, occupying an area approximately 4.5m square, is a natural
setting of boulders partly split by stone cutters.   The setting was clearly
incorporated in the monument in the manner of a tor cairn although the
proportions do not warrant the term here.
Maclean (a) in 1868 had the following to say about a cairn hereabouts ... "On
the top of Challowater, Blisland, there was a fine cairn a few years ago.   This
has now been removed and the stones used for making the new turnpike road which
skirts the parish of Temple".      (5)




AUTHORITIES:
 1.1st Edn OS 1:2500
 2.OS 2" MS drawing 1805
 3.F1 MHB 26 4 73
 4.Corn Arch 17 1978 15 (J E R Trahair)
 5.N V Quinnell FR 25 1 85
 5.a. History of Blisland 1868 p 24 (J Maclean)

RECORDERS




UP TO AUTHORITY: 0                    / /
```

Fig 8   Example of NAR record card: 'Brocka Barrow', SX 16057477

c *the vertical air photographs* from which the photogrammetric transcriptions were derived; also, a limited selection of obliques, and other verticals held by RCHME, to help with the interpretation of known sites.

d *the 1:2500 scale Ordnance Survey maps,* used mainly as a background of natural features and modern detail, but including some archaeology, into which the additional archaeological information generated by the survey might be inserted.

5 Procedures

As far as possible, individual sites and complexes

were dealt with in a single operation which might of necessity extend over a number of days or longer if the site was very large or complicated. Revisiting was kept to a minimum and in general took place only when unavoidable – for example, when snow or vegetation made field checking impossible, or when an initial visit indicated a need to bring in more powerful survey equipment to establish ground control.

The main field procedures were as follows:

a   The field check of the 1:2500 air photograph transcriptions

Checking was carried out on a sheet by sheet basis with the field recorders perambulating all the transcribed archaeological information both to verify its depiction and to classify it. Amendments and additions to the transcription were made using the same conventions and finalised for the archive in red (waterproof) ink to make them immediately apparent.

Before fieldwork proper began an accuracy test of the air survey was carried out. Measurements from a number of transcriptions were checked in the field using the most advanced survey equipment then at RCHME's disposal, a Wild T16 theodolite coupled to a Wild Citation Electronic Distance Meter. The test also included checks on selected parts of the transcription accurately enlarged to 1:1000 scale. The results were sufficiently impressive in all cases to warrant field survey on the basis that all transcribed detail be accepted as correct until proved otherwise. In fact the transcription was subjected to regular checks in the course of amending and adding information.

A variety of survey methods was used throughout the project. Normally the field recorders worked separately, using tape and offset survey to add to, or amend, the transcribed information. Where survey took place in areas with limited ground control the recorders worked as a team using, as appropriate, Electronic Distance Measuring (Wild Citation and Wild TO5 theodolite) or Optical Distance Measuring (Wild RK1 self-reducing microptic alidade) to record the archaeological detail and to establish its position within the National Grid.

A further element of the field check was the perambulation of areas where no archaeological detail of any sort was shown on the transcription. Four plans were selected for intensive quartering for statistical purposes, but the limitations of time required that the remainder be dealt with more summarily. Open, stone-free moorland could be covered relatively rapidly but areas of dense vegetation and clitter required altogether more intensive scrutiny.

Overall the archaeological content of the air photograph transcriptions proved to be very good indeed, with the field recorders adding a maximum of a further 20%. In the event of any similar exercise in the future one point, however, is clear. In open moorland, with little or no man-made detail to provide ground control, the inclusion of natural features such as rock outcrops, stream confluences, and isolated trees, can be of great assistance to the field surveyor and should be included wherever possible in the transcription.

b   The descriptive report

A report was compiled on each field monument within the study area at a level of detail that satisfied the needs both of the project and of the National Archaeological Record. Information was necessarily restricted to essentials but care was taken that it should be sufficiently comprehensive to stand independently of the transcription and at the same time allow the CAU to proceed towards its conclusions without the need for a further field visit. In general the individual reports compiled for all classes of monuments are primarily descriptive but inevitably involve a degree of analysis and an awareness of affinities. Every effort was made to correct errors and anomalies found in existing records.

As an indication of the content of the reports, round huts (perhaps more correctly round houses), for example, were measured and described individually except where they occur in large compact groups in settlements. In the latter instance the range of sizes and structural forms was noted, and in what proportions they were present, but only huts with exceptional features were described individually. Similarly, descriptions of fields and cultivation remains include the size of the fields, dimensions and types of banks, walls, and lynchets and whether they overlay earlier cultivation or were reused or incorporated into later enclosures; in particular, any association with huts and settlements was recorded. For sepulchral and ritual monuments full details of type, size, and form were recorded, supplemented by a large-scale graphic survey when textual description alone was inadequate.

In the interests of brevity some observations, especially on boundaries and cultivation remains, were recorded on Field Information Overlays (eg Fig 10). These consist of tracing paper gridded to conform to the 1:2500 air photograph transcriptions. They carry annotations essential to the understanding of the transcribed detail, explaining the reasons for any additions and amendments and, where necessary, distinguishing clearly between archaeological and non-archaeological information. The overlays were also used to carry the measurements of the very many peat platforms which are widespread on the Moor.

c   The large-scale graphic surveys

RCHME field reports of individual monuments are normally accompanied by a graphic survey at an appropriate scale, rarely less than 1:2500 and frequently larger. On Bodmin Moor each monument was viewed critically and a large-scale survey (1:1000 or larger), incorporating natural features such as clitter, was made when OS basic scale (1:2500) proved inadequate for the portrayal and understanding of very small or complex monuments. Such work

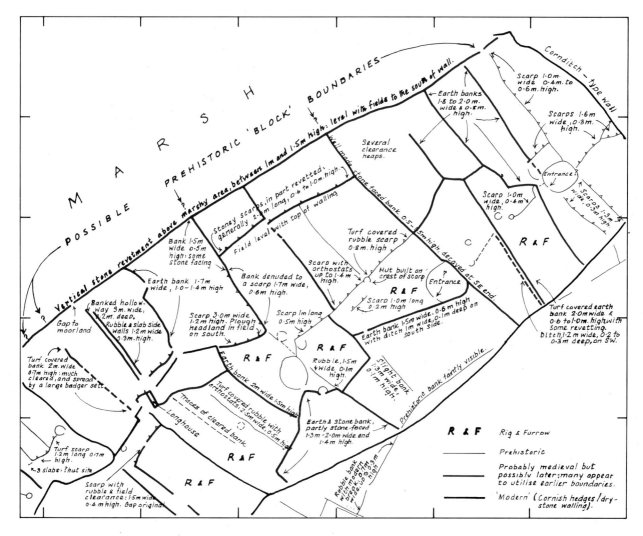

The figure contains the following labels:

MARSH

POSSIBLE PREHISTORIC 'BLOCK' BOUNDARIES

Corn ditch - type wall

Scarp 1·0m. wide 0·4m. to 0·6m. high.

Earth banks 1·8 to 2·0m. wide & 0·8m. high.

Scarps 1·6m wide, 0·3m. high.

Several clearance heaps.

Scarps, in part revetted; 0·6 to 1·0m high.

Stoney scarps, in part revetted, generally 1·2m long.

Field level with top of walling.

stone faced bank 0·5 - 1·5m high; decayed at S.E end.

Entrance?

Scarp 1·0m wide 0·4m. high.

Scarps 1·3m wide, 0·3m. high.

Vertical stone revetment above marshy area between 1m and 1·5m high; level with fields to the south of wall.

R & F

Bank 1·5m wide 0·5m high; some stone facing

Bank denuded to a scarp 1·7m wide, 0·6m high.

Turf covered rubble scarp 0·8m. high.

Scarp with orthostats up to 1·4m high.

Hut built on crest of scarp

Entrance

R & F

Turf covered earth bank 2·0m wide & 0·6 to 1·0m. high with some revetting. Ditch,1·2 m wide, 0·2 to 0·3m deep, on SW.

Earth bank 1·7m wide, 1·0 - 1·4m high

Banked hollow-way 3m.wide, 2m. deep.

Rubble & slab side walls 1·2m wide, 0·3m.high.

Gap to moorland

Scarp 3·0m wide 1·2m high. Plough headland in field on south.

Scarp 1m long 0·5m high

Scarp 1·0m long 0·2m high

Earth bank 1·5m wide, 0·6 m high: 0·1m deep on south side. Earth bank 1·5m wide with ditch 1m wide.

Turf covered bank 2m. wide 0·7m high: much cleared, and spread by a large badger sett.

Earth bank 2m wide 1·5m high.

R & F

Rubble,1·5m wide, 0·1m high.

R & F

Turf covered rubble with orthostats; 2·5m wide, 0·5m high.

Slight bank 1·3m wide, 0·1m high.

Prehistoric bank faintly visible.

Traces of cleared bank

Longhouse

Turf scarp 1·2m long 0·7m high.

3 slabs: ?hut site

Scarp with rubble & field clearance: 1·5m wide 0·4 m high. Gap original.

R & F

R & F

Earth & stone bank, partly stone-faced 1·3m -2·0m wide and 1·4m high.

Rubble bank 1·4m wide 0·8 to 0·9 m high.

R & F   Rig & Furrow

————   Prehistoric

————   Probably medieval but possibly later; many appear to utilise earlier boundaries.

████   'Modern' (Cornish hedges/dry-stone walling).

Fig 10   Rowden: the transcription in Fig 9 amended by fieldwork and with the addition of the field information overlay

was kept to a minimum but included examples of most types of monument, among them the more notable fort and settlement complexes. (For an example see Fig 11, end pocket).

d   The supply of archaeological information to the Ordnance Survey

In April 1983 RCHME took over the responsibilities of the Ordnance Survey Archaeology Division, whose primary task had been to furnish the Ordnance Survey with archaeological information to appear on its regular series maps and plans. The work involves the provision of copies of plans, generally known as 'antiquity models', at the appropriate OS basic scale (1:1250, 1:2500, and 1:10 000) for every antiquity that RCHME considers worthy of map depiction; each showing the antiquity in a form suitable to its map scale and accompanied by its distinctive name or relevant descriptive term. Antiquity models for Bodmin Moor were supplied at 1:2500, but it should be noted that the Ordnance Survey may not publish all the information at this

scale, preferring for certain areas to publish at 1:10 000 only.

4   Field survey, CAU

by Nicholas Johnson

The Unit surveyed 15sq km in the north-west part of the Moor, known to contain a wide variety of complex remains. The fieldwork was carried out between 1981 and 1985 as part of the countywide responsibility of the Unit; only during the last nine months up to May 1985 was the survey near-continuous. The method used has been fully described elsewhere (Johnson 1985) and only a digest relevant to the Bodmin Moor survey is presented here.

The survey method has been developed in direct association with the Sites and Monuments Record (SMR) and is used for all aspects of field survey throughout the county. The various stages or levels are illustrated on the flow diagram, Table 3. The information is recorded in several ways, finding its

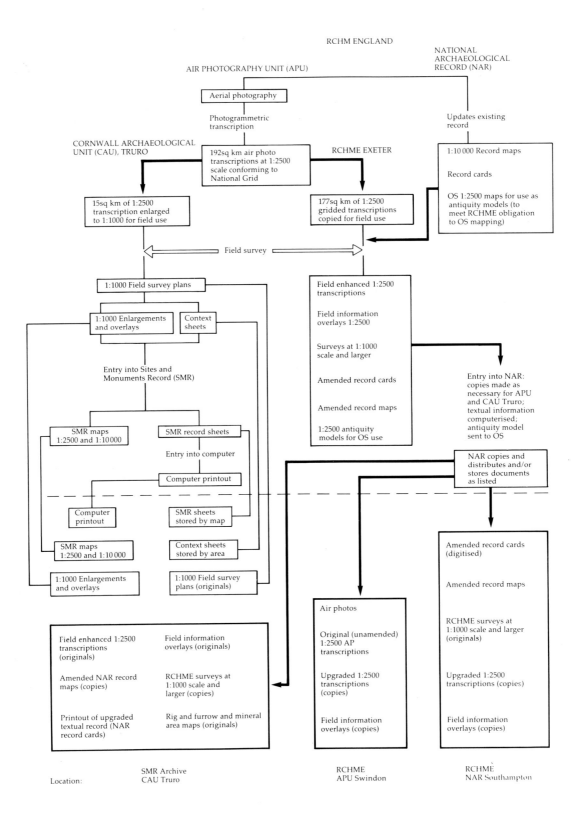

Table 3 The Bodmin Moor Survey: flow diagram showing the stages of pre-survey, survey and post-survey work
(The area below the dashed line represents the various types of record produced and indicates where they may be consulted.)

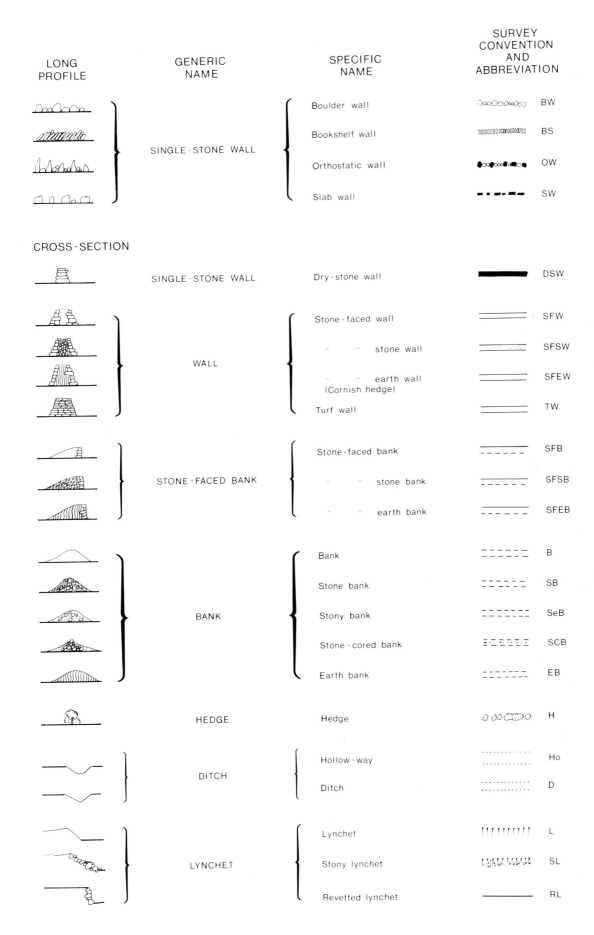

Fig 12   Cornwall Archaeological Unit field survey conventional signs

way into the SMR and National Archaeological Record (NAR), before final storage in the two archives.

1 Area

The main CAU effort has been concentrated on the area around Garrow Tor, Roughtor, Louden, Stannon Down, and Butterstor. For convenience this has been divided into smaller blocks – Stannon South, Stannon Down, Louden etc – delineated where possible by obvious features such as streams or intake walls. Such blocks serve as the basis for the context numbering and for the filing of the original field survey plans.

2 Scale

1:1000 was chosen, as at this scale it is possible to show the true dimensions and structure of the majority of features. Larger scales (1:200, 1:100 and occasionally 1:50) have been used to record individual structures such as cairns, huts, or longhouses.

3 Survey and mapping: method and conventions

The air photo plots enlarged to 1:1000 are copied onto pre-cut A2 × 50 micron drafting film and mounted on standard plane tables. Features are surveyed using microptic alidades for tacheometric survey and simple alidades and tapes for close work. Details are drawn to an agreed set of conventions, illustrated on Fig 12. Standard abbreviations are written beside features (eg DSW for dry stone wall) and, where necessary, small freehand cross-sections are added. Measurements for height are placed on the side from which they were taken, with an arrow marking the spot if needed. All measurements are identified by W for width, H for height, D for depth, and L for length. Relationships, clear or otherwise, are also noted.

All features, including modern walls, are drawn exactly to scale and stony and boggy areas are delineated. A standard system of conventions is used throughout. Some features are, however, shown differently in the field from on the finished drawings. Uprights, whether slabs on edge or orthostats, are shown as cross-hatched rather than solid, as on the finished drawings, to avoid smearing of the pencil work in field use; leaning stones are cross-hatched in the direction of lean on the finished drawings whereas in the field an arrow serves this purpose. Measured stones are marked with an M, those sketched by eye with an S (normally reserved for large-scale plans); earthfast boulders *in situ* are marked with a G for 'grounder'. Part-buried stones are marked by a solid line for the visible edge and by a dashed line for the presumed full extent.

The map conventions used here (see Fig 12) have been developed from the surveys carried out by CAU in West Penwith and are an attempt to standardise the description and representation of features found in the field. Many examples of the symbols are shown on Figs 14 and 15. Inevitably there are compli-

cations, eg a dry stone wall on or halfway down a lynchet, or a lynchet that includes uprights within it (as Feature D^I, Fig 15; also shown in detail on Fig 26 no. 7). In such cases the feature is represented as accurately as possible and a cross-section and description added to the plan and context sheet.

The system has proved to be very successful. It helps to eliminate the idiosyncrasies of individual surveyors and to present an acceptable version of the ground evidence to the reader unfamiliar with it. It has been developed as a shorthand for landscape survey where space for description on the survey board is very limited. Such a system would be difficult to implement on a complicated theodolite survey where measurements and descriptions are booked. However, a standard set of conventions would be very useful on the sketch plans to accompany such a survey.

4 The record: *context sheets (or 'record cards') and 'drawn-up' survey plans.*

a Context sheets (see Fig 13)

These are used in the field for structures such as huts and those features surveyed at a large scale. The measurements and structural features can be noted directly and the surveyor's comments are added with sketches to illustrate particular points. Other context sheets are filled in after the survey.

A context number from one to infinity is given to any feature or area within a survey block, ie Louden 6. The record, as shown on Fig 13, is divided into: (1) identification, location, and survey and record details (top third); (2) dimensions (middle right); (3) description (lower left) and sketch (lower right).

When all the contexts have been completed for a block the results are summarised to help with input to the SMR. Table 4 is an example of this for Louden. The hut and cairn numbers, for example, are brought together as 5 main numbers, encompassing 98 subsidiary context numbers. The summary context sheets are either existing contexts (eg on Table 4 nos 5, 6, 57, 100, and so on) or are new numbers (eg 188, 189, 190) added on to the end of the existing run. The summary gives an overall picture and provides the basis for allocating the final SMR numbers to the features. The original context numbers are referred to on the SMR sheets as the main source of information.

Large-scale surveys are copied onto illustration cards that accompany the context sheets, and small-scale maps indicate where the site or area is and to what the number refers. Copies of these, or the original illustration cards, are also filed with the SMR sheets.

b Grid plans and explanatory overlays

The surveys are drawn onto gridded pre-cut drafting film with the plans orientated to grid north. They are numbered/identified as with an OS map (SX 1491 NW – ie north-west corner of 1:2500 map no SX 1491), the scale is indicated, and also the survey blocks covered by the map (eg Louden, Roughtor N – this identifies the context numbers, where there may

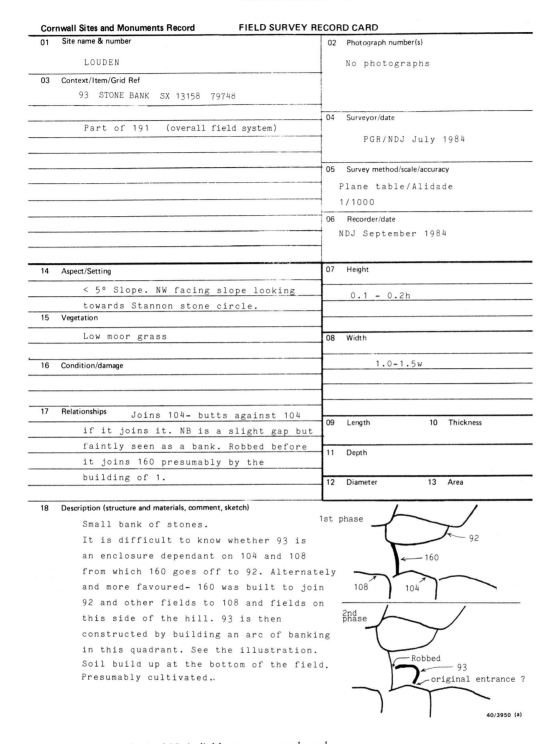

Cornwall Sites and Monuments Record   FIELD SURVEY RECORD CARD

01 Site name & number	02 Photograph number(s)
LOUDEN	No photographs

03 Context/Item/Grid Ref
93 STONE BANK SX 13158 79748

Part of 191 (overall field system)

04 Surveyor/date
PGR/NDJ July 1984

05 Survey method/scale/accuracy
Plane table/Alidade
1/1000

06 Recorder/date
NDJ September 1984

14 Aspect/Setting	07 Height
< 5° Slope. NW facing slope looking towards Stannon stone circle.	0.1 - 0.2h

15 Vegetation
Low moor grass

08 Width
1.0-1.5w

16 Condition/damage

17 Relationships Joins 104- butts against 104 if it joins it. NB is a slight gap but faintly seen as a bank. Robbed before it joins 160 presumably by the building of 1.

09 Length	10 Thickness

11 Depth

12 Diameter	13 Area

18 Description (structure and materials, comment, sketch)

Small bank of stones.
It is difficult to know whether 93 is an enclosure dependant on 104 and 108 from which 160 goes off to 92. Alternately and more favoured- 160 was built to join 92 and other fields to 108 and fields on this side of the hill. 93 is then constructed by building an arc of banking in this quadrant. See the illustration. Soil build up at the bottom of the field. Presumably cultivated..

1st phase

92
160
108   104

2nd phase

Robbed
93
original entrance ?

40/3950 (a)

Fig 13   Cornwall Archaeological Unit field survey record card

be two '6s', for example, when the grid covers two survey blocks). The surveys are drawn using the same conventions as in the field (see Fig 12 for the conventional signs). Figs 14 and 15 show parts of two grids that have been drawn up for the archive (not for publication) and are reproduced at scale (1:1000).

Fig 14 shows an area of Garrow Tor (SX 147782). The map conventions are those referred to above (3: *Survey and mapping*). Examples are a *dry stone wall* at A (top right); *single-stone wall* at B (bottom left); a *lynchet* at C (below centre); a *stony lynchet* at D (lower left); a *stone bank* at E (centre right); a *stone-faced wall* at F (above centre); a *stone-faced stone bank* at G (lower right); natural boulders have been surveyed on or transferred from the air survey. Evidence of clearance due to cultivation comes in two forms – stones placed on 'grounders' (earthfast boulders) as at H, and mounds of cleared stone as at J; the cultivation ridges have been transferred direct from the air survey and not resurveyed, although the presence of substantial headlands is shown at K. This is a complex landscape and the area as a whole

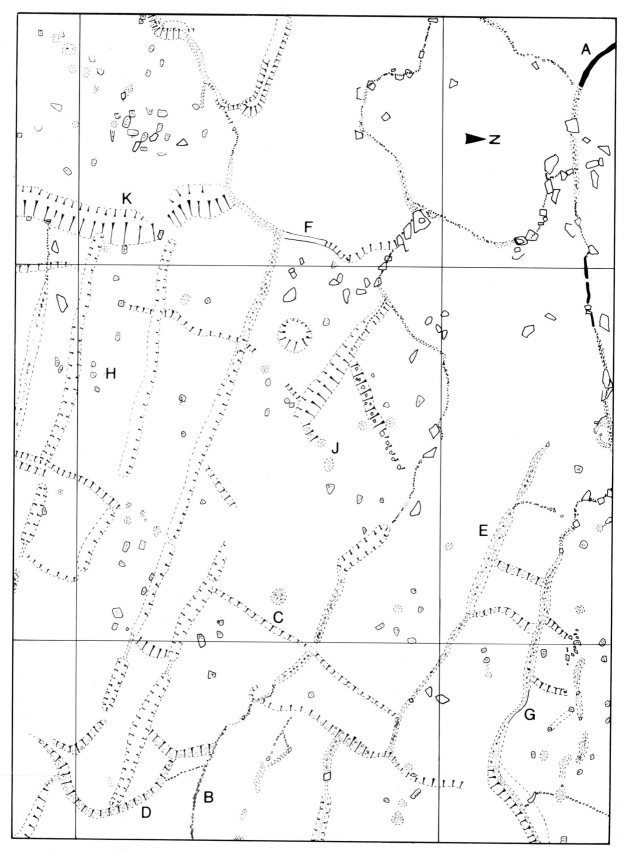

Fig 14   Garrow Tor, SX 147782: 1:1000 CAU archive plan (not redrawn for publication). Grid lines follow the National Grid. For lettering see text (p 19). Plan also part of Fig 5 (lower centre right)

is analysed in more depth in Chapter 5. There is much evidence of chronological and structural depth. Figs 15 and 47 show an area on the north slope of

Roughtor (SX 142815) with mainly prehistoric features present. In Fig 15, a medieval boundary at A is a *stone faced bank* with *ditch*, although for much of its

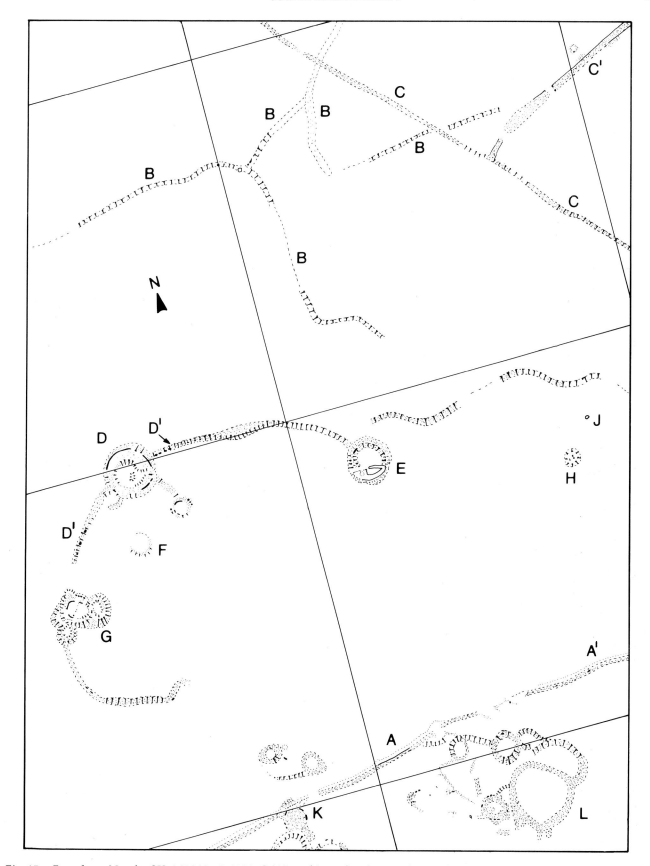

Fig 15   Roughtor North, SX 142815: 1:1000 CAU archive plan (not redrawn for publication). Grid lines follow the National Grid. For lettering see text. Area also shown as Figs 46 and 47

length it is just a bank with ditch (A^1). Originally it was a single *stone wall - bookshelf* (see Fig 12 for explanation) where the ditch material has been thrown on top. The fields at B which are defined by *lynchets* and *stone banks* have been cut by other prehistoric boundaries C and C^1. Boundary C is a

Table 4   Context summary sheet: Louden, St Breward

| CAU field survey–summary | Louden (St Breward, Bodmin Moor) |
| | 195 contexts |
Context main items	Subsidiary contexts

No		
5	Long cairn	
6	Boundary bank	
57	'Pillow Mound'	
100	Stone circle	
105	Stone setting	
114	Millstones	
126	Subrectangular hut	
185	Peat-drying platform	
186	Longhouse settlement	structures 21/1, 179, 10
		trackway 180
		longhouses 177, 178
		enclosures 12, 24, (11)
188	Field system (medieval)	Banks, stone-faced banks, and ditches 1, 2, 9, 12, 13, 14, 158
		banks, stone-faced banks 11, 12, 19, 22, 24, 175
		lynchets 27, 38
		clearance mounds 23, 187, (18?)
		ridge and furrow 176, (29?)
		trackways 180, 181, 182
189	Cairns	20, 21, 26, 53, 53/1, 74, 75/1, 75/2, 75/3, 75/4, 77, 78, 81, 82, 88, 102?, 110, 116, 117, 125, 127, 128, 129, 130/1, 130/2, 131, 132, 155, 168, 169, 170, 173
190	Boundary bank	stone banks 84/1, 85, 92/2, 106, 107/3, 111/1, 160, 160/1
191	Field system (prehistoric) (hut settlements 192–5)	stone banks/lynchets 3, 4, (17?, 18?, 19?), 25, (38?), 39, 40, 43, 44, 46, 47, 48, 60, 61, 67, 68, 69, 70, 71, 72(?), 73, 79, 80, 83, 84, 85, 86, 87, 89, 91, 92, 93, 95, 96, 104, 107, 108, 109, 111, 115, 118, 119, 166, 172(?)
		clearance mounds 75, 76, 90, 92/5, 97, 99, 101, (103?), (156?)
192	Hut circle settlement (field system 191)	platform ?41
		enclosure 52
		huts 42, 43, 49, 50, 51, 120, 121, 122, 123, 124, 171 (part of 194?); Stannon Down 1, 2, 3, 4
193	Hut circle settlement (field system 191)	enclosure/hut 98
		platform/hut 112
		hut circle 113
194	Hut circle settlement (field system 191)	huts 7, 8, 31, 32, 33, 34, 35, 36, 37, 54, 58, 59, 63, 64, 133, 134, 135, 136, 137, 138, 139, 140, 141, 142, 143, 144, 145, 146, 147, 148, 150, 151, 152, 163/1, 163/2, 163/3, 167, 184, 171?
		platform 155, 168 (cairn?), 183, (cairn?)
		enclosure 65
		stone bank/lynchet 30
195	Hut circle settlement (field system 191)	huts 15, 16

stony lynchet and boundary C^1 is a substantial ruined *stone-faced wall* that would originally have been an effective barrier. D is a kerbed platform cairn illus-trated on Fig 26 no. 7, with the kerb shown as a solid line; D^1 is a stony lynchet that built up along an earlier boundary of spaced orthostats, now leaning, that originally marked the boundary (the lynchet is secondary). E is a large hut that has had a small boat-shaped feature inserted into it, presumably a lambing shelter or a shepherd's hut (see Fig 52 no 2). F and G are huts, illustrated on Fig 35 nos 1 and 7. F is a robbed area and G is a cluster of structures, with the main hut having another annexe at the entrance and a later internal subdivision inserted. H is a small cairn with the remains of a cist but no kerb; J is a partially finished granite millstone; K could be a cairn slighted by the medieval boundary; the features at L are huts with enclosures attached. This area illustrates admirably both structural variety and chronological depth.

Both survey plans are accompanied by an explanatory overlay, as are all others; this is cut to the same size as the survey grid and laid over the top. All the context numbers, structural descriptions (SB – *stone bank*, etc) are noted beside each feature and the dimensions added exactly where they were taken. This ensures that the faded, smeared, and battered original survey plan is gutted of information. Stony and boggy areas are marked if relevant. These grids and overlays are the finished record and can be stored by map number. It is a great advantage that due to the accuracy of the air survey they can be placed on the National Grid. All such plans for Cornwall are stored in this way.

Larger-scale surveys are drawn up similarly, but on sheets (pre-cut to the same size as the grids) allocated to each survey area. Thus all Louden huts are drawn on the same sheets, all Louden cairns on another, and so on, with each structure orientated to grid north, accompanied by its context number. Different scales are drawn on separate sheets. Fig 16 shows the main settlement at Garrow surveyed at 1:200 scale and published here at 1:1000. The prehistoric huts lie at the top of the enclosure with the deserted medieval settlement below; Fig 16 F and K indicate the longhouse and associated outbuilding dug by Dudley (Dudley and Minter 1962–3). The farmhouse at Garrow, now used as a holiday cottage, is cross-hatched and the barn to the south-west is shown with solid walls. The explanatory overlay shows the usual information as well as an attempt at interpretation.

The RCHME field information overlays (see Fig 10), which give similar information to the CAU explanatory overlays, overlie the amended 1:2500 air survey plans (see Fig 9). They are the equivalent of the CAU Stage 4 (Table 3).

5 Entry into the SMR

The summary contexts are transferred, where suitable, to SMR record sheets for entry into the computer. The 1:1000 grids are transferred to 1:2500 SMR grids with SMR numbers added and stored. The survey grids described above are filed as well. This is the same level at which the NAR record sheets and 1:10 000 record maps are stored in Southampton, and CAU have copies of these.

a Garrow farmhouse   b Beehive hut

10   0   50 metres
10   0   50 yards

Fig 16   Plan of Garrow settlement, SX 146779: original CAU survey plan at 1:200 reduced to 1:1000 (not redrawn for publication). A, hut with concentric enclosure ('corridor house'), excavated by Dudley (MS, Royal Institution of Cornwall), see Fig 35 No 8; B, hut with entrance annexe or 'porch', see Fig 35 no 5; C, robbed hut stance; D, hut with boulder wall, see Fig 35 no 2; E, ?transhumance hut, see Fig 53 no 2; F, longhouse (excavated Dudley and Minter 1962–3), see Fig 54 no 1; G, longhouse, see Fig 54 no 7; H, corn drier, see Fig 56 no 3; J, longhouse, see Fig 54 no 4; K, barn, see Fig 56 no 7

6   Archive storage

a   The original field survey plans, of all scales, are brought together by survey blocks (context areas, eg Louden, Stannon Down) and stored.

b   The context sheets are stored in box files.

c   The handwritten SMR sheets, if still needed after computerisation, are stored in information files by 1:10,000 map number along with any other illustration cards, correspondence etc.

d   The 1:2500 air survey plans (amended by RCHME), together with RCHME field information overlays, are stored.

e   The large-scale finished plans of features such as cairns and huts are stored by context area.

4   The prehistoric landscape

by Nicholas Johnson

The survey undertaken attempted to identify and locate archaeological remains, and this report outlines the results. Chapters 4 and 5 are primarily a descriptive introduction and are not intended as a detailed account of the archaeological development of Bodmin Moor; the number and variety of remains identified and the severe lack of supporting dating evidence precludes such a detailed overview. Instead, it is hoped that these two chapters will form the basis for an overall strategy for future investigation on the Moor.

The remains identified from the air and recorded in the field have been summarised on Map 1. It has not been possible to show at this scale (1:25 000) all the individual huts and many of the field walls or small enclosures. The map does, however, give a very good impression of the prehistoric landscape as currently understood, within the survey area and in some instances immediately adjacent to it. On Map 2 the prehistoric remains are shown against the more boldly depicted features of the post-prehistoric landscape – frequently a close relationship, which makes it impossible in many cases to be sure whether certain features are prehistoric or later. The areas of bog, though approximate (many having been modified by tin-streaming), are shown boldly as a guide to their former extent. Major, well-known monuments are named, as are prominent topographical features such as tors, specific areas of moorland (ie East Moor), rivers, and streams.

The remains are discussed by type, but wherever possible the chronological sequence is outlined in more detail. All of the remains shown on these maps are referred to by site or area name or by grid reference. They have all been planned at a scale of at least 1:2500, and detailed plans and descriptions are stored in the Cornwall Sites and Monuments Record or in the National Archaeological Record, RCHME.

1   Long cairns (*Fig 17*)

Bearah Common

(SX 26307433) Linkinhorne, 285m above OD (Fig 17 no 2). Discovered in 1983 by Dr Gask of Cawsand and surveyed by N Quinnell in 1985.

The long cairn is a rounded trapezoidal platform, orientated almost due east–west. Part of the west end and south side has been disturbed by a recently improved (1983) quarry track. The mound is 28m long, 14.5m wide at the east end and c 5–6m at the west end, now reduced to 3m. It is 0.3m high at the west and 0.6m at the east end. Apart from one orientated slab, 0.5m high, on the north there is little to indicate any formal edge around the top of the platform perimeter.

Centrally placed within the east end, an area about 5 × 3m is occupied by stones of a collapsed and ruined chamber. Two post-like stones up to 1.3m wide and 2.4m long lean against an almost flat slab 1m wide and 2.7m long; north of this is an upright slab, 1m high, 2.7m long and 0.3m thick. A number of small recumbent slabs lie to the north–east, and south of the main structure are three upright slabs, protruding up to 0.4m, spaced around the west side. It is not clear what form the chamber took, except that it was probably box-like, being c 2.5 × 1.5m with a capstone on top. The millstone roughout a few metres to the south may have been made from it. Other upright and leaning stones may be the remains of an encircling kerb.

The structure is twice the size of the average Bodmin Moor cist and appears to demonstrate that at least here the chamber had always been a visible architectural feature. The latter, though ruined, does not appear to have been robbed. Apart from two pits dug in the mound, the cairn is essentially intact.

Catshole long cairn

(SX 17147828) Altarnun, 338m above OD (Fig 17 no 3). Discovered by P Herring (Herring 1983) in 1980 and surveyed by Herring and M Fletcher (RCHME) respectively.

The trapezoidal cairn is orientated north–north–east to south–south–west along the contour just below the crest of a fairly steep moorland hillslope, scattered with large granite boulders. The long cairn measures approximately 16m long by 3m wide at its south end and 5.5m wide at its north end. The cairn material is no more than 0.5m high. Unevenly spaced low orthostats and slabs (less than 0.55m high) define the two long sides. At the north end are the remains of a 'facade' of what originally would have been taller stones. Two central orthostats 0.95m high (one now fallen) are flanked by two taller (now fallen) orthostats some 1.6m long. In the middle section of the cairn are several upright stones, apparently defining a square compartment (4 × 4m), occupying the whole width of the cairn. A poorly defined turf-covered stony mound, which contains at least one large grounder, is evident towards the north end of the interior and may be all that remains of the cairn mound proper, or the remnants of what was originally the more substantial part of the long cairn at its facade.

A low boulder and stone bank no more than 0.2m high, perhaps robbed, approaches the cairn from the south and skirts its west side, having apparently turned sharply to meet the cairn rather than to avoid it. It continues for a short distance to the north. Twenty metres to the west is a substantial Cornish hedge (stone-faced earth wall) marking the parish boundary between St Breward and Altarnun parishes. It is likely that the cairn and adjacent bank have been extensively robbed to build and maintain this boundary.

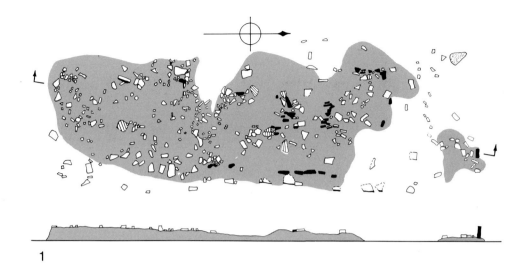

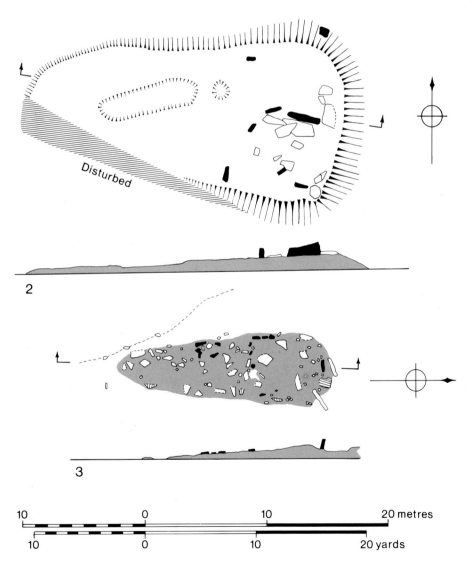

Fig 17   Long cairns: 1, Louden, SX 14018032; 2, Bearah Common, SX 26307433, chambered long cairn; 3, Catshole, SX 17147828 (Vertical scale enchanced × 2)

Louden long cairn

(SX 14018032) St Breward, 304m above OD (Fig 17 no 1). Discovered in 1976 by N Quinnell and reinterpreted and surveyed as a long cairn by CAU in 1984.

The long cairn is a low mound of stones orientated north–south along the contour on the lower edge of the north–east slope of Louden Hill. It lies close to the saddle linking Louden Hill to Roughtor, above the boggy head of a tributary of the De Lank river, and is conspicuous in the sense that it is overlooked by large areas of Louden Hill and Roughtor.

The mound is 30m long by 12m wide at the north and 8m wide at the south. The cross profile is asymmetrical because of the slope; on the east side it is 0.55m high but on the west it merges into the slope. The cairn can be divided into four sections, with remains of a kerb of upright slabs running for much of the eastern side set within the mound slope.

1   *South end*   Although mutilated at the end and in the south–west corner, the structure consists of a rectangular compartment (*c* 3.5 × 9m) defined on the west and east by low parallel banks with at least one edge stone, and on the north by stones on edge.

2   *Middle*   Part of the mound edge has been dug away (or it never existed) to give access to another compartment of smaller proportions (*c* 3.5 × 7.0m), also loosely defined by upright stones at the north end.

3   *North end*   An apparently mutilated area defined on the west by edging stones and on the south by an ill-defined jumble of upright or leaning stones.

4   *Transverse block*   This lies 6m north of the visible mound and slightly east of its central axis.

It is understandable that this was interpreted by the OS Archaeology Division and by the RCHME air survey as some form of twin structure, perhaps of medieval date. The Louden deserted medieval settlement lies only 200m to the west and two of its boundary banks pass each side of the cairn. The mound appears to be badly disturbed, but does not conform to known longhouse or associated structure types. Like the Catshole long cairn (Fig 17 no 3) it appears to have some form of internal structure, in this case two compartments, but this may be due to robbing for stone, as may be the gap on the east side.

In the absence of dating evidence, the mound is assumed to be a long cairn, with an internal structure of cellular form, but no apparent chamber. The detached transverse stone at the north end may be a form of blocking stone.

Discussion

The number of known long cairns in the South–West increased significantly in the early 1980s. Several were recognised on Dartmoor (Herring 1983), as well as the three new ones on Bodmin Moor. None produced any dating evidence but a date around 3000 BC may be inferred. There is increasing evidence for third-millennium and earlier activity on the Moor, notably from stray finds of Neolithic flints, particularly around Dozmary Pool and Siblyback Lake, but also from excavated evidence. Reassessment of the wartime excavations of C K Croft Andrew on Davidstow Moor (Christie 1988) revealed some sherds of Grooved ware under one of the barrows. Mercer (1970) found a greenstone implement in the earliest layer at Stannon Down. There has also been speculation (Johnson and Rose 1982; Silvester 1979; R J Mercer 1981b) that perhaps the enclosures of Roughtor and Stowe's Pound (called 'tor enclosures' by Silvester, 1979) could be of an early date, perhaps as early as the fourth millennium BC. Clearly there was a Neolithic presence on the Moor, with the Trethevy chambered tomb on the south–east edge at SX 25946881 (Barnatt 1982). The four monuments may form two groupings: (1) Trethevy and Bearah Common on the south–east edge of the Moor, Bearah 1.7km north–north–east of Stowe's Pound and Trethevy 3.8km to the south; (2) the north–west area of the Moor, with Louden 0.7km south–south–west of Roughtor and Catshole 3.5km to the south–east.

2   Miscellaneous ritual monuments
(*Figs 18–20*)

'Embanked avenue', Craddock Moor, St Cleer (*SX 24377208; Fig 18*)

This enigmatic structure was discovered during the Prehistoric Society's Summer Conference in May 1984. It lies immediately north–east of Siblyback Reservoir in a shallow valley in open moorland near the foot of a gentle south–west slope at 290m above OD. The feature is *c* 55m long and consists of two sets of twin parallel banks separated by a level turf-covered area *c* 4m wide. The monument is levelled slightly into the slope, in particular the area between the stone banks. For much of their length the banks comprise parallel stone 'rims' 3–4m apart and up to 0.3m high, with bands of small earthfast boulders and fist-sized stones. Gaps in the banks (mostly opening inwards towards the centre) and traces of transverse banks and some transverse kerb stones suggest 'compartments' reminiscent of internal structures at Catshole and Louden long cairns. At the south–east end the banks become twin terminals with signs of kerbing around the ends. At the north–west end the terminals have been disturbed by tin-working pits, although there are suggestions of a terminal bank on the southern of the two ends.

The whole may be interpreted in two ways:

a   Two parallel banks *c* 0.6m high and *c* 60m long with kerb stones around the edges of each of the banks. Buried within the banks were transverse walls of upright stones. These banks were then robbed, leaving the rims of stony material marking where the bank edges used to be. The slightly depressed internal 'compartments' are the result of this robbing. Whether the robbing was in antiquity, perhaps for material to build the small cairns in the vicinity, or of more recent occurrence, is unknown. Apart from a medieval field over 100m to the west, and a few tin-prospecting pits, there is nothing to suggest the reason for robbing.

b Two parallel twin banks with terminal mounds at either end. Each side consisted of two parallel stone banks closed at either end with terminal mounds. Kerb stones defined the edges all around the outside, and between the banks were transverse banks, some with upright stones defining several compartments. Two such structures lay parallel and 4m apart with a levelled area in between.

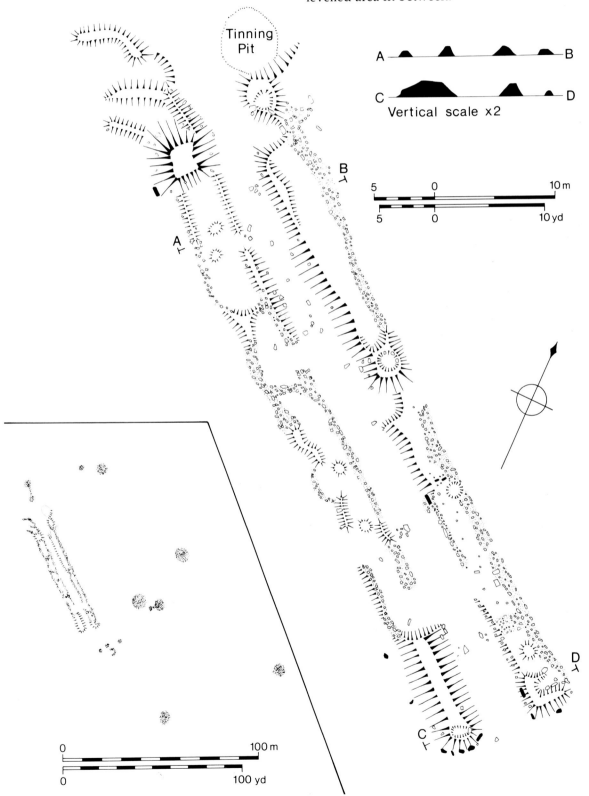

Fig 18   Embanked avenue, Craddock Moor, SX 24377208. It lies adjacent to a cairn cemetery and is partly disturbed by mining

The monument could have been massively disturbed, leaving only a gutted remnant, or alternatively, despite obvious disturbance in the past, what we see today is essentially its original structure. Whatever it may once have looked like, it is most unusual. It is unlike any medieval or post-medieval building found on the Moor and the medieval activity in its vicinity appears to be part of the outfield for farms along the Siblyback valley. No such structures are known in the industrial record for the Moor; and buildings connected with mineral and granite exploitation are sited close to extraction and processing areas. Although the area to the north–east around the Witheybrook valley and Caradon Hill has been intensively exploited, that in the vicinity of the monument has received only slight attention. Apart from slight indications of a hollow-way to the south, which presumably leads from the enclosed land to

the west out on to the Moor, there is nothing to suggest that it is not a prehistoric monument. In this context the presence of a cluster of cairns close by suggests a ritual function. The cursus monuments of Wessex perhaps form the closest parallels in plan, though not in scale. The monument has been called an 'embanked avenue', a term suggested by Professor T C Darvill (pers comm).

On the western slope below Showery Tor lies another monument (at SX 14728138) reminiscent of, though different in detail from, the Craddock Moor feature. It consists of two irregular banks over 90m long that point uphill towards the tor cairn at Showery Tor. The banks are between 3m and 8m apart and stand in places up to 0.7m high.

Here it may be tentatively noted that the Craddock Moor monument is aligned at right angles to the present north–east end of the Craddock Moor stone

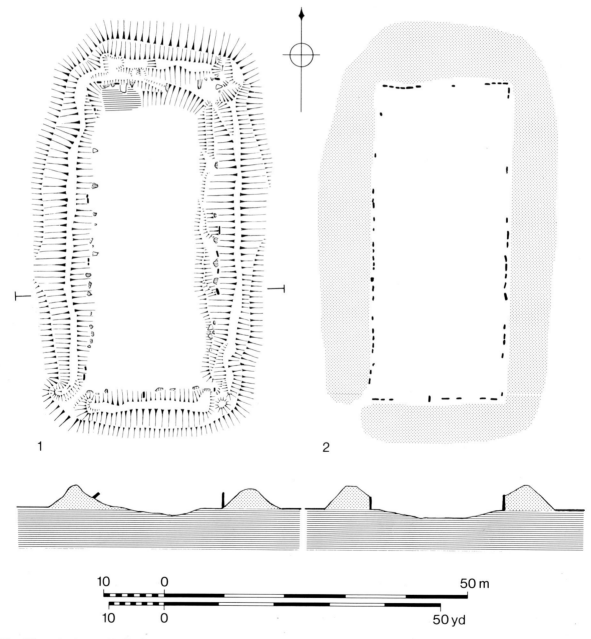

Fig 19 King Arthur's Hall, SX 12987765 (North top of drawing: vertical scale enhanced × 2) 1, field survey; 2, suggested reconstruction with fallen stones set upright

row (500m to the north–west), and to the south–west on the Craddock Moor stone circle; and beyond that to The Hurlers stone circles, and beyond that again to the summit of Caradon Hill, with its large barrow cemetery. This 'alignment' between five sets of perhaps broadly contemporary monuments is the only one that we have been able to identify, in addition to those already noted by Barnatt (1982), where stone circles and prominent tors are intervisible and align on cardinal points. The stone row is not visible from Caradon Hill, but Craddock Moor stone circle would have been visible on the skyline from the embanked avenue if the now recumbent stones had been originally upright. An alignment 3.6km long with very little deviation along its length is unusual and worth further study.

King Arthur's Hall, St Breward
(SX 12987765; Fig 19)

The monument lies just off the crest of an extensive moorland plateau on a slight southerly-facing slope at 262m above OD. The plateau continues as a flat ridge extending to the north–east towards the settlements and ritual monuments at Louden Hill.

A bank *c* 6m wide, 1m high externally, and 1.7m internally, with no sign of an outer or inner ditch, encloses a rectangular area 47 × 20m. The interior is lined by upright but not quite contiguous stones, now standing within the tail of the bank but originally forming a continuous retaining wall on the inside of the bank. In the centre of the south side, one of the upright stones is set transverse to the general line as if to mark a significant point. The equivalent place on the north side has been dis-

turbed and the stones removed. A number of retaining slabs stand to a height of 1.8m, but most are recumbent, leaning, or buried. A 2m gap in the south–west corner of the earthwork may be original, although it is not stone-lined and a slight rise here may indicate that the earthwork was originally continuous. The interior is dished, with traces of rough paving in the north–west corner, and presumably the bank material was dug from within. (Although above ground surface, the whole monument, in modern terms, has the appearance of an empty swimming pool.)

It has been suggested that this could be a manor pound (Herring 1986), lying as it does close to the boundary between the manors of Hamatethy and Blisland. Manor pounds are usually circular, and in Cornwall much larger (Professor A C Thomas, pers comm); also its construction seems unusually massive and unlike that of pounds elsewhere. Barnatt (1982, 196–7) suggests mortuary houses and Irish and Welsh henge variants as possible parallels. (See Ffynnod-brodyr, Dyfed: Grimes 1963, 140–1; Ffynnon Newydd, Dyfed: Williams 1984, 177–90). At present a medieval date seems more likely, though an earlier origin is possible.

Possible ritual enclosure, East Moor
(SX 22217784, Fig 20)

The structure is D-shaped, orientated north–north–west to south–south–east with maximum dimensions of 44.6 × 35m. It is formed of single stones, fairly consistent in their spacing at about 1.5m, but often erratic in alignment, being up to 0.5m off a reasonable curve. Forty-two stones are visible, almost all protruding only 0.1m above the turf; a similar number are visible only as turf humps. There is no obvious entrance, but the perimeter is broken for 16m in the extreme north–west by what appears to have been peat digging. The site does not resemble prehistoric field boundaries and is at least 1km from the nearest settlement; but it is within 150m of the East Moor stone row and 200m of a fine platform cairn at the summit of the spur. Its construction is reminiscent of stone circles and stone rows, and it has therefore been tentatively identified as a ritual enclosure.

3   Standing stones, standing stones in cairns, stone settings

(Some of these are illustrated in Fig 24, nos 33, 34, 35, 36, and Fig 25 no 15; and their locations are shown on Maps 1 and 3, Figs 29 and 30. Table 5 gives a list of these monuments on Bodmin Moor.)

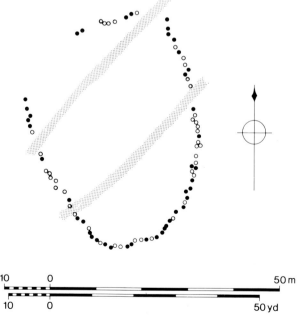

10   0   50 m

10   0   50 yd

Fig 20   Possible ritual enclosure on East Moor, SX 22217784. (Solid dots indicate visible stones; open circles, concealed stones; stipple, later trackways)

Deliberately set upright stones are familiar in the South–West. Menhirs or longstones are found in some numbers in West Penwith, Carnmenellis, the Lizard, Hensbarrow Downs, St Breock Downs and

Table 5   Standing stones and other variants

No	NGR	Parish	Width	Breadth	Height	Comment
Standing stones						
1	SX 11338197	Advent	1.0	0.6	3.0	
2	SX 14448182	St Breward	0.5	0.5	1.7	
3	SX 12437281	Blisland	1.3	0.3	1.6	
4	SX 19976953	St Neot	1.2	0.8	2.8	
5	SX 25717143	Linkinhorne/	0.4	0.3	2.0	
		St Cleer	0.4	0.3	2.0	
6	SX 23907113	St Cleer	0.6	0.4	1.3	
7	SX 24077384	St Cleer	0.9	0.6	2.4	
8	SX 21307952	Altarnun	1.15	0.9	2.5	
9	SX 20307725	Altarnun	destroyed			
10	SX 22157747	Altarnun	0.4	0.3	(2.7)	Recumbent
Standing stones in cairns or beside cairns						
1	SX 13707974	St Breward	0.8	0.2	1.4	Fig 24 no 33; 1 leaning, 1 upright in a slight mound
2	SX 17547787	Altarnun	0.4–0.7	0.1–0.4	0.2–0.4	Fig 25 no 2; 5 stones in line with a possible one on the cairn crest
3	SX 12527274	Blisland	–	–	0.4–1.8	A line of 3 (or 4) stones close by a cairn
4	SX 18016992	St Neot	1.1	0.1	0.9	2 large
			0.6	0.3	(1.6)	orthostats (one recumbent) in a stone mound
Stone settings						
1	SX 23027862	Altarnun				Fig 24 no 36
2	SX 12587292	Blisland				Fig 24 no 35
3	SX 12518007	St Breward				

Bodmin Moor (see Johnson 1980, 148, fig 2; Barnatt 1982, Appendix G, 259–61, for distributions). Standing stones within and buried by cairns or barrows are becoming more familiar (Miles 1975; Griffith 1984), but there are other forms, recognised on Bodmin Moor, that need explanation. There are six types on the Moor, perhaps not originally conceived as specific types but rather as variations on a theme of upright stones, as discussed here under the following headings:

a   Isolated standing stones
b   Standing stones with associated settings
c   Stone settings
d   Standing stones within and beneath cairns
e   Standing stones in the kerb of cairns
f   Standing stones protruding above the cairn mound

a   Isolated standing stones

These do not generally appear to be closely integrated with settlements and fields, but rather to lie on the edges of Barnatt's 'functional' areas, or deep within what he has termed 'sacred' areas (Barnatt 1982, 109); that is, those areas set apart from settlements – the plateaus, watersheds, and hilltops – that contain large burial and other ritual monuments.

The stones often stand just outside the settlement foci, and appear to mark the boundary edge of the settlement area. They could be markers to show the general line of access as, for example, stone crosses do in the medieval period. At SX 24077384 (see Map 1), a stone stands on the watershed between the Witheybrook valley to the east and the head of the Siblyback valley to the west. The Siblyback settlement lies adjacent, to the north. This gap is the only route northwards from Craddock Moor to the west

side of the Witheybrook catchment. At SX 14448182 (see Maps 1 and 3), a stone stands a little beyond the extensive fields and settlements on the northern slopes of Roughtor. There are no settlements for many kilometres to the north. The stone would act as a guidepost (several deep hollow-ways of presumed post-prehistoric date pass close by, giving evidence of a well-used track from Davidstow in the north towards Stannon, Louden, and all points south to St Breward) and a marker, lying close as it does to a variety of cairns and enclosures. Excavations elsewhere (Miles 1975, 10–12; Barnatt 1982, 95–102) can give no closer dating than the earlier part of the Bronze Age.

Many other stones, both on Bodmin Moor and elsewhere, are more clearly in 'sacred' areas. The standing stones around the Merry Maidens stone circle in West Penwith are part of a ritual landscape, the components of which include stone circles, standing stones, cists, barrows, and an entrance grave. Until the eighteenth century these ritual monuments were in moorland; the associated settlements were presumably located in the same area as the medieval farms, around the moorland edges. On Bodmin Moor a similar situation may be identified, with stones standing amongst cairns and ritual monuments along the more obvious watershed 'ridgeways' deep in the moorland zone. The menhirs on Trehudreth Common (SX 20307725) lie above and beyond the settlement zone, close to large cairns, stone rows, and other monuments. The stone at Spettigue (SX 21307952) lies on a ridge top, perhaps marking the east–west access across the moor, as in medieval times did the stone cross in the valley below, beside the modern A30. Standing stones have served many purposes in Cornwall in the past, from churchtown path markers to preaching places, from tinners' boundary stones to memorial stones; common sense demands a liberal interpretation of their prehistoric function which should encompass way-markers, boundary markers, memorial stones, and ritual foci.

b and c   Standing stones with associated settings, stone settings

More esoteric monuments might also have had a ritual function. On the slopes of Fox Tor (at SX 23027862), a setting of stones, upright and on edge, lies close to prehistoric huts (see Fig 24 no 35 for form and Map 3 for location); another setting of stones lies around the base of a 'truncated' menhir (SX 12587292) on Trehudreth Common (Fig 24 no 36), adjacent to the stone row, standing stones, and cairns; a setting of four stones (SX 1250480072) stands 84m north–west of Stannon stone circle and is probably associated with it (Barnatt 1982, 169).

d   Standing stones within and beneath cairns

Upright stones within mounds have been reviewed by Miles (1975), including the cairns of Caerloggas III and Trenance Downs on Hensbarrow; and Griffith has noted another – the centre of cairn CR.IVB at Colliford on Bodmin Moor (Griffith 1984). Wooden posts are sometimes found, but such features are invisible in the field.

e   Standing stones in the kerb of cairns

Two examples of stones standing within low plat-

forms occur on the Moor, at Louden (SX 13707974) and St Neot (SX 18016992), each with two standing stones set firmly in the platforms (see Fig 23 nos 33, 34). The Louden example lies close to a settlement but is also adjacent to a cairn cemetery.

f   Standing stones protruding above the cairn mound

Several cairns with kerbs have a substantial stone along the edge, a feature also noted in several cairns in west central Wales (Leighton 1984, 322). One at SX 22417761 (Fig 25 no 15) has slight traces of a kerb and a recumbent stone 2.2m long at its edge. The cairn lies close to the East Moor stone row and the enigmatic enclosure (Fig 20), a further reminder that so many of these features lie in ritual or sacred areas.

4   Stone circles and stone rows

(*Figures 21 and 22 show the relative size and structure of these monuments. The monuments are described and then discussed. Table 6 summarises the details for stone rows.*)

Stone circles (*Fig 21*)

Sixteen are now known, since the discovery of a second circle at Leskernick (Herring, report in preparation). The two at King Arthur's Downs (SX 13457751; SX 13487750) are adjacent, like the pairs at Tregeseal in Penwith and the Nine Maidens at Wendron; the triple circles at The Hurlers (SX 25827139)

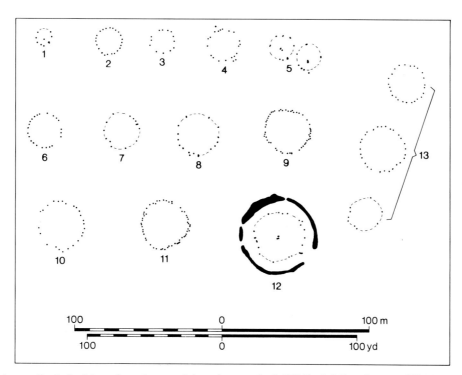

Fig 21   Stone circles on Bodmin Moor (north top of drawing, scale 1:2500): 1, Nine Stones, SX 23617815; 2, Leaze, SX 13677725; 3, Leskernick II, SX 18587992; 4, Leskernick I, SX 18567952; 5, King Arthur's Downs I and II, SX 13457751 and SX 13487750; 6, Goodaver, SX 20877515; 7, Trippet Stones, SX 13127501; 8, Craddock Moor, SX 24867183; 9, Stannon, SX 12628001; 10, Louden, SX 13207949; 11, Fernacre, SX 14487998; 12, Stripple Stones, SX 14377521 (henge bank blocked in); 13, The Hurlers, SX 25827139

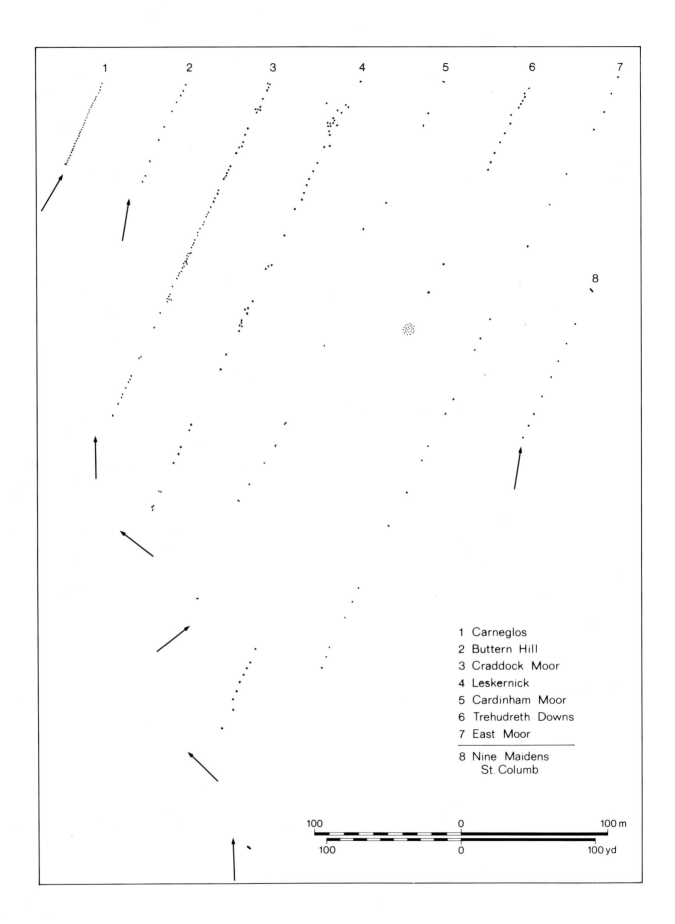

Fig 22   Stone rows in Cornwall (Leskernick after P Herring). All are on Bodmin Moor except Nine Maidens, St Columb. (Arrows denote north; see table 6 for details.)

are unique in Cornwall. The shape, build, and alignment of the circles have been examined by Burl (1976), and more recently by Barnatt (1980, 3–16; 1982, 51–75; 1984, 197–216). The Leskernick II circle is not easy to fit into the general picture as the scatter of surface stones makes identification difficult.

Of particular note is the circle henge known as the Stripple Stones (SX 14377521). The ring consists of four upright stones and the remains of nine others, with a large recumbent stone at the centre. Outside the ring of stones is a ditch with an external bank, both cut by a single entrance. The Trippet Stones circle on the moorland plateau below to the west is visible through the entrance, looking from the centre stone. The henge sits on a southerly spur 25m below the summit of Hawk's Tor, within an area defined by streams and bog to the east and west. The nearest settlements are on Brockabarrow Common, over 1 km to the south–east, and on Carkees Tor, 1km to the north. The henge lies in a sparsely populated area along the route that divides the Moor north to south. As with the presumably earlier long cairns, it is entirely uncertain whether there is associated settlement in the vicinity, as yet unrecognised, or whether the monument reflects use of an area of the Moor by a group based further away.

The Bodmin Moor circles are both regular and irregular. Barnatt (1982, 84) identifies two groups in the western part of the Moor:

a *Irregular circles*: Stannon, King Arthur's Downs, Fernacre, Stripple Stones
b *Regular circles*: Louden, Leaze, Trippet Stones

He suggests that one group may have replaced the other, although the sequence remains unclear.

Stone rows (*Fig 22*)

Since Fletcher discovered the stone row on Cardinham Moor in the 1970s (Fig 22 no 5), a further

six have been found, either through the survey (East Moor, N Quinnell; Carneglos, N Johnson; Trehudreth, P Rose and A Carter; Craddock Moor, M Fletcher) or work by others (Buttern Hill, F Griffith; Leskernick, P Herring). Table 6 gives their details. Bodmin Moor is now an important area for these monuments, but we must look to Dartmoor for a recent study of stone rows (Emmett 1979, 94–114). The main differences between the Bodmin and Dartmoor rows may be summarised thus:

a The Bodmin rows are generally longer

b The spacing between the stones is generally greater

c The rows lie on flat or nearly flat land, or along the contours

The Bodmin Moor rows, like the Dartmoor examples, are orientated in the north–east to south–west quadrants and exhibit certain noteworthy characteristics:

a If they are on a slope, however slight, the lower end is the southerly end.

b Six of the seven rows have taller stones, transverse stones, or other structures at the southern terminal. (These are listed in Table 6.)

c There are two distinct types of row: (1) those with small stones and small gaps between the stones (Fig 22 nos 1–4, 6); (2) those with larger stones and larger gaps between the stones (Fig 22 nos 5, 7).

A row at Longstone Farm, Lezant (SX 36258038), discovered a few years ago by Miss G King (CAU SMR), has now been destroyed so details are not available. The Nine Maidens, St Columb (Fig 22 no 8), consists of large stones with wide gaps between them, and a standing stone (the Magi stone) several

Table 6 Stone rows in Cornwall

No	Name	NGR of ends	Length (m)	Alignment	Average height of stones (m)	Average distance between stones (m)	Topographical setting	Terminal features
1	Carneglos	SX 19887737–19877743	59	N–S	0.15	1.6	level along contours	tallest stone at S end
2	Buttern Hill	SX 16938158–16958165	77	NNE–SSW	0.45	3.5	level valley watershed	tallest stone at S end
3	Craddock Moor	SX 23967203–24087224	244	NE–SW	0.3	0.9	very slight slope, S end lower	
4	Leskernick Hill	SX 18707986–19017991	317	ENE–WSW	0.2	4.5	level plateau	? stone setting at S end
5	Cardinham Moor	SX 12997155–12817189	380	NW–SE	1.3	14.0	very slight slope, S end lower, ends not intervisible	tallest stone at S end
6	Trehudreth Downs	SX 12497295–12837306	460	ENE–WSW	0.25	4.5	very slight slope, S end lower, ends not intervisible	transverse stone at S end
7	East Moor	SX 22377785–22577822	560	NNE–SSW	1.0	10.0	crosses a slight plateau saddle	
8	Nine Maidens	SW 93636754–93696763	107	NNE–SSW	1.6	12.5	shallow watershed	? large standing stone 600m to NNE

hundred metres to the north may have been a terminal. This is at the northerly or uphill end.

The rows do not appear to point to any significant visual landmarks; no astronomical investigations have been undertaken. It may be significant that stone rows, like stone circles, divide clearly into two distinct types: those consisting of large stones spaced wide apart, and those in which many more but smaller and more closely-spaced stones were used. It is not clear if this difference is due to local custom or simply to the varying availability of large or small stones. Like stone circles, however, rows lie outside settlement areas in broadly similar locations, along or slightly below the watersheds in areas easily accessible from settlement along the valley sides. Only one row is very close to a settlement: at Craddock Moor (Fig 30) the row runs into an area of prehistoric fields; a medieval enclosure surrounds the row and cultivation ridges cross it. It seems, however, that the prehistoric fields encroach upon its north-east end. Here we may have an example of a field system encroaching upon a redundant monument.

5   Cairns (*Figs 23–7*)

Introduction

All cairns on the Moor have been surveyed and measured; the diameters, heights of stones and mounds, and structural features have been noted. As illustrated here, the vertical scale has been doubled to show more clearly the cross-section. Structural features have been incorporated on a 'presence or absence' basis: thus if part of a kerb has been noted, then a kerb is drawn as if it existed around the whole of the cairn. Cists, grounders (natural boulders *in situ*), and tors have been shown by standard conventions. Selected examples surveyed at scales greater than 1:500 are drawn as measured plans. The cairns illustrated represent the majority with obvious visible structure; those which are simple mounds or have only cists have not been included. The cross-sections are intended to given an indication of the variety encountered and to provide a starting point for a more comprehensive typology for the South–West. Excepting those cairns that are drawn with ground plans, all the cross-sections are illustrative sketches and whilst the horizontal measurements are accurate the vertical measurements are estimates only. The structural details are likewise also sketched for clarity.

The most recent survey of cairns on Bodmin Moor (Trehair 1978) identified 225 monuments; 15 more were subsequently identified by the Ordnance Survey Archaeology Division, and the present survey has identified a further 114, making a provisional total of 354. This substantial increase includes an unexpected number of large cairns, although most are small, in many cases less than 5m in diameter.

Trehair's classification is based on that developed by Lynch (1972) for Welsh monuments, but in the light of detailed fieldwork is not readily assignable to Bodmin Moor. In part this is due to reinterpretation

of known cairns and in part to the identification of forms that do not fit such a typology. In addition, sustained damage has often made interpretation difficult.

Excavations at Crowdy Marsh (Trudgian 1977a), SX 14018342; Draynes (Wainwright 1965), SX 209693; on Stannon Down (Harris *et al* 1984), SX 13448101; on Davidstow Moor (C K Croft Andrew's excavations, published by Christie (1988), SX 155845; on East Moor – Clitters Cairn (Brisbane and Clews 1979), SX 24147821; at Colliford (Griffith 1984), SX 176710; and in other parts of Cornwall, and also in Devon, have shown the many structural forms that exist beneath apparently unimpressive exteriors. The majority have some form of inner kerbing, in many cases several such rings, whilst small cairns cover burial remains. Quinnell has reviewed the evidence for the presence of ring cairns (Miles 1975), and it is clear that for most the external appearance gave no indication of what lay inside. Therefore, although it is possible to give a factual account of the many forms that can be seen on the Moor, it must be remembered that in most cases the surface appearance represents only the last structural phase.

The many structural elements encountered can be summarised as follows, bearing in mind that many cairns possess a combination of several elements:

1   *Mounds*
bow-shaped, slightly domed, flat-topped
central or offset on platforms
large flat-topped mounds – (platforms)

2   *Kerbs*
delimiting a mound
set just inside the mound
internal kerbs, in some cases several kerb rings
kerbs of stones that are contiguous or open
kerbs of uprights, slabs on edge, boulders, or coursed walling
kerb stones that are vertical or deliberately tilted inward or outward
kerbs that edge rim banks, or banks set well within the rim

3   *Cists*
central or offset
above ground within the mound material or sunk into the ground
visible as an upstanding feature
buried beneath the mound surface

4   *Ring banks*
with no internal mound (ring cairn)
on the rim of a platform (rim bank)
set inside the edge of a platform

5   *Cairn foci*
cists
standing stones
grounders (natural boulders *in situ*)
tors

Two hundred and fifty cairns have been surveyed at

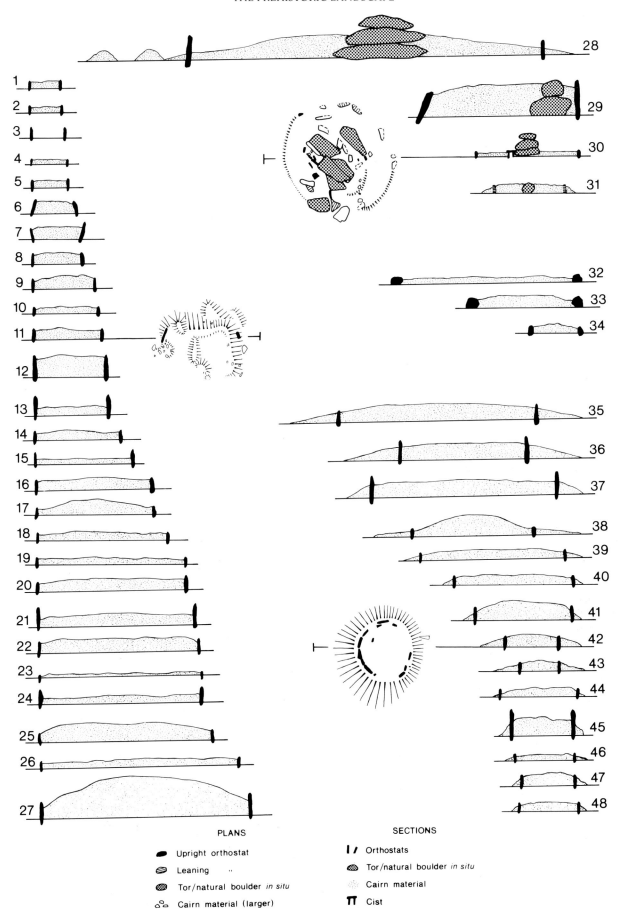

PLANS

Upright orthostat

Leaning "

Tor/natural boulder *in situ*

Cairn material (larger)

SECTIONS

Orthostats

Tor/natural boulder *in situ*

Cairn material

Cist

Fig 23   Cairns on Bodmin Moor (1): 1–27, slab or orthostatic kerbs; 28–30, kerbed cairns with central tor/rock; 31, as above, but with coursed kerb; 32–34, boulder kerbs; 35–48, internal kerbs. (Scale: horizontal 1:300, vertical ✕ 2; see Appendix 2 for locations)

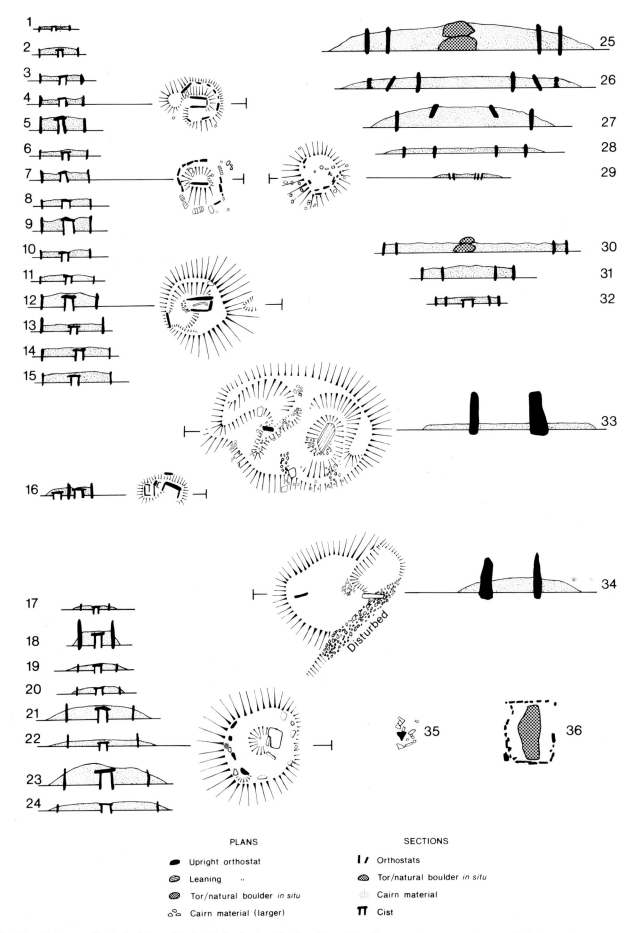

PLANS

- Upright orthostat
- Leaning   "
- Tor/natural boulder *in situ*
- Cairn material (larger)

SECTIONS

- Orthostats
- Tor/natural boulder *in situ*
- Cairn material
- Cist

Fig 24   Cairns on Bodmin Moor (2): 1–15, kerbed with cist; 16, with adjacent cist; 17–24, internal kerb with cist; 25–29, multiple internal kerbs; 30–32, multiple kerbs; 33–34, platforms with standing stones; 35, standing stone with stone setting around it; 36, grounder (earthfast boulder) with kerb. (Scale: horizontal 1:300, vertical ✗ 2; see Appendix 2 for locations.)

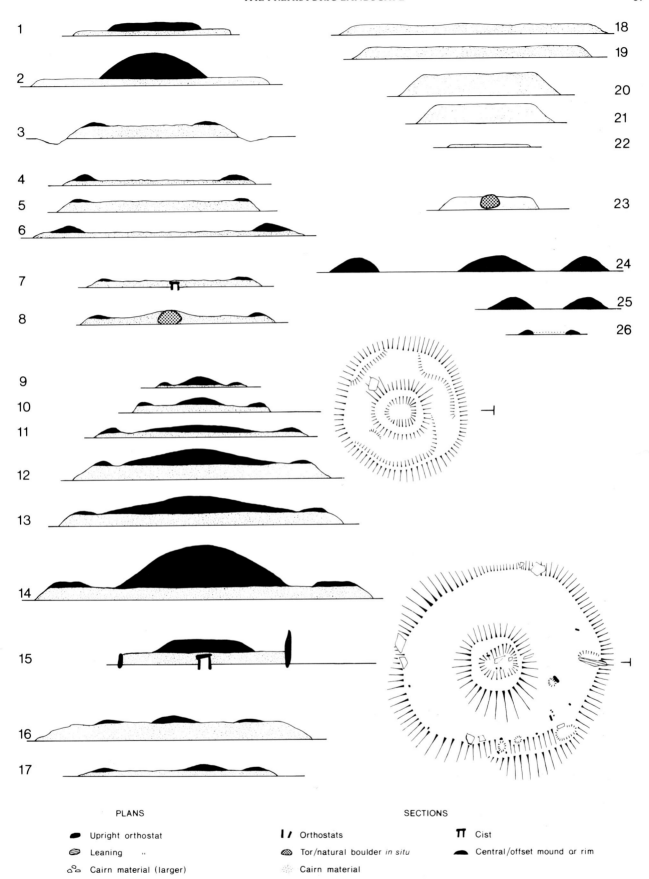

Fig 25 *Cairns on Bodmin Moor (3): 1–2, platform with central mound; 3–8, rimmed platform; 9–14, rimmed platform with central mound; 15, kerbed, standing stone, central mound, cist; 16–17, other rimmed platforms; 18–23, platforms; 24–26, ring cairns. (Scale: horizontal 1:300, vertical × 2; see Appendix 2 for locations.)*

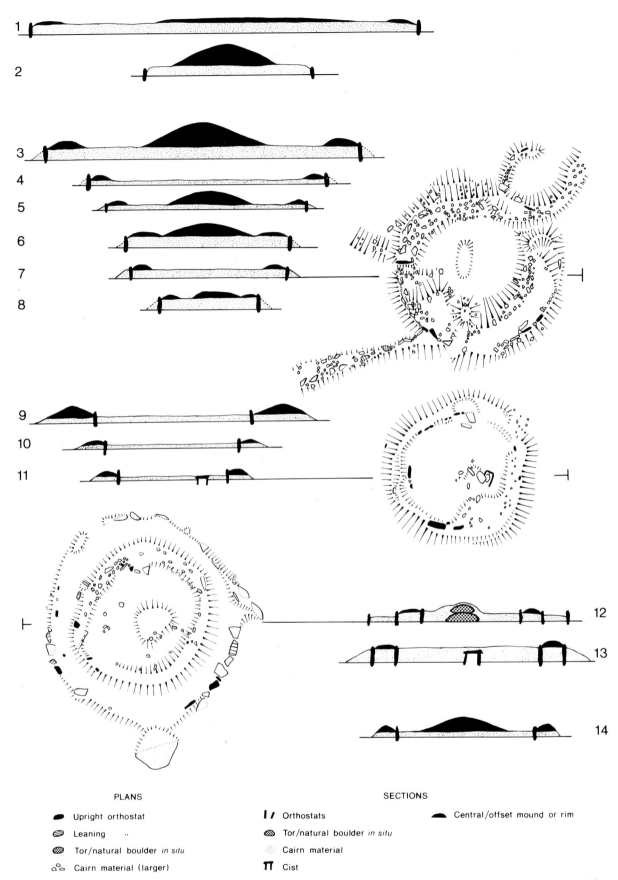

Fig 26   Cairns on Bodmin Moor (4): 1, kerbed, rimmed platform with offset mound; 2, kerbed platform with central mound; 3–8, kerbed, rimmed platform with or without central or offset mound (cairn material outside the kerb); 9–11, rimmed platforms with internal kerb; 12–13, rimmed platforms with central features and multiple kerbs; 14, rimmed platform with internal kerb and central mound. (Scale: horizontal 1:300, vertical × 2; see Appendix 2 for locations.)

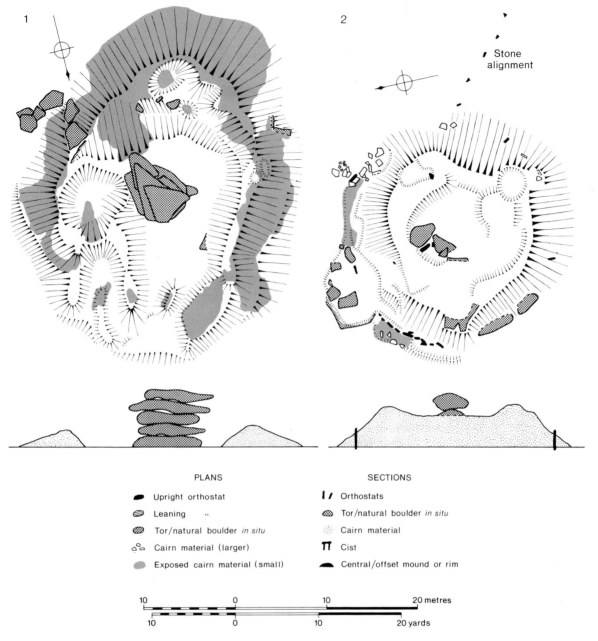

Stone alignment

PLANS

- ⬛ Upright orthostat
- 🫓 Leaning "
- ◍ Tor/natural boulder *in situ*
- ⚬°⚬ Cairn material (larger)
- ⬤ Exposed cairn material (small)

SECTIONS

- I / Orthostats
- ◍ Tor/natural boulder *in situ*
- ⋮ Cairn material
- π Cist
- ◣ Central/offset mound or rim

10   0   10   20 metres

10   0   10   20 yards

Fig 27   Cairns at Showery Tor and Tolborough Tor: 1, Showery Tor, SX 14928131; a substantial stone bank surrounds the tor; 2, Tolborough Tor, SX 17547787; a rimmed platform surrounds and overlies part of the tor. An alignment of five upright stones approaches the cairn from the south-east (top right). The shaded areas are exposed stone rubble. (Scale: horizontal 1:400, vertical × 2)

1:2500, with detailed measurements noted on the record sheets; 30 at 1:1000; and 70 at 1:250, 1:200, 1:100, or exceptionally at 1:50; 4 lie outside the survey area or have been destroyed.

Structure

The majority of cairns have no visible structure (166=47%); a further 24 (=7%) have only cists visible; and 2 (=0.6%) show evidence of a surrounding ditch (one of these is Triple Barrow, SX 13628346, where three conjoined barrows are surrounded by a single ditch). Small cairns are largely unstructured (apart from cists) or are single-kerbed cairns (with or without cists). Large cairns are also unstructured, or

have multiple kerbs, or belong to the various types of platform cairn. With the exception of the simple cairns, the larger the cairn, the more likely it is to be complex.

Cists

Trehair identified 15 cists on the Moor, a figure now increased to 58. Many are indicated only by slight traces of sidestones. It is assumed that numerous others are buried and invisible within cairns. The cists measure *c* 0.75 × 1.5m internally and are orientated up and down slope. The size of the cist stones is probably dependent on what was readily available, with single rather than several slabs being preferred for the sides. The cists' floors are not paved with slabs. The majority may originally have been buried in the mounds, or visible merely as flat slabs on the surface. A few cists, however, must have been prominent architectural features clearly visible above their mounds. A good example is at Louden (SX 13297986), where a large cist of almost megalithic proportions sits in a very low mound. Downhill to the east in a cemetery of small cairns is a kerbed cairn with central cist (SX 13887976, Fig 24 no 16), with a second smaller cist adjoining the side outside the kerb. At present it seems that cist orientation is too variable to be significant, and apart from the repeated presence of five stones for making a cist (capstone and four sidestones), the only general characteristic shared by the majority is their rectangular shape.

Kerbs

Many cairns have single external revetment kerbs, or kerbs just within the cairn margin (Fig 23 nos 1–48; Fig 24 nos 1–24). The majority are orthostatic or slab kerbs, but some are boulder kerbs (Fig 23 nos 32–4) and one a coursed wall kerb (Fig 23 no 31). Those enclosing cists are all less than 10m in diameter.

A number of cairns have single external kerbs incorporating tors or grounders as foci (Fig 23 nos 28–31).

Eight cairns have two or more internal kerbs (Fig 24 nos 25–32), either as concentric rings (Fig 24 no 29) or as double or triple rings with some of the stones deliberately tilted inwards or outwards (Fig 24 nos 26, 27).

A variety of cairns contain or incorporate standing stones, either in pairs within the mound (Fig 24 nos 33–4), or as part of the kerb (Fig 23 no 15).

Ring cairns (*Fig 25 nos 24–6*)

These comprise circular banks with no build-up inside. A spectacular example, Showery Tor cairn (Fig 27 no 1), one of the largest and most prominent cairns on the Moor, has a most attractive tor in the centre (similar to, though much larger than, the one on Rippon Tor, Dartmoor).

Platform cairns (*Figs 25, 26*)

These are all over 10m in diameter and comprise the following types:

a *Simple cairns*

b *Kerbed cairns*

c (1) *Rimmed platform cairns*
   (2) *Kerbed rimmed platform cairns*

d *Ring cairns*

e *Tor cairns*: any of the above incorporating a natural outcrop

All are with or without additional mounds, kerbs, cists, grounders, or tors. Quinnell has noted the existence of platform barrows, referring to them as enclosure barrows where the enclosure had been infilled but not overlain by the mound (Miles 1975). The 'ring cairns' on Davidstow Moor and at Botrea, Sancreed, in West Penwith are of the ruined platform cairn type. Much more fieldwork needs to be done in the South–West before a satisfactory typology is evolved. The descriptive terms given above for the various structural forms (eg kerb, rim, platform) have been kept as simple as possible and are not intended to be immutable. A satisfactory nomenclature must include both field and excavated structural evidence. It is clear, however, that the various types of platform cairn are common on the Moor, and in their most developed form are reminiscent of the disc and bell barrows of Wessex.

Dimensions

Simple cairns (*160*)

These vary between 2m and 34m in diameter and from less than 0.5m to 2.5m in height. Of those recorded, 92 are less than 10m in diameter, as are 23 out of 26 with visible cists. With the exception of a few massive cairns (the Brown Willy summit cairns, Carburrow cairns, Brown Gelly cairns, and the Rillaton Barrow), the majority are not bowl-shaped, except for several at the smaller end of the range, but have a flattened profile. This may simply be due to the lack of sufficient available stone; the larger mounds would require enormous quantities. General disturbance, robbing, and collapse has also reduced the cairn profiles.

Kerbed cairns (*50*)

The majority (30) are less than 10m in diameter, as are all those with cists (24).

Multiple-kerbed cairns: platform cairns

The majority of the former and all the latter are larger than 10m in diameter.

Dating

There are radiocarbon samples from nine cairns on Bodmin Moor, eight of whose mean dates range from 2162 to 1746 Cal BC (tabulated in Christie 1988, 164). This would appear to provide the principal date range of cairn building on the Moor. Some may be earlier, as at Davidstow (Christie 1988, 164) where site xxvi (22) gave a mean date of 2740 Cal BC. The date range for settlements is likely to be longer.

Location

Large cairns (over 10m in diameter)

The majority of large cairns lie on watersheds (plateaus and hillslopes or hillcrests) and in 'sacred' areas (as identified by Barnatt, 1982), some distance from settlement. In general there is no obvious preference for particular types of large cairn in any one area; two or more such cairns close together are often of varying type, as the following example indicates:

Carkeet, SX 225727: 2 simple, 1 platform
Caradon Hill, SX 272705: many simple, 2 kerbed,
   3 possible platforms, 1 tor
Sharptor, SX 256737: 1 kerbed, 2 simple
Manor Common, SX 129742: 1 kerbed, 1 simple
Bray Down, SX 189821: 2 kerbed (1 tor), 1 platform
Buttern Hill, SX 175816: 1 platform, 1 simple,
   1 kerbed, 1 ring cairn and 1 small simple
High Moor, SX 163811: 1 platform, 1 simple
Brown Gelly, SX 196727: 4 simple, 1 platform

In some areas, however, specific types of *large* cairn are preferred, for instance:

Treswallock Downs, SX 117784: 3 kerbed (2 with
   multiple kerbs)
Central East Moor, SX 224777: 2 platforms
Ridge, East Moor, SX 242780: 2 kerbed
Tresellern, SX 230764: 2 simple
Catshole, Tolborough, and Codda, SX 170784,
   SX 175778, SX 172785 (all kerbed)
The Beacon, SX 197793: 2 platforms

Many cairns lie in visually prominent positions visible for miles around, for example: Brown Willy (SX 159797); Roughtor (SX 146809); Alex Tor (SX 118788); Brown Gelly (SX 196727); Sharptor (SX 256737); Buttern Hill (SX 175816); Carburrow Tor (SX 155708); Pridacoombe (SX 162771); Brockabarrow (SX 159751); Blacktor (SX 157736).

Some large cairns are not prominent and lie on flat land, perhaps only visible locally. These tend to be in 'sacred' areas – Trehudreth Downs and Greenbarrow Downs (SX 125729); Cardinham Moor (SX 135711); East Moor (SX 224777); King Arthur's Downs (SX 126779).

A few large cairns lie adjacent to ritual monuments, as at Trehudreth Downs stone row, East Moor stone row, Goodaver stone circle, and Leskernick stone circles and stone row.

Elsewhere there are no large cairns in the immediate vicinity (within 100m) of ritual monuments. Cairns are scattered throughout the Craddock Moor and Stowe's Pound area, not concentrated around the stone row or stone circles. There are no large cairns adjacent to the Buttern Hill, Cardinham Moor, or Carneglos stone rows, or to the Trippet Stones circle, Stripple Stones, Nine Stones, Stannon, Fernacre, King Arthur's Downs, or Leaze circles.

Many of the more prominent rocky tors do not have cairns on them (ie tor cairns using the tor as the focus), for example Brown Willy, Louden Hill, Fox Tor, Trewortha Tor, Kilmar Tor, Newel Tor, Sharptor, Bearah Tor, Smallacoombe Tor, Hill Tor, Colvannick Tor, and Lamlavery Rock. In fact, of those mentioned, only Brown Willy has any cairns on it, although Sharptor and Bearah Tor have cairns on

their spines at a distance from the tors themselves. It seems strange that the most famous of all the Bodmin Moor tors, the Cheesewring (SX 258724), should have no tor cairn; perhaps it was robbed to build Stowe's Pound, or Stowe's Pound itself was a sufficient focus.

We are left with no obvious patterns beyond a few simple observations:

a   In areas devoid of surface stone (eg Cardinham Moor) many of the cairns seem to be of the simple variety.

b   The larger cairns generally lie outside the area of settlement, and are located on ridges and plateaus.

c   Where large cairns cluster they are often of different types, with no obvious indications of degrees of importance, beyond the complexity and size of the monuments.

d   Excavated cairns invariably show a more complex internal structure than surface appearance indicates.

e   Many prominent locations clearly held no significance as cairn sites.

Small cairns (less than 10m diameter)

These concentrate on the edges of or within areas of settlement or cluster around ritual monuments. Those around ritual monuments are of the simple bowl type whilst the others are more variable.

The cairns near settlements and fields are concentrated in a few areas: the north–west corner of the Moor – Treswallock Downs, Stannon South, Stannon Down, Garrow Tor, Louden Hill, Butterstor, and Roughtor; Leskernick Hill; Twelve Men's Moor; Langstone Downs and Craddock Moor, Little Care Hill, Blacktor, Wardbrook (one small kerbed cairn below the fields, SX 253732), Muttons Downs. Such concentrations may be the result of differential survival. Many of the settlements that have no cairns are on the edge of enclosed land where cairns provide a most convenient source of walling stone. In addition, many prehistoric fields have been reused and cultivated in the medieval period and the cairns perhaps removed. In other areas mineral working may have destroyed cairns.

The cairns also occur in areas with clearance mounds. If a simple mound is particularly small and is clustered with others, it is tempting to call them clearance mounds, as for example at Codda Tor. In several cases there are no obvious fields nearby (eg Twelve Men's Moor, SX 247755), or the mounds occur in open moorland on one side of a boundary and in fields on the other (eg East Moor, SX 242783), or they occur in some fields but not in others equally stony. At Codda (SX 179793) the mounds lie outside a small area of huts and fields and have been regarded as clearance mounds only because they are small and have no structure.

The distinction between 'clearance cairns' and 'cairns' is often difficult to make. Some small mounds may have been the product of clearance before field boundaries were defined, others of later clearance where stone was dumped in piles for convenience; yet others could be of ritual significance (stone clearance perhaps perceived as being related to the success of a field). The many hundreds of clearance mounds found in areas of rig and furrow, however, served an obvious function, where immovable boulders were used as bases upon which to heap cultivation debris. In West Penwith there are many areas (eg Bosigran in Zennor, and Bosiliack in Madron) where clearance cairns of apparent prehistoric origin lie on boulders. This does not normally appear to be the case on Bodmin Moor.

Cairns in the landscape (*Figs 28–30*)

Three areas are shown in these Figures to illustrate the main differences: Leskernick, the Roughtor area, and the Craddock Moor, Stowe's Pound area.

Leskernick (*Fig 28*)

This well-preserved settlement occupies the southerly slope of a stony hill. A large cairn lies on the hilltop, and below the settlement is a ritual complex comprising two circles, a stone row and a large cairn. The larger cairns, including the two platforms to the

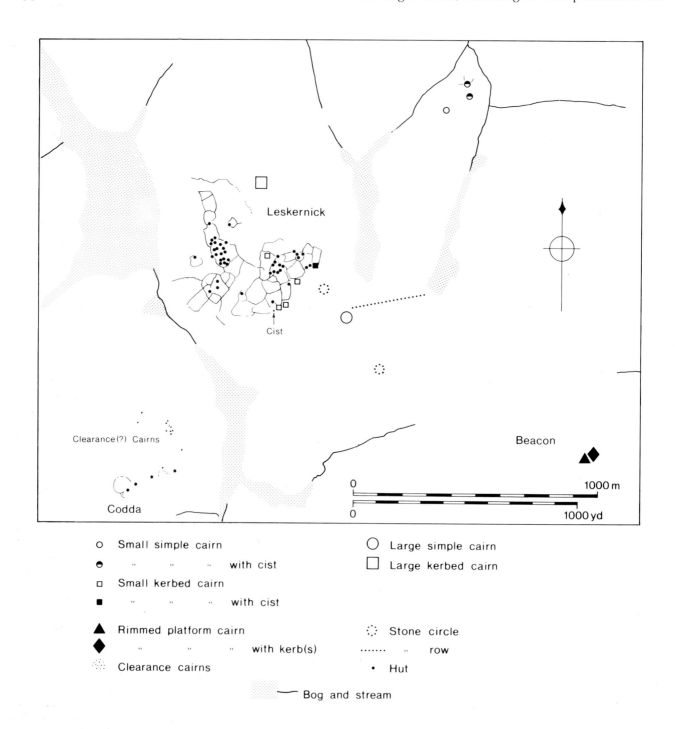

○ Small simple cairn	◯ Large simple cairn
◕ " " " with cist	☐ Large kerbed cairn
▫ Small kerbed cairn	
▪ " " " with cist	
▲ Rimmed platform cairn	⬭ Stone circle
◆ " " " with kerb(s)	⋯⋯ " row
Clearance cairns	• Hut

— Bog and stream

Fig 28   Cairns, ritual monuments, and prehistoric settlement around Leskernick Hill, SX 185799

south–east on Beacon Hill, lie apart from the settlement. Associated with the settlement are a cist and a number of very small cairns, less than 3m in diameter, which sit within the walls or immediately adjacent to them.

To the north–east, along a small spur between two streams, at SX 191807, are three small mounds, two of which have cists. Small lengths of wall appear to be associated with at least one of them. Comparable instances recur elsewhere. One of the cairns excavated (Harris *et al* 1984) on Stannon Down – SX 13408095, cairn 3 (see below, the Roughtor area, point D) – was associated and contemporary with an enclosure, and early air photographs show at least one other such enclosure now under the china clay tip. At Bunning's Park (SX 185718), a small length of walling immediately south–east of the Stuffle enclosure (prehistoric in its earliest phase) has two small cairns at either end and a hut close by; on the ridge between Louden Hill and King Arthur's Downs are two cairns with a wall between them (SX 132791); several other examples of small cairns and enclosures occur on the northern slopes of Roughtor, some of which have been noted elsewhere (Johnson 1980, 158 and fig 6).

The Roughtor area (*Fig 29*)

This area contains the majority of the small kerbed cairns, kerbed cairns with cists, and small simple cairns on Bodmin Moor, many of which cluster in cemeteries as at Louden, Stannon Down, Fernacre, and the north–west part of Roughtor. In addition there are numerous larger cairns of all types, not only in the cemeteries but spread evenly throughout the whole area, the largest and most elaborate lying on the Roughtor summit and the tors along its ridge. No clear pattern emerges as the complex of settlements and fields seems to include both large and small cairns.

The few examples of clear relationships between boundaries and cairns on Figure 29 are as follows:

A   The boundary fades away as if robbed on either side of a large cairn.

B   The boundary to the north appears to fade away as if robbed before it reaches the large cairn.

C   The boundary to the south butts against the kerb of the large cairn (see also Fig 15 feature D; Fig 25 no 7; Figs 46, 47).

D   As mentioned above, this cairn is contemporary with its small enclosure.

E   The three small kerbed cairns are part of the structure of the north–west entrance to the Roughtor enclosure (see Fig 31). Two other cairns lie adjacent to the south entrance.

Elsewhere on the Moor, cairns lie on the line of walls with no evidence of robbing on either side, suggesting that the cairns are earlier, as at Clitters cairn, SX 24147821 (Brisbane and Clews 1979); or are contemporary, as at Stannon Down, cairn 3 (see above). To complete the range of examples, two cairns adjacent to the boundary that runs up to Bearah Tor (SX 25337430, SX 24637441) show conflicting evidence: one appears to rob the boundary, while the other has been robbed to build the boundary.

There are clearly several phases of land allotment in this area. The larger cairns are set apart from the settlements but sometimes lie amongst the fields. The cemeteries of small cairns either stand alone, apart from settlements, or are associated with small enclosures. We would prefer to think of these as an early phase associated with the early accreted curvilinear fields. Gradually many cairns were absorbed within an expanding farming landscape. The larger cairns appear to represent the more impressive focal or prestige markers; the small ones are humble in appearance and may have a more local significance. The differences in size and complexity may reflect social importance, but in an area so intensively occupied it is difficult to believe that the precise location of cairns was not significant. Although many cairns, large and small, lie in unprominent positions, it was noticeable that some of the cemeteries appear prominently on the skyline but only when viewed from certain areas and settlements, not necessarily adjacent to them. In contrast, the Roughtor summit cairns are not only complex but very prominent, as if to mark or acknowledge the importance of the place.

Craddock Moor/Stowe's Pound (*Fig 30*)

Figure 30 shows the more typical arrangement of large cairns lying adjacent to or within 'sacred' areas outside the settlement zone, with the smaller cairns clustered around the embanked enclosure and also between it and the Craddock Moor stone circle. Other small cairns lie closer to fields on Tregarrick Tor, and two areas of 'clearance mounds' occur in the Craddock Moor fields and below the west entrance to Stowe's Pound. A kerbed boulder (Fig 24 no 36, marked as an open square on Fig 30, left, below centre) lies immediately outside the Craddock Moor field system.

The large cairns are almost all in prominent places, along ridges or clustered around the ceremonial monuments (see p 41). Rillaton Barrow is visible from many locations. Plundered in the nineteenth century, it contained Early Bronze Age material (gold cup, Camerton-Snowshill type dagger, a metallic rivet, pieces of ivory or bone, and a few glass beads perhaps of faience – all save the gold cup are now lost: Barnatt 1982, 213–4). The cist was secondary, giving the barrow an early second millennium BC date. It is tempting to identify the remains with a prominent inhabitant of Stowe's Pound.

This area can be seen as a 'sacred' area as defined by Barnatt. The large area of moorland containing only barrows and ritual monuments stretches from Craddock Moor to Caradon Hill to the south–east and Stowe's Pound to the east (see Map 1). Enclosed land has encroached along the south and west margins, removing any traces of settlement, but a field

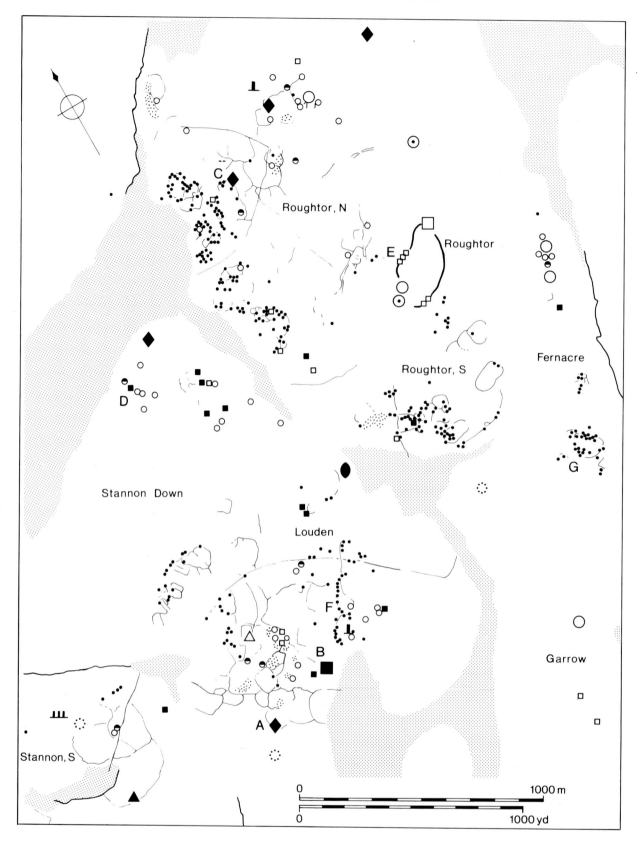

Fig 29   Cairns, ritual monuments, and prehistoric settlements in the Roughtor area, SX 140812 (letters are referred to in text, p 43: for key, see Fig 30.)

Fig 30   (Opposite) Cairns, ritual monuments, and prehistoric settlements in the Craddock Moor, Stowe's Pound area, SX 245725

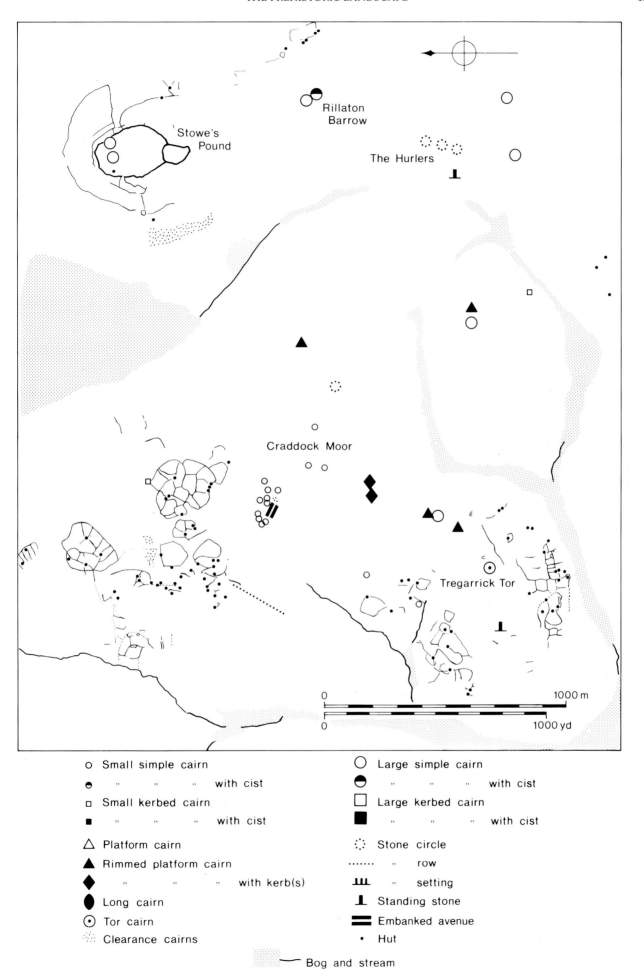

Stowe's
Pound

Rillaton
Barrow

The Hurlers

Craddock Moor

Tregarrick Tor

0   1000 m

0   1000 yd

o Small simple cairn	◯ Large simple cairn
◓ " " " with cist	◖ " " " with cist
□ Small kerbed cairn	▢ Large kerbed cairn
■ " " " with cist	■ " " " with cist
△ Platform cairn	⦂⦂ Stone circle
▲ Rimmed platform cairn	······· " row
◆ " " " with kerb(s)	⊥⊥⊥ " setting
⬤ Long cairn	⊥ Standing stone
⊙ Tor cairn	▬▬ Embanked avenue
⦂⦂ Clearance cairns	• Hut

Bog and stream

system still survives in the east below Rillaton Barrow and Stowe's Pound, and there are others around Tregarrick Tor and on Craddock Moor in the west and north. The small kerbed cairn, above centre right in Figure 30, marked as an open square, is Wollagate Barrow, excavated by C K Croft Andrew (SMR archive and photographs). It may indicate the former presence of a settlement in the enclosed land to the west or be related to the huts to the south. The two large cairns immediately to the north may be markers for this small territory lying between the two small streams.

It seems likely that the ritual monuments on Craddock Moor 'belong' to the settlements evenly spread around its margins. The same may be said of Leskernick (Fig 28).

The impression given generally, despite particular relationships suggesting the contrary, is that the large cairns, especially the isolated ones, are early features of the land division, no matter how informal, of the Moor. They may have functioned as territorial boundary markers, in the boundary edge sense (Spratt 1981, figs 7.5, 7.6). As settlement expanded in some areas, the original limits were moved and the cairns absorbed within the settlement or utilised zone. The smaller cairns served a more local cemetery function and some of these may also have been absorbed within the enclosed landscape, but as an original rather than a later development. The dates from Stannon Down and Colliford may represent, within a few centuries (c 1700–1900 BC), the principal cairn-building phase, with the settlement pattern evolving for some time after, before contracting towards the 1st millennium BC.

6   Defended enclosures

Early enclosures

The two large enclosures at Stowe's Pound (SX 25777260) and Roughtor (SX 147808) are complex features built around the rocky outcrops of the two tors and contain extensive evidence of habitation.

Roughtor Hillfort (Fig 31)

At 400m above OD Roughtor is the highest part of an elongated north–east to south–west hill with a flattish top and moderately steep sides. The defences join Roughtor to Little Roughtor, encompassing an area of 6.5ha, 350m long by 210m at its widest, and for the most part set below the crest at about 370m above OD. The defences consist in part of stone walls, apparently constructed of orthostats front and rear with rubble between; outer lines consist of lines of large orthostats or slabs, many now fallen, with no other rampart material, giving the appearance of jagged teeth. On the north side there are up to four defensive lines and two entrances. The more northerly entrance is defined by two walls that continue beyond the outer defensive line. The southerly entrance is more substantial, with a deep hollow-way passing through four stone lines that bulge outwards around the entrance. Three small kerbed cairns are built into the entrance (one on the north and two on the south). A small ruined corbelled chamber lies between the ramparts on the south side; it may be related to the entrance or a medieval or post-medieval structure used by herdsmen, similar to other structures dug into cairns on the northerly slopes of the tor below. The defences on the south are incomplete at the northern end closest to Little Roughtor; elsewhere there are two lines of piled stones between rock outcrops and areas of dense stone clitter. A third entrance on the south has a staggered approach between the ramparts with a third rampart added at this point. Several small attached stone structures lie close to the entrance.

Within the hillfort there are two groups of 'hut scoops' or platforms. One group, centred at SX 14668076, lies inside the south–west entrance, the other at SX 14668090 lies inside the more southerly of the north entrances. The south–west group (11 in all) appears as cleared grassy patches in clitter, mostly oval or subrectangular in plan, with no evidence of an entrance; three other structures are set against the ramparts close to the entrance, two on either side of it. The northerly group of seven consists of closely-spaced, roughly circular platforms, all cut back into the north–west slope; four have no build-up on the lower side and merely fade into the slope. The platforms within the enclosure range from 3.5m to 12m in diameter and probably represent stances for wooden houses.

The cairns that crown the hilltops are complex in structure and very large. The Little Roughtor cairn in the north surrounds the tor top with a platform edged by large coursed stones with a wide mound of stones spreading down the side. The cairns on Roughtor appear to be attempts at complex platform cairns set amongst the uneven outcrops, with a large pile of stones set against the southern base of the central outcrop. In the medieval period a chapel to St Michael was set within the cairn in a similar fashion to St Michael's chapel at Chapel Carn Brea in West Penwith. The cairns almost form a continuation of the enclosing defences amongst the tor outcrops.

Stowe's Pound (Fig 6 and front cover)

Close to the Cheesewring a massive stone bank, in places 12m wide and up to 1.5m high internally and 5m externally, encloses the highest part of Stowe's Hill (c 1ha). In places coursed stonework is visible, but in the southern section, where the rampart has been partly removed by quarrying, two lines of substantial orthostats show that the rampart was faced on both sides. The structure and dimensions are very similar to Carn Brea (R J Mercer 1970 and CAU 1:500 survey 1985). Attached to this enclosure on the north is a larger enclosure (c 5ha), encompassing the whole of the rest of the hilltop. The ground slopes fairly steeply on all sides. This rampart is faced with coursed walling in places but does not appear to have had an orthostatic construction. Fig 6 shows that several other stone banks are attached on the north and east side with flanking walls defining two opposed entrances on the west and east sides. The eastern entrance has various flanking works with two banks or 'antennae' forming a long funnel with a mound in the middle (in modern terms, suggestive of a dual carriageway entrance). The southern bank turns southwards along the hillside and joins a field system and settlement partly overlaid by dumps from the quarry and from mining. The northern bank turns and curves round the north and west side of the hill until it meets the track which extends downhill from the west entrance. It contin-

ues southwards beyond this before becoming lost in the clitter and stone-splitting debris. The west entrance is approached through a large annexe. The track is defined on one side only at first and then on both sides as it approaches the entrance. It develops into a deep hollow-way as it passes through the entrance and into the central area of the enclosure. At the bottom of the western side of the hill a small enclosure lies on the line of the flanking bank; just outside the area shown in Fig 6 is a hut circle, and a short distance beyond, a cluster of small stone mounds. Set within the enclosure bank (not shown

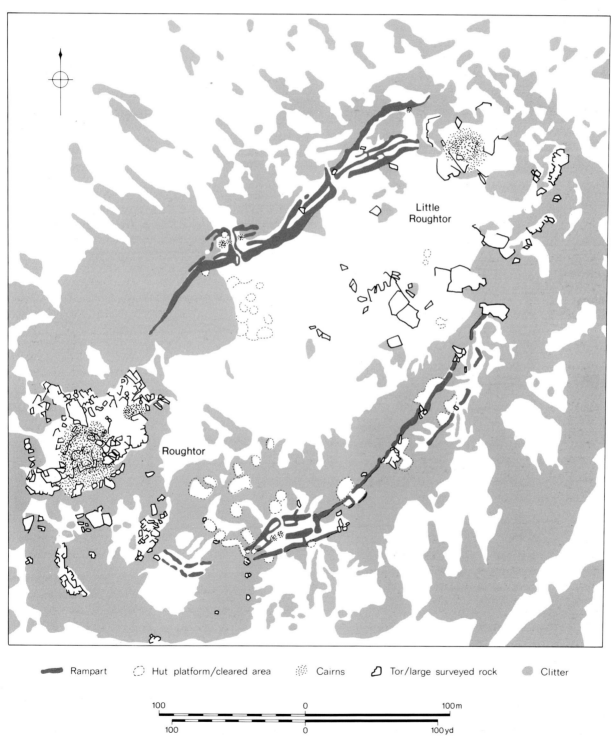

| Rampart | Hut platform/cleared area | Cairns | Tor/large surveyed rock | Clitter |

100   0   100m
100   0   100yd

Fig 31   Roughtor Hillfort, SX 147808

on Fig 6) are many narrow defined gaps that appear to be deliberate entrances of a simpler type than the two main ones. Inside the large enclosure are numerous (c 80) cleared areas or platforms clustered in two groups. One faced stone hut lies to the north of the west entrance. Two tumbled cairns stand at the north end of the hill within the enclosure.

Discussion

The two enclosures differ in appearance and location from other prehistoric enclosures in Cornwall, and it has been suggested elsewhere that they may be of earlier date (R J Mercer 1981b; Silvester 1979; Johnson and Rose 1982; National Archaeological Record record cards). The following characteristics reinforce this view:

1   The altitude and extreme exposure of the sites

2   The apparently casual nature of the defences around parts of Roughtor – there are no signs of any enclosing work to the south of Little Roughtor; the outer lines on the north flanks are merely upright stones acting as a fence rather than a defence

3   The apparent integration of the kerbed cairns of Bronze Age date within the entrance structure of Roughtor

4   The presence of very many hut stances for wooden structures, suggesting that large amounts of timber were easily available in the vicinity

5   The presence of many small entrance gaps in both enclosures, reminiscent of the multiple entrances at Carn Brea (CAU survey archive)

6   The scarcity of evidence of later prehistoric activity in the vicinity of the enclosures (NB no excavation has taken place in the enclosures and no finds of any date have come from them.)

7   The practice of facing the ramparts, front and back, with very large orthostats, which is very similar to the Neolithic ramparts at Carn Brea

8   The presence of much Bronze Age settlement around the enclosures.

Although no excavations have taken place within the enclosures, there are certain specific areas where excavation could provide important evidence of relationships with Bronze Age features: (1) the cairns at the entrance of the north side of Roughtor; (2) the point where the southern flanking entrance bank of Stowe's Pound meets a field system below the Cheesewring quarry dumps (when the dumps were disturbed in 1984 this crucial relationship was preserved; it now survives as an unimpressive isolated scarp, but may still indicate the chronological relationship of the fields to the flanking bank); (3) the excavation of some of the hut stances; and (4) the excavation of a small section of the ramparts.

Evidence of tin streaming is visible in areas of bog on all sides close to Roughtor, and marshy areas close to Stowe's Pound have certainly been disturbed,

perhaps by the same processes. Smith suggests (Balaam et al 1982) that exploitation of streamed tin was an important factor in supporting second-millennium BC settlement in the Plym valley on Dartmoor. It has already been noted that evidence of pre-Roman tin streaming has been found in the St Neot valley (S Gerrard pers comm); perhaps tin exploitation was important on Bodmin Moor, and these enclosures may be related to it. Such an hypothesis does, however, add another dimension to the examination of bog samples, where prehistoric workings are likely to lie completely buried by later peat development, as at St Neot. The Witheybrook valley below Stowe's Pound provides an ideal area for exploration. (It is hoped to examine the possibilities of prehistoric tin working in a second volume of the survey.)

Berry Castle (see below) is possibly a further member of this class. Another example was discovered in 1989 at De Lank (SX 10057523) by Peter Herring, (and surveyed in 1992 by the Exeter Office of RCHME). An area of approximately 0.25ha on a narrow ridge is enclosed mostly by a single slight wall, but with a stretch of triple rampart at the entrance.

Roughtor and Stowe's Pound have been surveyed at 1:1000 and Carn Brea and Helman Tor, two Neolithic enclosures, at 1:500. The only other comparable site is Trencrom Hill, a hillfort that stands at the entrance to the Penwith peninsula south of St Ives and is yet to be surveyed. All the surveys so far completed reinforce the view that we are dealing with pre-Iron Age enclosures.

Later enclosures (*Figs 32, 33, 50*)

by Peter Rose

There are two main types of such enclosures in Cornwall: univallate enclosures, or rounds (sometimes with annexes), not normally in strong defensive positions; and hillforts, multiple enclosures and cliff castles, more strongly defended because of their siting or multiplication of defences. Excavated examples of the latter have a date range from perhaps the fourth century BC to the first century AD. The rounds are probably as early but continue later, through the Roman period and in some cases to the sixth or seventh centuries AD (Johnson and Rose 1982).

Bury Castle and Berry Castle (Figs 32; 33) are strongly defended, whilst the others are of round type. Bury Castle (SX 135696), located at the south end of a ridge, is a multivallate hillfort with an outwork to the north. Berry Castle (SX 197689) is a univallate hilltop enclosure containing nine hut circles, with a small annexe and a larger but incomplete outwork attached to the south, covering the entrance. The site has been tentatively proposed as a further example of an early prehistoric defended enclosure or 'tor enclosure' (Silvester 1979, 189), and this remains a possibility.

The rounds found within the survey area show

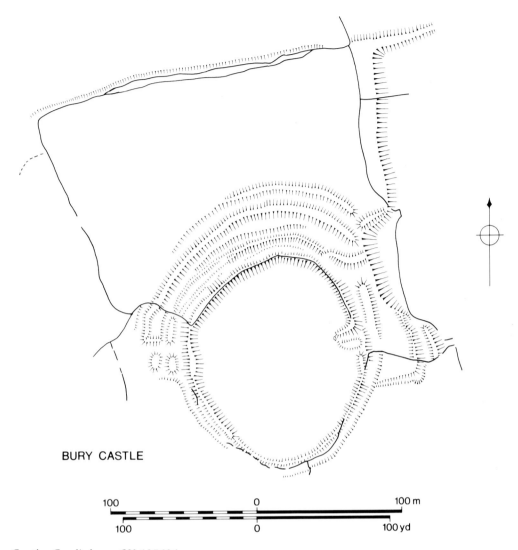

BURY CASTLE

100   0   100 m

100   0   100 yd

Fig 32   Bury Castle, Cardinham, SX 135696

some of the variety that is seen throughout Cornwall (Johnson and Rose 1982). Internal dimensions range from 32m (Carburrow, SX 15467050) to 120m by 80m (Allabury, SX 25747694). Most are curvilinear, but one (Lestow, SX 17146771) is rectangular. Rounds generally survive as ploughed-down earthworks (Higher Langdon, SX 20747330, Lestow) or incorporated into the present field pattern (Allabury, where the substantial rampart is mostly intact). As it is very rare to find sites with undisturbed interiors, the two moorland examples on Bodmin Moor – Bray Down and Carburrow – are particularly important. The small circular enclosure at Carburrow contains a single large hut circle (10m in diameter). The apparently defensive character of this site is quite unlike that of other small prehistoric enclosures on the Moor. The adjacent medieval farm, Carburrow, contains the place-name element *ker* (fort, round: Padel 1985, 50) which may refer to this site.

The enclosure at Bray Down (SX 19068258), on a steep north slope, contains two cleared platforms, presumably for timber rather than stone buildings. Their elongated form could suggest a Romano-British date (see Quinnell 1986). Outworks set both uphill and downhill of the enclosure, perhaps unfin-

ished, may have been intended to form a large defensible enclosure for stock.

Other associations are less certain. A rectilinear field system close to the Bray Down enclosure is not necessarily contemporary, and the same is true of the large number of hut circles and fragmentary fields at Carburrow. There are slight traces of a lynchetted field system adjoining the round at Higher Langdon. At Carburrow and Bray Down the lack of obvious associated field systems suggests a pastoral emphasis; seasonal use is a possibility.

The pattern and development of settlement on and around the Moor at this time is discussed further at the end of the chapter (p 72–6).

7   Prehistoric huts

We have used the term 'huts' to describe prehistoric buildings in preference to 'houses' because the latter term implies a habitation, and in architectural terms a certain status. The well-built double-faced huts were undoubtedly dwelling houses, and handsome ones at that, but there is a wide range of smaller structures, both circular and non-circular, where the

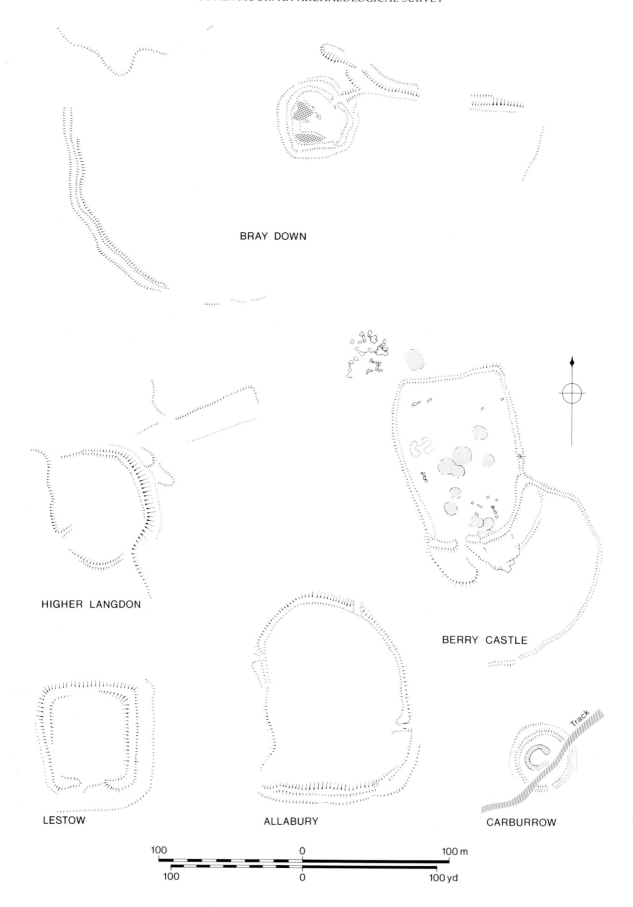

Fig 33   Defended enclosures, Bodmin Moor: Bray Down, SX 19068258, stippled areas indicate hut platforms; Higher
Langdon, SX 20747330; Berry Castle, SX 197689, huts stippled; Lestow, SX 17146771; Allabury, SX 25747694;
Carburrow, SX 15467050, hut stippled

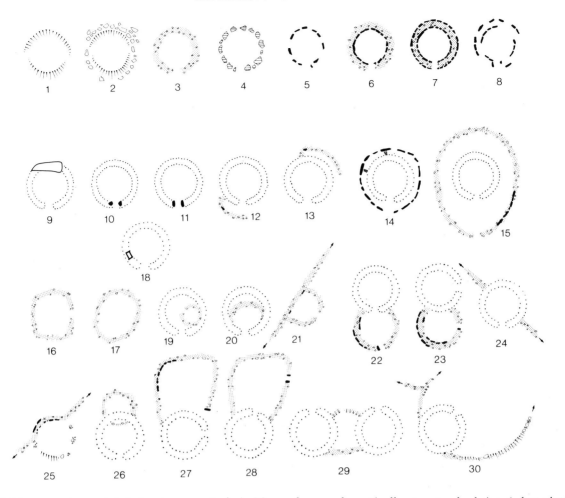

Fig 34   *Hut types and associated structures on Bodmin Moor, shown schematically at a standard size. 1, hut platform; 2, stone-cleared hut stance or sometimes a platform; 3, stone bank; 4, single boulders; 5, single uprights (no bank visible); 6, single face; 7, double face; 8, double uprights (no bank visible); 9, large rock incorporated into hut wall; 10, orthostatic door jambs; 11, transverse slab door jambs; 12, 'porch'; 13, attached, partially concentric annexe away from entrance; 14, concentric ring of slabs (or bank) with occasional radial subdivision; 15, concentric enclosure; 16, subrectangular, subsquare; 17, subcircular, oval; 18, cupboard or recess in hut wall; 19, hut within hut; 20, subdivided hut; 21, hut attached to wall; 22, conjoined huts mutually dependent; 23, conjoined huts mutually exclusive; 24, walls abut hut; 25, wall robbing and overlying earlier hut; 26, hut slighting hut; 27, attached enclosure with separate entrance; 28, hut opens into attached enclosure; 29, structure between two or more huts; 30, hut opening onto associated fields or enclosures. Although not illustrated here, several huts have external ditches, most notably on Twelve Men's Moor.*

function is not so clear. There are many huts of less than 4m diameter which may have been for animals, fodder, tools, or implements. In a medieval context, many of the habitable buildings of non-longhouse type may have been no more than the seasonal dwellings of herdsmen and therefore huts rather than houses.

Fig 34 attempts to illustrate the forms of hut encountered on the Moor, as well as the more common relationships with other features. The drawings are schematic and indicate how the huts now look in the field, rather than how they might have looked when in use. Whilst further variations may be revealed in future, what has already been found provides a sound basis for the development of standard descriptive terms (as has been developed for boundaries: see Fig 12). The materials used, the style and complexity of construction, size, shape, and relationships with other features, together with the

general and specific location of a building, are all that we have from fieldwork to help indicate status, function, date, and length of use. The survey has tried to identify the different elements and where they occur, and by simplifying them (Fig 34), to begin to identify diagnostic features towards which specific questions may be directed.

Structural and other features
(Fig 34, 1–30: the features shown are described here in detail.)

Simple platforms

1   *Hut platforms* no stone structure visible, perhaps indicating wooden construction. These are not com-

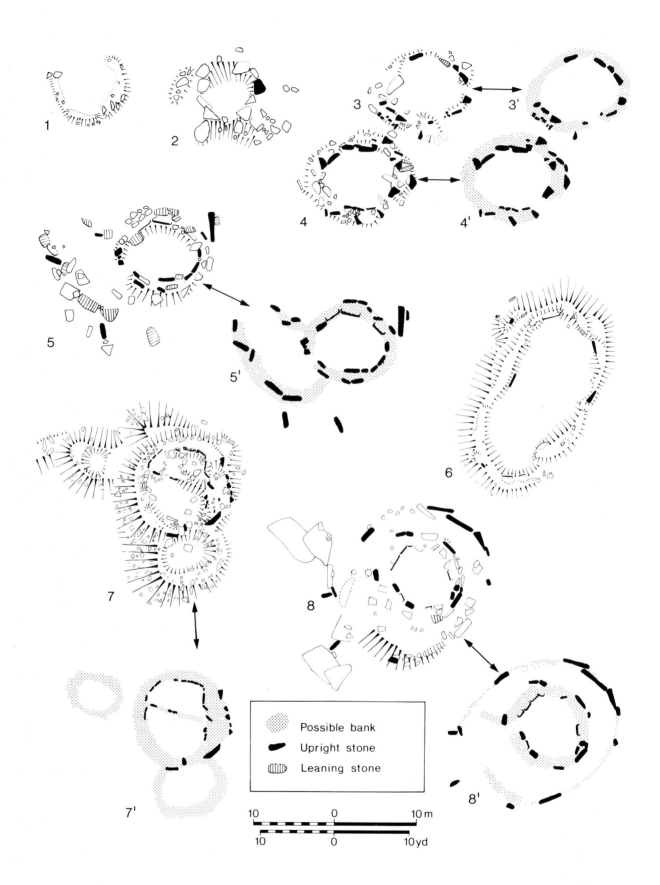

Fig 35   Examples of hut types (surveyed) with some structural simplifications: 1, robbed platform; 2, platform with a boulder wall, see Fig 16D; 3, hut with both single and double facing; 4, hut with double facing; 5, hut with entrance annexe or 'porch', see Fig 16(B); 6, subrectangular hut; 7, subdivided hut with two adjacent huts; 8, hut with concentric ring ('corridor house'), see Fig 16(A).

mon, but examples occur within the Roughtor enclosure (Fig 31) and on Cardinham Moor (SX 14407109).

2 *Hut stances cleared of stones* The stones have been moved to one side and do not appear to be part of any wall construction. Stances have been found only within the enclosures at Roughtor and Stowe's Pound and again suggest wooden buildings.

Walls: structural details

3 *Stone banks* (Fig 35 no 1) Hut walls with no apparent internal or external facing stones.

4 *Hut walls of single boulders* with no apparent facing (Fig 35 no 2).

5–8 *Huts with wall facing* Numbers 6 and 7 are common types, with facings on the inside or both inside and out and associated bank material (eg Fig 35 nos 3, 4). Facings are normally of upright slabs, but occasionally coursed walling is found, probably because of the lack of suitable facing slabs in the vicinity. Where there is an outer face it is generally less substantial and less continuous than the inner face, and may merely have acted as an edge to the hut bank. Numbers 5 and 8 are further examples of such walling with no associated bank material, suggesting perhaps a turf/earth infill that has eroded away, or a stone infill that has been deliberately removed.

9 *Large rocks* are sometimes incorporated into the hut wall. There are good examples at Roughtor South, Leskernick Hill, and on Garrow Tor (see Fig 36 hut nos 6, 7, 10, 11).

Non-circular huts

16 *Sub-rectangular or sub-square huts* occur in many of the settlements; some may be wrecked circular huts, but many were clearly deliberately built in this form. Several such huts have been identified on Brockabarrow Common (SX 15637466; see Fig 11). Their wall structure is the same as that of the other huts in the settlement and some have facing stones. The huts are mostly squarish in plan with rounded corners and range internally from 3m to 4m across. Other more markedly sub-rectangular huts are attached to enclosure walls. Their function is obscure, but they may have served as store houses, animal houses or tool sheds. It is not inconceivable that, like those on the east side of the hill, they may have been post-prehistoric seasonal huts. Another sub-square hut at Louden (not illustrated) sits isolated below the main prehistoric settlement (SX 13757970), and although slightly larger may have had a similar function. The hut at Stannon shown in Fig 35 no 6, almost oval in plan, is very different from circular huts nearby. It resembles most closely the Romano-British houses at Grambla near the Helford River (Saunders 1972), Castle Gotha (Saunders and Harris 1982), and Trethurgy (Miles and Miles 1973).

17 *Oval and sub-circular huts* are found at many settlements. Some may be misshapen through robbing or lateral spread of material downslope, but the majority appear to have been deliberately built in this shape. Like those in type 16 above, some may be late prehistoric or post-prehistoric in date.

Entrances

10–11 *Entrances* comprise simple gaps, orthostatic door jambs, or slabs set on edge; a number cannot be clearly distinguished. In at least one place on Roughtor North only the jambs survive from a robbed hut. In some cases the hut walls become broader at the entrance, with a strong outer face here but nowhere else on the perimeter.

Internal features

18 *Cupboard-like recesses* have been found within the walls of excavated huts (Stannon, hut 4, R J Mercer 1970, fig 9), and several were noted at other sites during the field survey.

19–20 *Internal sub-divisions* Many settlements have huts, usually the larger huts, with internal subdivisions of some form. It is often not clear if such divisions are primary or secondary.

External structures, attached and free-standing

12 *'Porches'* at hut entrances to protect doorways from wind and weather are common (Fig 35 no 5; Fig 36 no 7; Fig 37 points A–D). At Stannon Down, R J Mercer (1970, figs 8 and 9) found evidence of wooden porches, whilst more visible stone ones were found at Poldowrian on the Lizard (Smith and Harris 1982, fig 21) and attached to some of the huts in enclosure 15 on Shaugh Moor, Dartmoor (Wainwright and Smith 1980). Worth notes many others on Dartmoor (eg Grimspound: Worth 1945, plate 7, fig 1).

13 *Annexes* At Blacktor (SX 15717326; Fig 39, points A), small annexes concentric to the hut wall, but away from the entrance, are found on seven huts, a feature not noticed widely elsewhere on Bodmin Moor. These may be stores or pens of some sort and do not appear suitable for habitation. Worth notes structures of similar character on Dartmoor, although they are nearer the entrance (Worth 1945, 227, fig 7).

22–3 *Conjoined huts* In complex settlements many huts are conjoined, forming a sort of 'kitchen' extension, but in few cases do they use a common entrance. There is a good example of type 22 at Roughtor South (Fig 49 point D, although the print does not show it very clearly.)

21 *Structures attached to walls* are common features within enclosures, as at Brockabarrow Common (Fig 11). They are also found attached to field boundaries, as at Leskernick (Figs 3, 4) and elsewhere to major boundaries where the boundary was used as the back wall. The five small structures attached to the exterior of the wall of the southern enclosure at Garrow Tor (SX 14707841, Fig 5) appear to have served a different function from the huts confined within the enclosure.

24 Walls abutting huts Where the walls butt against a hut the relationship can form the basis for establishing the chronology of a site.

29 Inter-hut structures The function of inter-hut structures set among some huts is presumed to be non-domestic, serving as lean-to sheds or small stores or byres. (Several examples can be seen at Garrow Tor, Fig 36.)

14 Huts within concentric rings D Dudley (MS, Royal Cornwall Museum) found several examples of this curious arrangement on Garrow Tor and excavated one of them (Fig 35 no 8; Fig 16 point A). Although examples are known from elsewhere, they are not common. A concentric ring of slabs lies close to the exterior of the hut wall defining a narrow area, sometimes subdivided by small walls or banks. The structure could be for storage or penning, or alternatively for keeping animals away from the hut and its roof which, if thatched, would have been susceptible to nibbling. For other examples on Garrow, see Fig 36 huts 1–5.

15 Huts within small enclosures There are half a dozen examples on Garrow Tor (Fig 37, stippled enclosures between 12m and 25m across), but they are not found widely elsewhere.

27–8 Huts with attached enclosures Both types can be seen at Brockabarrow and many other sites of this type of settlement. The enclosures appear to be yards, or perhaps garden plots, and are directly associated with the attached hut. At Brockabarrow (Fig 11) the northern enclosure has two huts that face away from the enclosure, which is subdivided, presumably between them.

30 Huts integrated with contemporary field systems and enclosures The enclosures at Brockabarrow (Fig 11) appear to be of the same build and date as the associated huts, and this is true for many of the settlements with fields.

25–6 The slighting of huts by other huts is common, especially in complex settlements, although robbed huts are a common feature generally. They often appear as scatters of boulders or slight scoops abutting well-built huts. Examples of huts, robbed to build walls, can be seen at Leskernick (Fig 5 point D) and at Roughtor (Fig 15; Fig 48 points B).

Figures 36 and 37 show evidence of many of the features mentioned above and demonstrate the extreme complexity of the settlements on this part of the Moor, where the huts have been extended and altered. Evidence of hut construction has often been compromised by robbing, either in antiquity or more recently. There is no doubt that many hut walls had a facing of some sort, many both inside and out; often all that remains are a few inner and outer liners. Whilst undoubtedly the larger huts are double-faced, so too are some of the smallest. There are many examples of double-faced huts less than 3.5m in diameter. Hut construction may be significant in identifying ancillary buildings for storage or for animals, where double facing may be regarded as an extravagance. This may also be so for structures that may never have been roofed or were roofed only

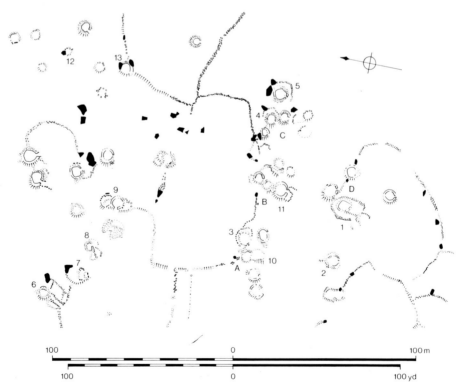

100   0   100 m

100   0   100 yd

Fig 36   Settlement on Garrow Tor (1), SX 14107820. An area of complex huts, described on p71. A, B, C, D, clusters of huts; 1–5, huts with concentric rings ('corridor houses'); 6–11, huts with complex entrance-annexes or yards, 12 and 13, huts with large rocks incorporated into their walls. NB: hut 1 was excavated by Dudley (Dudley MS, Royal Cornwall Museum).

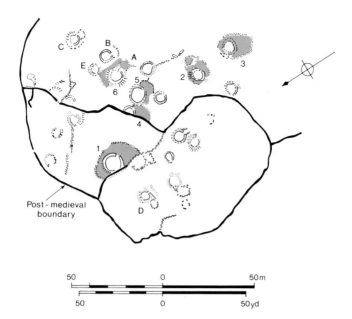

50   0   50m
50   0   50yd

Fig 37   Settlement on Garrow Tor (2), SX 14527803: huts with different types of annexes and enclosures, described on p53–4. 1–3, huts with concentric enclosures; 4–6, huts with yard-like enclosures; A–D, huts with entrance annexes or 'porches'; D, E, 5, and 6 are huts with evidence of reuse. The shaded areas are the enclosures associated with six of the huts.

temporarily. Seasonal huts, such as those discussed in Chapter 5, are usually sub-rectangular in shape and do not have faced walls. Small shelters of the type used for young lambs, or for the herdsmen, could have had cloth roofs or covers of branches and bracken. Some have substantial walls, others weak drystone walls set against large boulders or set within an earlier structure such as a hut or cairn.

Despite these exceptions, however, wall construction is not a good guide to differences in settlement type. The size and shape of the structures and the complexity of associated buildings do begin to show a variety, the significance of which is by no means clear. When this is set against the variations in associated fields and enclosures, it is clear that local factors are important.

Dimensions

Most huts are 5–7m in internal diameter, giving a range of roofed living space of 20–39sq m. This is a similar range to that found in medieval longhouses, from the 18.5sq m of the small excavated longhouse at Garrow (Fig 54 no 1) to the 40sq m of the larger longhouses at Brown Willy (Fig 54 nos 8, 9); one or two others may be larger. The many prehistoric huts larger than 7m in diameter would have had substantial floor areas ranging from 39 to 120sq m. These differences are enormous. Huts above 8m in diameter have a greater total floor area than the ubiquitous one-up one-down cottage (c 50sq m or less) so common in Cornwall until the twentieth century; and the very largest huts exceed the total floor area of longhouses, including the shippons (byres). But large huts required substantial numbers of roof timbers 8m or more in length, as well as large areas of thatch. The impact on the local woodland of a settlement such as Blacktor, with more than 90 huts, must

have been considerable, even though all the huts are not necessarily contemporary.

The much smaller huts, particularly those less than 4m in diameter, seem hardly capable of housing a family, and may have been dwellings for individuals. If the 'notional number of occupants' cited by Bradley (Bradley *et al* 1980, 254–5) is used, then a diameter of between approximately 6m and 8m could house 4–5 adults. The average Bodmin Moor hut could support a small family, but a diameter of less than 5m drastically reduces the space available for comfort and use.

8   Settlements

The survey has recorded a large number of prehistoric settlements and it is unlikely that many more will be found, although no doubt many huts lie hidden in the gorse and bracken, amongst the rocks and buried beneath the peat. Since the last revision by the Ordnance Survey Archaeology Division in the 1960s and early 1970s, it is sad to report that upwards of 50 huts have been destroyed, due in part to gradual but increasing agricultural improvement. This process has been most damaging on Smallacoombe Downs, where forestry plantation has removed the remains of a once extensive curvilinear field system above the deserted medieval settlement of Smallacoombe at Trewortha Marsh.

Examination of the results is still at an early stage. At a general level it is possible to identify a large number of presumed Bronze Age settlements scattered along valley slopes, also a number far into the moorland in very exposed areas. On closer examination it is clear that within these settlements there is great variety of hut form and in some instances very complex developments of hut clusters, annexes, and subdivisions.

Map 1 shows the distribution of settlements. It is noticeable that in some areas there are general scatters of huts with concentrations of less than ten huts representing a common feature; in others, as on Brockabarrow Common (SX 157746, Fig 11), Blacktor (SX 157732, Fig 39), Higher Langdon (SX 204734, Fig 76), and Brown Gelly (SX 201727, Fig 38 no 5), there are settlements with 40–90 huts. The area of Garrow and Roughtor includes both the greatest concentration of settlement, and the greatest variety in huts and associated structures. Here, in less than 10% of the Moor, lie at least one-third of all the huts and cairns.

The variety of fields and enclosures associated with settlements is illustrated by the range of examples below.

Unenclosed hut settlements

The settlement at Catshole Tor (SX 16717873, Fig 38 no 1) is isolated and not associated with any fields or enclosures. It lies in a bleak and stony area of the Moor and consists of six huts and six other structures. A post-medieval enclosure and field barn may have damaged part of the site.

Huts A and F appear to have only one face, whilst the others (B, D, G H) are double-faced. They range from 9m in diameter (B) to only 2.7m (G). F and B have been subdivided, with a small hut built inside hut F. Four other non-faced structures (C, E, J, K) are small, between 2.2m and 3.4m in diameter, although C is squarish in shape. It is tempting to see these as the outhouses belonging to each habitation, and as there are no obvious fields or enclosures in the area they may be related to pastoral activity. There are, however, other groups of isolated huts that do not have such associated structures. The group at Stanning Hill (SX 16787570), although robbed, shows a similar range of huts (4.5–9.6m in diameter) with only a single enigmatic D-shaped structure attached to a few low upright slabs. On Twelve Men's Moor (SX 24937559), an open settlement covering 6ha has been robbed in places to build nearby intake walls. Of the 16 huts more or less visible, 7 show evidence of outer ditches, a feature rarely encountered elsewhere on the Moor. Some of the huts are very large (10.5–12.6m), and another 6 are over 7m in diameter; the others are robbed platforms or smaller huts as little as 4.7m in diameter. Again there are no associated fields or enclosures and only one conjoined hut. Close by is a cluster of stone mounds, and several cairns lie in the vicinity. These three settlements, superficially similar in character as open settlements, display great variation in hut size and structure, although the presence of facing is a common feature.

Whilst the hut variety is great, perhaps the most significant feature is the high ratio of huts or structures of less than 4.5m diameter to huts of greater size in the Catshole Tor settlement (8:4), indicating, perhaps, a need for many small ancillary non-domestic buildings. This does not appear to be so marked at Stanning Hill or Twelve Men's Moor. There are other isolated settlements that fall broadly within this range of variability; yet others have probably been absorbed within later settlements, or lie within improved modern fields and are thus difficult to identify.

Huts with small enclosures (*Fig 38*)

At Brockabarrow Common (SX 157746, Fig 11), the settlement of 61 huts and 7 enclosures is concentrated within an area of 4ha, with a few outliers. There are 22 structures less than 4.5m in diameter, 17 over 7m, and 22 in between. Some 13 of these, having perhaps been robbed to build others, are defined only by platforms or by a few stones. (Alternatively they may have been stances for non-domestic structures, possibly even rickstands.) There are several larger huts with 'porches' or concentric annexes that lie away from the entrances (this also occurs at Blacktor; see p 53). Seven are roughly square in plan and resemble the huts on the east side of the hill, possibly shieling houses of later date (see Chapter 5). There are seven enclosures or yards. None contains freestanding huts; instead, the huts adjoin the enclosure walls, either on the inside or the outside. The walling of the enclosures is similar to that of their associated huts. In those huts where entrances are discernible, the majority do not open into the enclosures. This is by no means the rule elsewhere; at Colvannick Tor (SX 12577158), for example, a 7.4m diameter hut looks into a small enclosure. The Brockabarrow settlement appears to be very complex, containing a wide variety of hut types and associated structures. This suggests a long period of use but within a pastoral context. Only one substantial hut opens into an enclosure, so perhaps the smaller huts within the enclosures are non-domestic. Brockabarrow is a pronounced example of a superficially simple settlement which on close examination at 1:1000 scale reveals great complexity. Taking medieval longhouse settlement as an analogy, it is not altogether surprising to find that the larger huts are associated with smaller (ancillary) buildings in a ratio of 3 to 1.

It is difficult to identify other undamaged settlements for comparison, although those at Lower Candra (SX 11797769), Brown Gelly (SX 201727, Fig 38 no 5), and North Langstone Downs (SX 24307436, Fig 38 no 3) may qualify. Others within the CAU survey area will be discussed below.

At Lower Candra a small settlement of ten huts lies within an area of later prehistoric and medieval fields on an extremely stony hillside (Johnson 1980, fig 5). Six of the huts are small and only one is larger than 6m in diameter. Associated with them are four enclosures, within which three of the huts are freestanding apart from connecting walls. In this sense the settlement is different from Brockabarrow. The other two settlements are more directly comparable. At North Langstone Downs, out of 28 huts only 6 are small; 10 of the remainder are very large, with 5 over 8m and one possible hut 15 × 13.5m in diameter. Small enclosures are attached, with the majority of huts facing away from them. At Brown Gelly, west and uphill of the main settlement, are at least 13 small structures mostly less than 4m in diameter, below which a complex arrangement of huts and

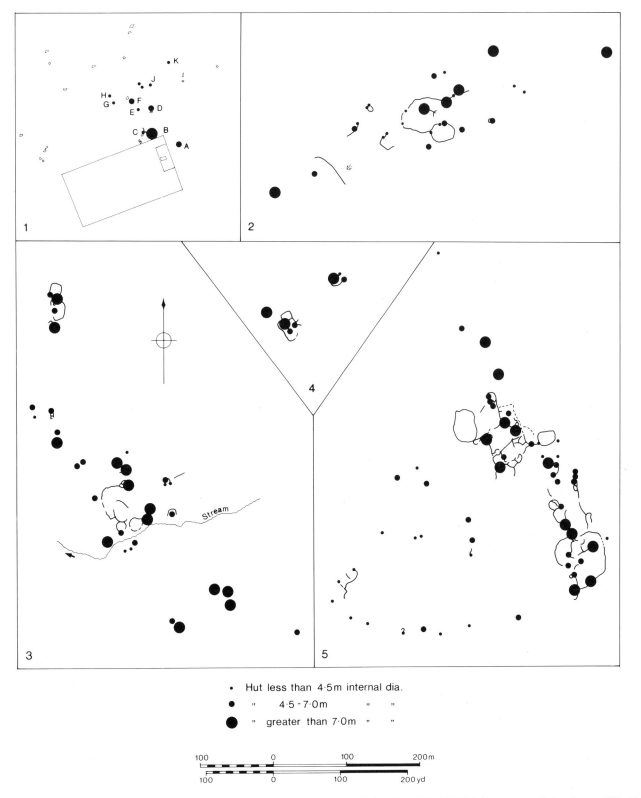

Fig 38 Hut settlements and settlements with enclosures: 1, Catshole Tor, SX 167787 (letters explained on p56); 2, Hawkstor, SX 255761; 3, North Langstone Downs, SX 243743; 4, Trewortha Tor, SX 246761; 5, Brown Gelly, SX 201727 (North top of page)

small enclosures extends for 350m along the hillside (Johnson 1980, fig 2). Twelve huts greater than 7m in diameter are scattered evenly through the settlement, with slightly smaller ones adjacent or connected to them, forming enclosures, or with enclosures attached. The whole complex of some 51 huts may

have comprised one coherent group with the smaller ancillary buildings clustered slightly apart from the main domestic area, as at Catshole Tor, but it is more likely that there were two settlements, separate both in function and date: the upper, where the huts cluster around a central semi-enclosed area, being seasonal; and the lower, where lengths of walling connect huts to form enclosures, which is similar to those discussed below.

The settlement at Hawkstor (Fig 38 no 2) is scat-

tered and disturbance by medieval cultivation has probably removed some of the enclosures. The two small clusters on the northern flanks of Trewortha Tor (Fig 38 no 4) are smaller and more compact

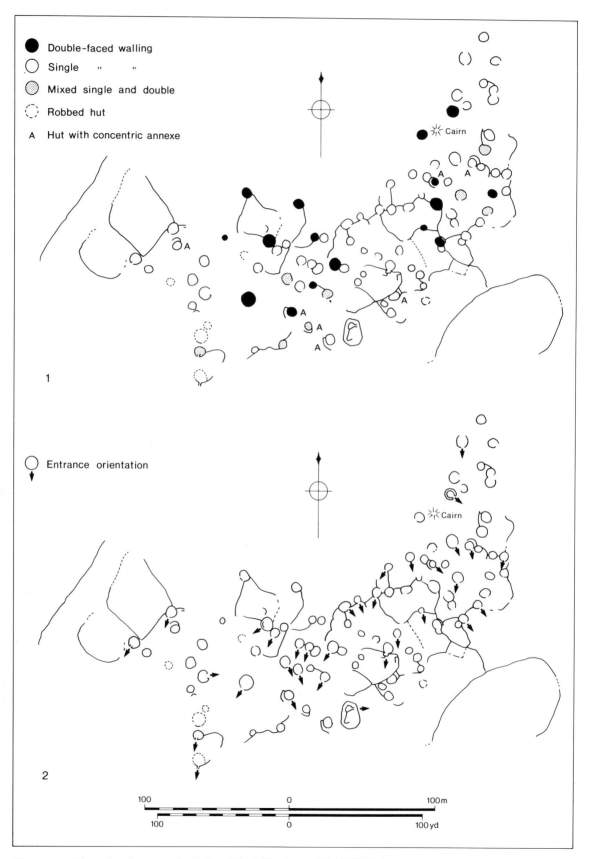

Fig 39   Hut types (1), and entrance orientation (2) at Blacktor, SX 15717326

versions of this general type. The huts vary in size and the impression is of two distinct settlements with small associated paddocks or yards and an area of common grazing.

Enclosures with huts around the edges and within (*Fig 39*)

The most spectacular of these is Blacktor (SX 15717326, Fig 39). Within an area of only 3 hectares lie 96 huts. Only a few have double-faced walls, the rest being single-faced (on the inside), some with traces of a double face on the uphill side, and some robbed. Figure 39 no 1 is the only illustration showing hut build in a settlement and it shows no particular pattern, with the double-faced huts being scattered throughout the area. There is no apparent difference between the size range of the double-faced huts and the others (3.5–7.5m in diameter). In general the huts are small, mostly less than 5.5m in diameter. Figure 39 no 2 shows the entrance orientation of huts where this is visible. The double-faced huts are turned away from the enclosures whilst many of the others open into them. The enclosures are formed by joining many of the huts with short lengths of walling. The huts are located on the uphill or north side of the enclosures with their entrances looking south–west and south–east. To some extent the position of the enclosures relative to that of the huts is determined by the common desire to face away from the bitter north–easterly winds; the enclosures tend to be south of the huts.

Whilst the Brockabarrow settlement may be a collection of separate family units with enclosures, the impression here is of communal enclosures. Similar settlements are found at Louden (SX 137798, Fig 29F), Fernacre (SX 149799, Fig 29G), and Carburrow (SX 15557060), where huts, mostly of 5m diameter or less, cluster like strings of beads, with others free-standing within these segmented enclosures. The function of these settlements is unclear as they have a very large number of huts for the small area enclosed. The enclosures do not seem like the 'yard' type enclosures at Brockabarrow or the more 'domestic' type enclosures at Lower Candra, which may have served to prevent animals from coming too close.

It is noticeable that on Bodmin Moor there are very few enclosures or pounds within which large numbers of huts are enclosed with others lying outside as on Dartmoor (cf the Plym valley; Balaam *et al* 1982). Other settlements on Dartmoor, such as Standon Down (Johnson 1980, fig 6), more closely resemble the Blacktor type.

Huts and fields (*Figs 40–4*)

It is difficult to be sure when an 'enclosure' should properly be regarded as a 'field' to denote both pastoral and arable land that is defined in some way – by walls, hedges, or even marker stones, or simply by agreement. Although this is not the place to explore in depth such contentious definitions, we have used 'field' to mean defined areas where cultivation and controlled grazing can take place. 'Enclosures' are defined as areas where the more intensive processing, sorting, and corralling of animals takes place; where animals are protected, and the domestic areas (including garden plots) are in turn protected from the animals. On the ground such functions may be suggested by the size of the enclosures and the form of their boundaries, but a clear distinction between 'field' and 'enclosure' cannot always be made.

Many of the field systems have been absorbed within areas of medieval settlement – Figure 40 shows a particularly fine example at Little Siblyback. Here the medieval settlement probably known as Newhall has reused many of the curvilinear prehistoric boundaries, leaving small areas of cultivation ridges visible in the moorland. Later use of the fields in connection with the more recent settlement known as Little Siblyback (A) has retained some of the prehistoric boundaries and one of the huts (B).

Prehistoric fields on the Moor are typically curvilinear and accreted, having developed organically from one or more foci. It is possible at both Craddock Moor (Fig 30) and Leskernick (Figs 3, 4, 28) to identify the sequence of accretion, although it is not possible to tell how long the process may have taken. The general impression on Bodmin Moor is that of small farms scattered along valley sides, and in the case of the Fowey Valley (see Map 1) at regular intervals, separated by small areas of moorland. Settlements were gradually being established, but with no obvious pattern in their locations: only in certain areas did farms give rise to continuous enclosure. We can begin to see concentrations on Craddock Moor, Langstone Downs, at Higher Langdon and in the north–west sector of the Moor; and it is in these areas that there are very large numbers of huts, suggesting a complex and lengthy chronology.

The farms range in size between the smallholdings of a few hectares, as at Carneglos (Fig 41 no 2), to the larger systems as at Leskernick (21ha). The huts tend to be 5m or more in diameter, with few structures smaller than this, in contrast to the wide range of huts that are free-standing or associated only with enclosures. The ratio of huts to enclosed land falls broadly within the range of 1–2 huts per hectare. This is in marked contrast to the huts and enclosures that range from at least 10 huts to as many as 30 huts per hectare of enclosed land. At the lower end of the scale are the rectilinear field systems on East Moor and Buttern Hill (see Map 1) which have 0.26 and 0.32 huts per hectare respectively. The possible presence of undetected wooden houses, huts, and structures means that any density statistics relate only to the visible remains: it is likely, however, that they are a reasonable guide to the relative differences between settlements.

Generally the fields are between 0.25 and 0.5ha in area, although some of those at Stannon South (Fig 29) and Butterstor are greater than 1ha. The huts lie scattered within the fields or are concentrated into certain areas as nucleated groups.

The settlement at Leskernick (Figs 3, 4) includes several nuclei as well as individual huts scattered

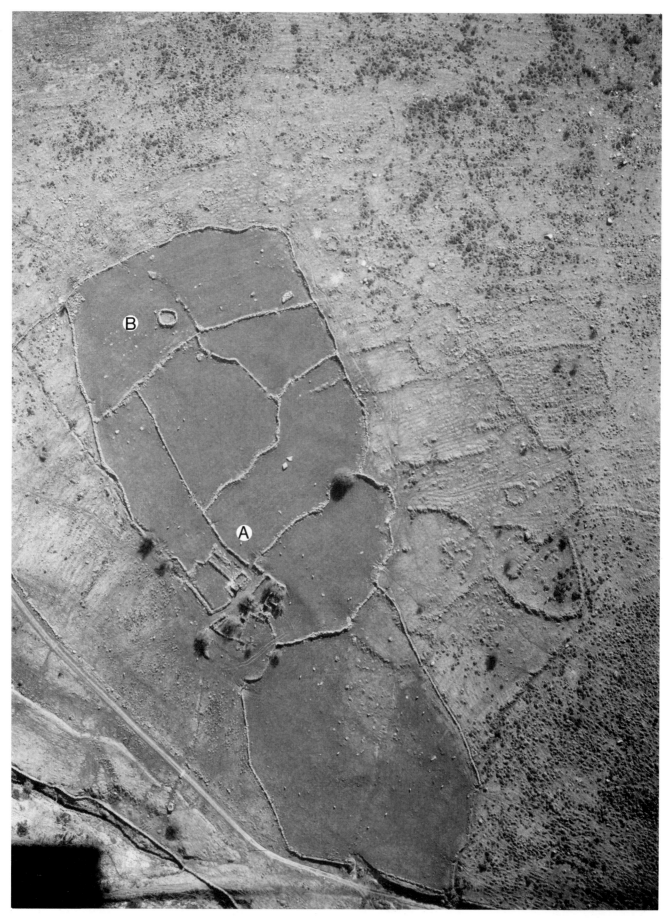

Fig 40   Little Siblyback, SX 240740, looking south-west with slope rising from bottom left to centre right: a multiphase landscape. Prehistoric fields and huts (B) lie in the moorland above and are fossilised by post-prehistoric boundaries. Cultivation ridges are visible within the prehistoric fields in the moorland. The post-medieval settlement of Little Siblyback is at A. (Photo NMR SX 2473/1/56, 21 April 1980; Crown Copyright Reserved)

Fig 41   Accreted field systems: 1, Twelve Men's Moor, SX 256755; 2, Carneglos, SX 200768; 3, Lady Down, SX 104763; 4, Kerrow Downs, SX 114751. (Letters explained on p62–3)

through the fields and is a good example to describe as it has not been disturbed by later activity and appears to have a long chronology. The huts in the north–west part of the system are within a very stony area and are enclosed by two straggly walls; 13 of the huts are very small, less than 4.5m in diameter. Most are within a focal field or enclosure and may be the remains of an earlier settlement, similar to Catshole Tor (Fig 38 no 1), that has been absorbed within a

later accretive field system. A series of large huts (greater than 7m in diameter) form perhaps four smallholdings in the western sector with little groups of fields associated with each. The eastern half of the settlement (Fig 4), joined to the western by only one wall, is agglomerated, consisting of two nuclei in the northern part and several other large huts within fields in the southern part. It is also significant that it is only here that the small cairns occur. The association between small cairns (often with kerbs and cists) and this type of accreted field system has been noted above (see p 43).

A trackway leads from one of the nucleated settlements out to the moorland to the south, as does a similar trackway at Craddock Moor (Fig 30), although at the latter the gateway has been blocked. Leskernick seems to represent a series of separate small-holdings that have coalesced to form a block of enclosed land, probably with communal grazing on the surrounding open land. Within this community each farmer or group of farmers had identifiable enclosed units or smallholdings, not necessarily held in common.

The settlements at Twelve Men's Moor and Carneglos (Fig 41 nos 1, 2) are smaller, with no such

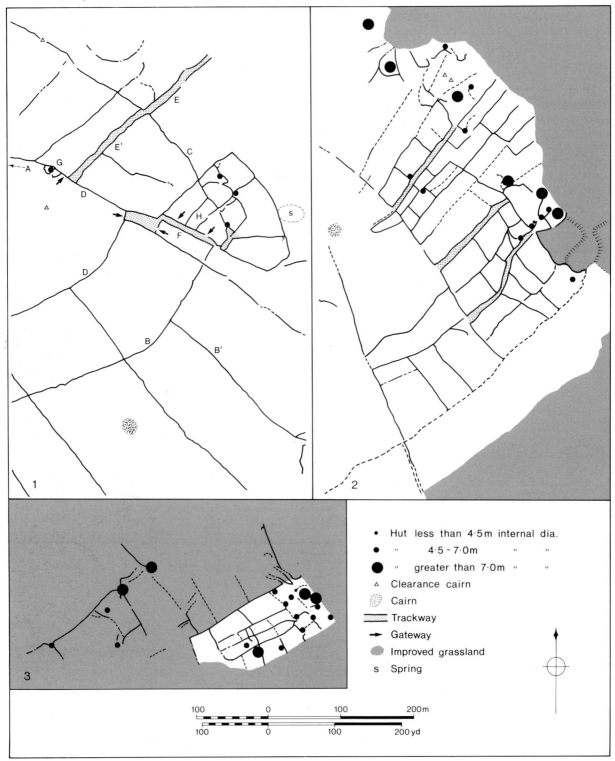

Fig 42 *Coaxial and rectilinear field systems: 1, East Moor, SX 244781: A, cairn excavated by Brisbane and Clews (1979), off plan to W; B B¹, C, and E, early phase; D and E¹, later extension; F, trackway to settlement (later phase); G, hut and enclosure attached to later phase extension; H, cultivation ridges sampled by Brisbane and Clews; this area is shown on Fig 43; 2, Curne Downs, SX 203818; 3, Watergate, SX 118813*

clear subunits or smallholdings. The fields at Lady Down (average field size 0.25ha) and Kerrow Downs (average size 0.5ha) are different in shape (Fig 41 nos 3,4). Those at Lady Down related to a long boundary bank that extends for 870m before disappearing in an area of stone robbing. There is still a curvilinear element at Lady Down, with the huts scattered about the system, generally on the edges of the fields and, at A and B, (Fig 41 no 3) with small enclosures or plots attached. Most of the huts are greater than 5.5m in diameter, although many have been disturbed. There are at least four clearance cairns within the fields; and a large cairn is either an earlier or early element of the system. At Kerrow the fields are more rectilinear though still accreted; a large platform cairn lies adjacent but with no clear relationship to them. A sub-square hut appears to have robbed one of the walls at A and may have been a later feature.

There are comparatively few examples of coaxial field systems on the Moor, although the systems on East Moor (SX 244781: Fig 42 no 1, and Map 1) and Sharptor (SX 258734) are similar to the Dartmoor systems. There is an element of land allotment by larger boundaries, but no coherent plan of watershed or contour layout. The division of the landscape into blocks occurs in areas of great concentration of activity in the Stannon, Louden, and Roughtor areas, with little evidence of fields developing to any degree within the blocks. The East Moor, Sharptor, and Treswallock systems do not have such large boundaries and the terminal banks are often no larger than the subdividing banks within the fields.

Figure 42 shows three different systems that are rectilinear in form but are different in scale and density of settlement. The East Moor system may have stretched from Bohayland in the south (see Map 1) as far north as Eastmoorgate and Tregune, a moorland edge of c 3.5km divided by two streams and bounded at either end by streams. There is a hint that the system continued in the south over Carey Tor. Seven settlements lie within the area (c 300ha) and some of them appear earlier than the system itself. The settlement shown on Figures 42 no 1, and 43 lies at the eastern corner of the system, where it changes direction abruptly, around the northern flanks of the Moor. Brisbane and Clews (1979) have already discussed some elements of the chronological development and this plan can enlarge

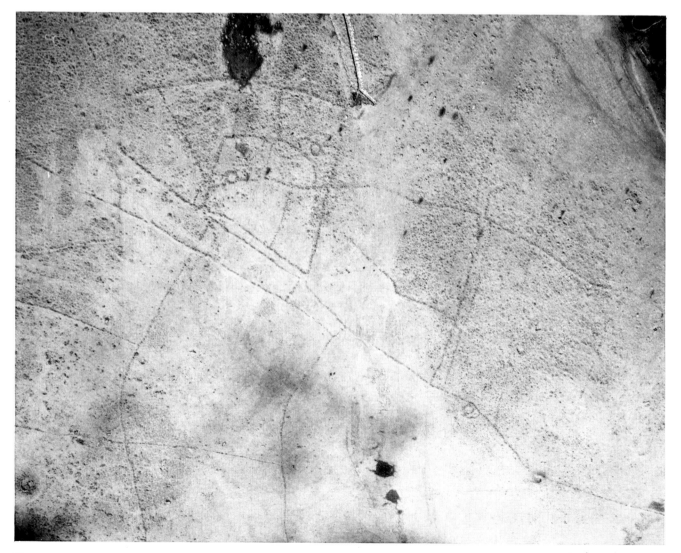

Fig 43   East Moor, SX 244781, looking north-east: settlement and coaxial field system. Details are shown on Fig 42 no 1. (Photo NMR SX 2478/3/190, 8 April 1976; Crown Copyright Reserved)

upon that discussion (Fig 42 no 1). The boundaries are later than the two cairns in the area. The cairn at Ridge lies within the fields, and Clitters cairn, shown by excavation to be earlier (Brisbane and Clews 1979), lies on the line of the moorland boundary a few metres off the plan, in the direction of the arrow at A. An earlier terminal boundary B, with at least the dependent boundary B^1, appears to be related to the settlement, and boundary C is earlier than the settlement enclosure, suggesting that the settlement was remodelled when the fields were extended. The extension boundary D has many dependent boundaries that in part overlie the former moorland boundary B. Trackway E has been extended to E^1 and the trackway at F created to serve the enclosed settle-

ment. It is a very organised layout with gateways (arrowed), defined by low gateposts, giving access to the houses as well as the small paddocks within the settlement enclosure. A hut and small enclosure have been added to the moorland boundary at G with an entrance through to the field nearby. Much of the area was ploughed in the medieval period. Brisbane and Clews felt that the ridges in field H were prehistoric, partly because they were covered by peat, but we have no evidence from excavation that any cultivation ridges on the Moor predated post-prehistoric boundaries. The cultivation ridges at Colliford (Griffith 1984) also had a slight cover of peat, although here it was suggested that this was due to post-medieval peat development. Until firm dating is

Fig 44   Sharptor, SX 258734, looking north: lynchetted field system overlain by modern fields. (Photo CUCAP AFE 41, 7 June 1962; Cambridge University Collection, Copyright Reserved)

established to demonstrate to the contrary, the cultivation ridges have been assumed to be post-prehistoric in origin.

Some of the boundaries show slight lynchetting, and clearance cairns lie scattered both within and beyond the fields; but a predominantly pastoral context for the East Moor system seems appropriate, with controlled grazing in the fields and common grazing beyond.

At Carne Downs (Fig 42 no 2) a more compact set of fields is defined by two moorland boundaries, with three trackways leading to the settlement nuclei. The fields are much smaller, 0.15–0.6ha, than at East Moor. The huts are large, with five over 7m in diameter. The land to the north–east and south has been improved, so that the extent of the fields in these directions is not known. The main terminal boundary, however, extends westwards around the hill to meet other fields on the slopes opposite Bray Down.

The fields at Watergate (Fig 42 no 3) are different again; they are small and, unusually, lie along the contour. As at Carne Downs there is evidence of lynchetting, suggesting that parts of the system were cultivated. A less compact set of fields to the west is associated with huts slightly larger (over 6.5m in diameter) than those in the small fields. Again, due to later enclosure, it is unclear how large these systems were, especially on the south.

The other main field-type on Bodmin Moor has relatively substantial lynchets and resembles those, so common in West Penwith, which are associated with courtyard-house settlements and are presumed to be of later prehistoric or Romano-British date. The fields at Watergate may possibly be an early development of this form. The fields are found at three places on the Moor: Carwether (SX 095790); Berry Down (SX ·198685), and Sharptor (SX 258734). The air photograph of the fields at Sharptor (Fig 44) serves to illustrate their form: roughly square fields, 1ha or less in size, heavily lynchetted. At Sharptor and Carwether they appear to have evolved from part of an earlier and larger field system. They are shown on Map 1 and Fig 50, and it can be seen on Map 2 that those at Sharptor also lie within a later enclosure, suggesting that their use extended into the medieval period.

A search of the enclosed land surrounding the Moor may reveal traces of other lynchetted field systems of later date. The search may also reveal traces of coaxial field boundaries running into the post-prehistoric farms, as they so evidently do at Bohayland on East Moor (see Map 2) and Dartmoor.

9 Cornwall Archaeological Unit survey area (Map 3)

by Peter Rose and Nicholas Johnson

In this section the main archaeological components of the various survey blocks are outlined prior to discussion in section 10 below. The names of the survey blocks are marked on Map 3 as a location guide.

Louden

1 (SX135800)   An accretive system of irregular curvilinear fields extends over 30ha on both sides, and over the top of the hill. The fields are generally 0.25–0.75ha and are defined by low stone banks, slight lynchets and occasionally by single stone walls. The system has probably developed from three separate foci: SX 13307997, SX 13307975, and SX 13657995. A few scattered huts are probably associated. There are three areas of clearance cairns: one lies within a field, but two groups are not within fields and may represent an early stage in field development.

2   Two cross-ridge boundary banks cut the field system. The southern was laid out by enhancing the line of the existing system with a more substantial stone bank, robbed from adjoining boundaries. Fig 45 shows a section of this boundary with three stages of development:

a   component 1: accretive curvilinear fields;
b   component 2: the cross-ridge boundary reuses part of component 1;
c   the medieval tenement boundary of Louden partly reuses components 1 and 2.

Neither bank is particularly large and evidence for facing is rare. The northern boundary has a small hut attached towards the west end. The boundaries appear to run between areas of bog or stream on either side of Louden Hill.

3   (SX 13137982 and SX 13347998)   Two enclosures appear to be later than component 1 and the southern one is probably contemporary with component 2.

4   (SX 13707980)   On the east side of the hill a settlement of c 30 huts extends along the contour in association with a lynchet which cuts the northern cross-ridge boundary. The huts are mostly small (77% are less than 5m in diameter), with little facing apparent. A hut at SX 13868000 has robbed the northern boundary and further up the hill two huts (SX 13728008) of similar type appear to have robbed the northern cross-ridge boundaries.

5   (SX 13308010)   On the west side of the hill is a smaller group of 14 huts, half of them greater than 7m in diameter (only one is less than 4.5m), and generally well built with a clear inner facing of slabs. A small enclosure is linked to one of them. The huts do not have associated enclosures and their place in the sequence is unclear; they could be contemporary with component 1 or 2 or with neither. They are similar in size range to huts on Stannon Down and resemble the settlement at North Langstone Downs (Fig 38).

Stannon South

1   (SX 12707990)   An accretive system of at least four large curvilinear fields defined by low stone banks, each of 2–3ha and covering a total of c 9ha. The fields may be associated with two or three very robbed huts lying on the north edge, but there is no

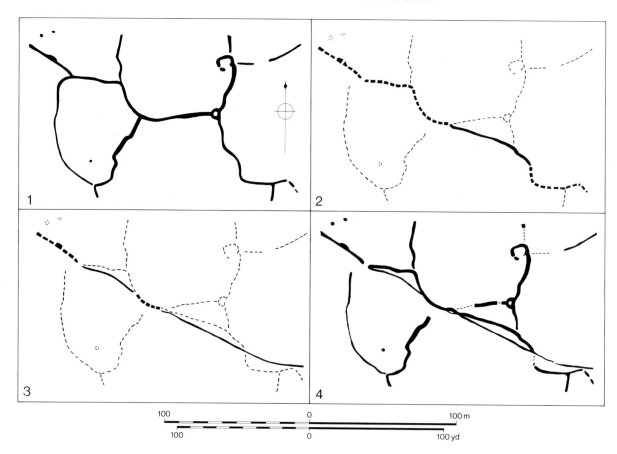

Fig 45   Multiple-phase boundaries on Louden, SX 13317971: 1, early curvilinear accreted system with two huts; 2, system overlain by later prehistoric boundary bank, which reuses part of the earlier field boundaries; 3, medieval boundary of Louden tenement, reusing parts of earlier boundaries; 4, appearance today

direct relationship, nor with the Stannon stone circle which lies adjacent. The boundary nearest the circle is incomplete. Although it is unlikely that the boundary was robbed to build the stone circle, as the stones used are very different in type, it nevertheless seems likely that the fields are earlier than the circle and that the field closest to the circle was slighted. Alternatively the fields were contemporary with the circle and the boundary closest to the circle was constructed as a fence.

2   The field system is cut by a cross-ridge boundary, in its original form a substantial stone-faced stone wall up to 1.5m wide.

3   (*SX 12748004*)   A substantial elongated hut with rounded ends (13 × 5.6m), is perhaps of Romano-British date (Fig 35 no 6).

Stannon Down

1   (*SX 13658094*)   A system of irregular curvilinear fields of unknown extent. The area is in part peat-covered. There are cairns in the immediate area and two possible huts, but their relationship with the fields is not apparent.

2   A scatter of enclosures of varying size, now largely destroyed. Some of these include cairns in their boundaries (Harris *et al* 1984).

3   (*SX 13208030*)   A settlement of *c* 25 huts, some of

them excavated (R J Mercer 1970). The huts are large, 5.5–10m in diameter, and comparable to component 5 at Louden, which can perhaps be regarded as an extension of the same settlement. Fields are almost certainly associated, but the picture is confused by medieval reuse. The settlement may have two phases with two or three smaller and more ruined-looking huts associated with three to four curvilinear accreted fields, as in the north–east part, and a large number of bigger and better-preserved huts, perhaps associated with more rectilinear fields. Mercer's site plan (R J Mercer 1970, fig 6) is difficult to reconcile with the remains on the ground. The many narrow strip-like fields appear to be wider, shorter, and fewer than shown, some boundaries probably being medieval cultivation ridges. The fields lie almost entirely within the later fields of the medieval tenement of Stannon, with several of the boundaries certainly being of this date. There is evidence of much cultivation, with clearance mounds and slight ridges showing in many of the fields. Nevertheless some of the rectilinear fields appear to be associated with the prehistoric huts.

Roughtor North (*Figs 46–8*)

1   (*SX 14308160*)   An accreted system of irregular curvilinear fields, *c* 34ha, is defined by low stone banks, sometimes with single stone walls, and is associated with a few slight huts (part shown on Figs

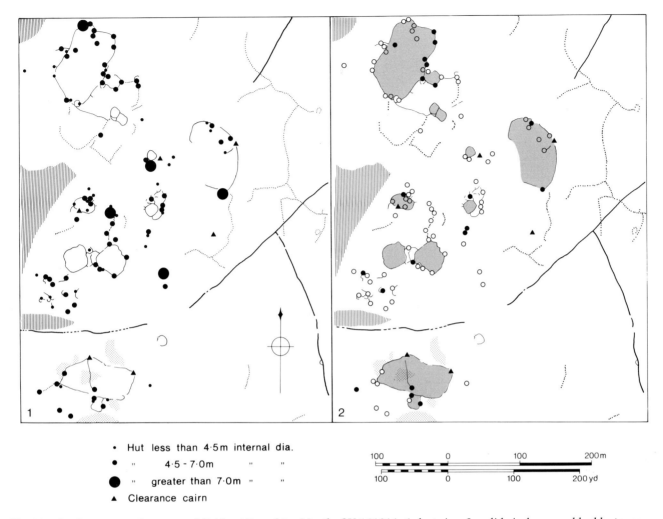

Hut less than 4·5m internal dia.

" 4·5 - 7·0m " "

" greater than 7·0m " "

▲ Clearance cairn

100   0   100   200m

100   0   100   200yd

Fig 46   Settlement, enclosure, and fields at Roughtor North, SX 141814: 1, hut size; 2, solid circles, unrobbed huts; open circles, robbed huts. The shaded enclosures appear to have been cultivated and/or maintained, and are relatively substantial. The area is illustrated on Figs 47 and 48, and discussed on p66–8. The early-phase curvilinear fields, shown as dotted lines, are cut by later boundaries, in bold line. Vertical shading, bog; regular stipple, clitter; triangle, cairn

15 and 47). In places the system is incomplete, perhaps reflecting its original character as well as robbing. There are clearance cairns where the boundaries trail off in the north, perhaps suggesting early stages in field formation. To the south, occasional isolated lengths of bank and patches of clearance suggest cultivation over an extensive area, perhaps as far as Roughtor South.

2   *(SX 14508105)*   A field system consisting of small accreted fields together with two examples of parallel banks following the contour, in one case entering and crossing an exceedingly stony area of clitter. There are cairns on two of the boundaries and three huts lie close by. It may be another aspect of component 1.

3   A few individual enclosures are associated with cairns. The enclosures tend to be open at one side, and defined by substantial stone banks, sometimes strongly lynchetted. Their relationship with component 1 is not certain.

4   A series of substantial boundary banks cut through the field system (Fig 47 points A1–4, Fig 29,

and Map 3). The northernmost is very substantial (Fig 47 point A1); in its present form a stone bank 5–7m wide and up to 1m high, but originally a stone-faced stone wall 2–3m wide. Although this is a considerable barrier, at the north–west it fades out as if either unfinished or continued in some other way (eg by ending on an area of dense vegetation or continuing as a fence). Attached to the south–east and upper end of the wall is a much less substantial boundary (Fig 47 point A2), a stone bank generally less than 0.4m high and 1m wide. The difference in character is remarkable for two boundaries which are presumably serving a similar function in a single boundary system. Halfway along the larger boundary a straight stony lynchet extends at right angles from the wall (Fig 47 point A4). A third major boundary ends on the second and runs uphill to end in clitter at the foot of Roughtor (Fig 47 point A3). This is 0.3–0.7m high and was originally a stone-faced stone wall 1.5m wide. Two possible structures (4 × 2.5m internally) appear to have been built on to the west side of the boundary, but they are very rough and may be the result of disturbance to the bank.

Fig 47   Roughtor North, SX 142815, looking south-south-east: ground slopes down from left to right; multiphase prehistoric landscape. A1–4, block boundaries (p67) overlying curvilinear accreted fields, top and middle left; B, post-medieval shelter built into hut circle, Fig 52 no 2; C, kerbed platform cairn, Fig 26 no 7; D, hut with internal subdivision, Fig 35 no 7; the medieval tenement boundary of Stannon runs through the settlement on the right-hand side from top to bottom. Middle right area shown in more detail on Figs 15, 46, 48. Two people acting as convenient scales are walking from D towards the bottom right corner. (Photo NMR SX 1481/18/325, 28 February 1979; Crown Copyright Reserved)

Further south, a fourth boundary (SX 14218065) extends from the clitter downhill to a stony area above the bog (see Fig 29, centre of drawing). It is a stone bank 1.5–2.5m wide, 0.3–0.6m high, with little indication of facing. A small oval structure defined by low stone banks (4.6 × 2.3m internally) is attached end on to the north side of the boundary.

5   *(SX 14008140)*   A settlement (or settlements) of 103 huts is spread out for 850m along the hillslope. Part of this is shown in more detail on Figures 46–8. At least two phases of boundary are apparent: (1) slight and often fragmentary banks which may be an extension of component 1; (2) a series of enclosures, defined by more substantial stone banks, some of which appear to use elements of the curvilinear field system (component 1); the enclosures are confined to the northern two-thirds of the settlement. In the south of the settlement is a third element, not neces-

sarily a different phase. It is more compact and better defined as a field system than the slight and sprawling component 1 fields.

The huts are of at least three phases: (1) a large number throughout the settlement are of slight appearance or have been robbed to provide material for the enclosures, into which some have been incorporated (Fig 46 no 2 and Fig 48 points B show the robbed huts); (2) a smaller number of better preserved huts, many of which are associated with enclosures (Fig 46 no 2); (3) three small structures 2.5m in diameter adjoining the outside of the southernmost enclosure (Fig 46 no 1).

Roughtor South (*Fig 49*)

The settlement straddles a very stony area around the southern slopes of Roughtor. Much of the eastern

Fig 48 Roughtor North, SX 140814, looking north along a slight slope: huts and enclosures. A large number of huts have been robbed (examples at B) and more substantial huts and enclosures maintained or constructed (components 1 and 2, p72). Slight traces of fields are visible at A (part of component 1, p66). The medieval tenement boundary of Stannon cuts through a prehistoric hut at C. The photograph shows the middle left section of Fig 46. (Photo SX 1481/24, date unknown; Crown Copyright Reserved)

part is taken up by a block of medieval fields that have obscured or destroyed much of the earlier pattern (Fig 67).

1 (*SX 14258051*) An area of fields defined largely by edges of clearance and a few clearance heaps that may be associated with a small number of badly robbed huts along the uphill edge.

2 (*SX 14688062*) A scatter of six or more huts of slight and rough build lie to the south of the south-

ern entrance of the Roughtor enclosure. There are no associated boundaries.

3 (*SX 14508030*) At least 42 huts within an area of 6ha, some of them associated with a system of curvilinear, irregular fields (Fig 49, bottom left), which extends through the stony area. It is possible that components 1 and 2 are an extension of this and all bear some similarity to the southern part of Roughtor North. The huts are not generally large.

4 Two probably contemporary boundaries are of

Fig 49 Roughtor South, SX 143803, north at top of page: multiphase landscape. A, large boundary; B, group of huts cut by boundary A: C, D-shaped enclosure attached to boundary A; C^1, hut cut by enclosure C; D, hut cut by later enclosure; E, subrectangular structure attached to boundary A; F, peat-drying platform; G, complex hut (p74); H, animal shelter built against a large rock, Fig 52 no 4. (Photo NMR SX 1480/34/297, 28 February 1979; Crown Copyright Reserved)

similar build – stone-faced stone walls; that on the west (SX 14308037) was originally up to 2m wide, that on the south–east (SX 14678020) 1.5m wide. The western boundary (Fig 49 point A), cuts a group of huts in component 1 (Fig 49 point B), and runs from the Roughtor clitter to Garrow Marsh (Fig 49 point A, bottom to top of photograph). Attached to it is a substantially built D-shaped enclosure (Fig 49 point C) that cuts a hut circle (Fig 49 point C^1) and therefore also postdates elements of component 3. The south–east boundary (Fig 29 and Map 3) appears

to connect two roughly oval enclosures: the western one cuts a hut of component 3 at point D (Fig 49). They are of similar size to the D-shaped enclosure (point C). All are possibly of similar date and function. It is not clear which huts, if any, are contemporary with this phase. A sub-rectangular structure (4 × 2m) at point E is attached to boundary A.

5   Two or three small structures (eg SX 14438038) are perhaps comparable to those on Brown Willy identi-

fied by Herring as early medieval transhumance huts (Herring 1986).

Butterstor

Two separate field systems (Map 3) are divided by an area of stones:

1 (*SX 15057745*)   An accretive system of curvilinear fields *c* 10ha in extent with generally large fields (1–2ha). The boundaries are slight stone banks and lynchets. Nine huts up to 9m in diameter are scattered through the system.

2 (*SX 15097830*)   A fragmentary accretive system of curvilinear fields *c* 13ha in extent. Only one possible hut was found.

Garrow Tor

1   Two linked enclosures adjoin the east side of Garrow Tor (Fig 71):

(*SX 14657855*)   A sub-oval enclosure, 110 × 60m (Fig 71, point A), containing *c* 15 huts, 3.5–5m in diameter. Five have complete or partial concentric rings around them (see Fig 34 no 14). They are likely to be contemporary with the enclosures and have no associated fields.

(*SX 14657843*)   A large sub-oval enclosure, 170 × 100m (Fig 71, point B), containing 20 huts, 2.0–5.5m in diameter. Eight of the huts are smaller than any in the first enclosure. Six huts have dependent enclosures (see Fig 34 no 15) and one a concentric ring (Fig 34 no 14). They are likely to be contemporary with the enclosure and have no associated fields.

2 (*SX 14517801*)   Nine huts, in a close group immediately above the medieval settlement (Fig 16; Fig 35 nos 2, 5, 8), are similar in character to those in component 1 but slightly larger; four are over 4.5m in diameter. One hut has an elaborated entrance (Fig 16 B; Fig 35 no 5) and four have concentric rings. One of the latter (Fig 16 A; Fig 35 no 8), excavated by D Dudley (MS at Royal Cornwall Museum, Truro), was thought to be Late Bronze Age.

3 (*SX 14527803*)   Twenty-five huts lie on the summit of the southern spine of Garrow Tor, of which eleven are under 4.5m, and the rest up to 7.8m in diameter (see Fig 37). Later medieval and post-medieval boundaries run through this tight group, robbing some of the huts. There are three concentric enclosures (Fig 37 nos 1–3), one of which has two small structures added to the inside of the enclosure (no 2). Three huts appear to have small yard-like enclosures similar to Figure 34 no 28 (Fig 37 nos 4–6). Three or four have porches (Fig 37 points A–D), and four show evidence of reuse (Fig 37 points D, E, nos 5, 6). The huts with associated enclosures and porches are more substantially built; the remainder appear to have suffered more robbing. There is no clear association with fields.

4 (*SX 14277819*)   Ten or eleven huts, 3–5m in diameter lie in a stony area on the hilltop with several enclosures or part-enclosures and some fragmentary curvilinear boundaries which extend eastwards over the brow of the hill. It is unclear whether the fields are associated with this settlement or with two turf-covered hut platforms to the north–east and south–east. Three of the huts are more substantial, perhaps suggesting phasing.

5 (*SX 14407789*)   Twenty-three huts lie amongst 3.5ha of enclosures and small fields in a generally stony area on the south–east side of the hill. The south–eastern half of the settlement has been incorporated in the medieval field system; though robbed, many huts are still visible. The huts are not elaborate and all but a few are less than 5m in diameter. The fields are all less than 0.4ha, reflecting the stoniness of the area, and the whole is similar in character to Roughtor South (component 3; Fig 49), and perhaps Carneglos (Fig 41 no 2).

6 (*SX 14177765*)   Four huts lie inside an enclosure and a fifth adjoins the exterior of an enclosure appended to the first. The enclosures are within an area of medieval fields. The huts within the main enclosure are substantial though not large (3.5–6m) and have been excavated (Dudley 1957–8, 47–8). Bronze Age and Iron Age material was found, including a glass bead of the third century BC (Silvester 1979).

7 (*SX 14167763*)   Up to five very slight huts or platforms, 3.2–5m in diameter, some of them conjoined; not obviously associated with any boundaries.

8 (*SX 14107820*)   An extensive area of settlement covers at least 13ha and contains *c* 62 huts. The area is shown in part on Figures 5 and 36. It includes a system of curvilinear accreted fields, 0.2–0.5ha, possibly developed from a series of individual fields and enclosures. It is not always clear which huts are associated with them. Stony areas define some of the unbounded edges. They may be part of a system that spread eastwards over the hill to incorporate component 4 and others.

The huts exhibit a great variety. Slight huts are scattered throughout the system, but there are also distinct clusters of generally more substantial huts, notably in the southern part at A, B, C, D in Figure 36 which shows part of the settlement. At B the huts appear to be grouped around a small yard. Hut 1 (Fig 36), excavated by Dudley (Dudley MS, Royal Cornwall Museum), produced pottery said to be of the second century AD; it was selected for excavation because it somewhat resembles the Romano-British courtyard houses of West Penwith. The hut sits within a subdivided concentric enclosure similar to those identified as numbers 1–3 on Fig 37. In Figure 36, the group at 6–9 display an unusual degree of complexity and anomaly. Hut 6 in particular, with associated small enclosures, superficially resembles a courtyard house but differs considerably in scale and detail. The apparent discovery of Romano-British pottery from hut 1 may suggest that these structures and clusters are indeed part of a later prehistoric tradition. The only other example of similar complexity in the area is at Roughtor South (Fig 49 point G).

A rectangular structure (Fig 36 no 7) 1.7 × 2.5m is associated with two small enclosures and may well be post-prehistoric in date.

Huts 1–5 have concentric rings (type 14, Fig 34). There is a very good example a little to the north, SX 14037841. Other huts have elaborated entrances (6–7).

10   Discussion

by Peter Rose and Nicholas Johnson

CAU Area 1:1000 survey

The detailed survey of this area was intended to provide a framework of settlement type and chronology that could be applied to the remains elsewhere on the Moor. First, it was possible to identify a broad range of settlement and land use types:

1   Curvilinear accreted fields associated with cultivation and potentially permanent settlements.

2   Potentially permanent settlements with more limited areas of fields or with enclosures, some with cultivation; here the emphasis is likely to be on pastoralism.

3   Large boundaries dividing the landscape into blocks.

4   Small huts which occur singly or grouped in settlements, presumably associated with seasonal pastoral activity.

There is, however, much local variation in the form of settlements, even within the relatively small area examined in detail. The very large numbers of huts, ritual monuments, and cairns, as well as the enclosure at Roughtor, suggest that this is an unusually important part of the Moor.

Second, in reviewing the chronology of the remains, it has been possible to distinguish evidence of phasing, although the examples given below are not necessarily sequential.

1   At Stannon South, Louden Hill (Fig 45 no 2) Roughtor North, and Roughtor South, large boundary walls cut across accreted curvilinear fields (see Map 3 and Fig 46).

2   At Roughtor North (Fig 46) many huts have been robbed and are earlier than the present form of the enclosures. It is not clear, however, whether the robbed huts were associated with the earlier curvilinear fields, or whether they belong to a phase of huts and enclosures coming between the fields (dotted on Fig 46) and the later enclosures (shaded).

3   At Roughtor South a D-shaped enclosure (Fig 49) attached to one of the large boundary walls, and at

least one other enclosure, are later than the underlying field system. Both are presumably related to the boundary phase.

4   At Garrow clusters of huts (Fig 36) with annexes, concentric enclosures, and concentric rings of stones appear to be later than the straggly curvilinear fields in the area.

5   A settlement of small huts (Fig 29 point F) at Louden (generally less than 4.5m in diameter) are strung along a looping lynchet that cuts through a cross-ridge boundary bank.

6   On the west side of Louden, an enclosure (Map 3) at SX 13357997 slights and partially uses an accreted curvilinear field system. Another enclosure (Map 3) at SX 13137982 appears to have developed to its present substantial form after the building of the cross-ridge boundary.

In addition, certain assumptions have been made when considering fields and settlements, based on field evidence alone, and they must be viewed with circumspection.

1   Potentially permanent settlement is indicated by the presence of large huts, greater than 4.5m internal diameter, but more particularly 6m upwards, often associated with a range of smaller structures. Seasonal settlement is indicated by concentrations of smaller huts; sub-rectangular or sub-square huts may indicate a later form.

2   Curvilinear fields, cleared areas, clearance cairns, and lynchetting within fields and enclosures, indicate cultivation.

3   Long boundaries, especially the stone walls (ie features faced on both sides), indicate the control of stock, and define grazing areas.

4   Enclosures, if lynchetted, may indicate areas of cultivation from which animals were excluded; and enclosures with no lynchetting, but with gates and/or well-built banks or walls, may indicate stock enclosures.

The clearest and commonest relationship is between the substantial block boundaries and the extensive systems of accretive fields. What cannot immediately be demonstrated, however, is the phase of settlement with which such block boundaries are associated. The options are:

1   that the boundaries are not contemporary with nearby settlement, but represent extensive control of grazing by settlements located elsewhere. Structures attached to some of the boundaries might be shelters or stores associated with this phase of land use.

2   that contemporary settlements be sought in the area of the boundaries themselves; one possibility is the suggested Romano-British structure at Stannon South (component 3, p 66). The boundaries would, however, have required a considerable investment of labour; the preferred option is that individual settle-

ments at Roughtor, Stannon, and Louden should be related to each of the defined blocks.

With all these points in mind, it is possible to construct a tentative picture of the chronology of land use within the area.

Phase 1

Farms of huts and accreted curvilinear fields developed throughout this part of the Moor, concentrated in the following areas:

Stannon South (SX 127798)
Stannon Down (SX 135810; close to the cairns and extending south under the clay tips)
Louden Hill (SX 133798)
Garrow Tor (SX 141781)
Butterstor (SX 150775 and SX 151786)
Fernacre (SX 151801)
Roughtor South (SX 144803)
Roughtor North (SX 143815)

The majority of small cairns may be contemporary with these settlements, although those associated with enclosures, as on Stannon Down (SX 135810) and Roughtor North (SX 145816; SX 131820), may be earlier, perhaps contemporary with the pre-settlement phase at Stannon Down (R J Mercer 1970).

Phase 2

The large-scale cultivation phase ended, perhaps because of land exhaustion, and was replaced by pastoral activity. Of course, pastoralism could have taken place alongside cultivation, or separate from it, in phase 1. We do not know if there was a phase of huts-and-enclosures associated with pastoral activity that preceded the next phase – the dividing of the landscape into pastoral blocks. This could have been possible, the robbed hut phase at Roughtor North (see Fig 46) perhaps representing a settlement and its associated enclosures directly overlooking an area of 'common' pasture defined by natural features (clitter, rivers, and bog) or, possibly, fences or hedges.

Phase 3

Large boundaries divided the area into blocks:

(1) Roughtor North block 1 (centred SX 140815)
(2) Roughtor North block 2 (centred SX 140810)
(3) Stannon Down block (centred SX 137805 from Stannon Down to the foot of Roughtor)
(4) Louden Hill block (centred SX 134797).

Within each block is a series of huts and enclosures, including a number of huts with enclosures that show evidence of cultivation.

The enclosures shaded on Figure 46 at Roughtor North indicate that the two blocks had small areas of cultivation; the southern part of the settlement is associated with a small field system rather than

'enclosures', probably reflecting local variation that can be expected from settlement to settlement. At Stannon Down, only one of the enclosures now survives, incomplete, at SX 13528044; a slight negative lynchet at its upper edge suggests it was once cultivated. The two enclosures described above (see p 65), within the Louden Hill block both appear to have been cultivated.

The three enclosures at Roughtor South, one of which adjoins the boundary wall, may be examples of enclosures outside a controlled grazing block (ie the Stannon block). The attached enclosure (Fig 49 point C), which has at least one gate, is well built but not certainly associated with any of the huts that lie within it. As at Roughtor North, however, some huts are clearly in better condition than others. The middle enclosure at SX 14508022, part shown on Figure 49 at point D, has opposed gates, while the third, now within an area of medieval fields (Fig 67, kidney-shaped enclosure, centre), has one well-defined gate visible on its north side. These entrances are evident as upright posts or transverse slabs defining gaps between 1m and 1.7m wide.

It is not clear whether some of the huts and fields/enclosures in the settlement are similar to those in the later phase at Roughtor North; if so, this area defined on the west and south by substantial two-faced walls may be a further block, making a total of five for the area.

Outside the Roughtor, Louden, and Stannon areas the sequence is less clear. The two linked enclosures adjoining the eastern side of Garrow Tor appear to have been stock-proof, but they were probably refurbished in the medieval period. Furthermore it is unclear whether the huts inside, which are all small, were contemporary or later. The small concentric enclosures (Fig 34, type 15) and the concentric ringed huts (Fig 34, type 14, Dudley's 'corridor houses') both seem to suggest that animals needed either to be kept away from buildings or corralled within the small enclosure. There is no evidence of any large boundaries defining Garrow, although the southern wall at Roughtor South could conceivably be a northern boundary. Although it does not entirely cut off the northern approach, Garrow is in effect an island of land defined on three sides by streams and bog. It may therefore form another block within which there was similar activity to that of the other blocks.

The Butterstor field system appears to have been abandoned at an early stage and the Stannon South system was divided (p 66) and similarly abandoned. The Stannon South boundary wall may have been related to settlements to the west, off the present area of the Moor.

Within this subdivided landscape, cultivation was taking place (the cultivated enclosures), but on a more restricted basis. It must be significant that the area of large curvilinear fields such as those at Butterstor, Louden, perhaps Stannon Down, and the south–west and north–west slopes of Roughtor have been demonstrably overlain by the boundary banks or abandoned. These earlier systems have fields that are generally larger than those elsewhere on the Moor. We can therefore suggest that cultivation was taking place within enclosures or smaller fields during the large-boundary/pastoral block phase and that fields on the southern half of Roughtor North and within the southern Roughtor block, the more rectilinear fields at Stannon Down, and perhaps some at Garrow Tor, represent the field rather than the enclosure element of this period. We have no way of knowing whether all the other curvilinear accreted field systems on the Moor can be phased in this way.

At some stage, perhaps contemporary with or even before the phase of large boundaries, seasonal pastoral activity developed. It may have started earlier in the bleaker areas of the Moor, and may have been a feature of the earliest settlement of the Moor, as has been suggested for Dartmoor (Fleming 1978), but in this area it was perhaps later, towards the end of the second and the beginning of the first millennium BC. This may be suggested by the settlement on the east side of Louden (component 4), which is demonstrably a later phase. The considerable numbers of small huts in some of the Garrow settlements (particularly components 1 and 2 – see p 71) suggest a similar function, although not necessarily a similar date. Land use of this type may have continued into the medieval period (see Chapter 5).

On Garrow, Dudley found Iron Age pottery (Silvester 1979; Dudley MS, Royal Cornwall Museum, and CAU SMR record) in the pound settlement (SX 14177765) and in an enclosed hut (Fig 36, site 1). Although the huts are small they are well built, and it seems probable that they represent permanent settlement of the 1st millennium BC at the head of the De Lank valley. The huts in this area, with the addition of another at Roughtor South (Fig 49 point G) within one of the three enclosures, do not have obvious local parallels; it has already been suggested in the section on hut types (p 49) that they may all represent a form of proto-courtyard-house development, using the term in a general rather than specific sense. This development may also be seen in West Penwith, for example, at Bosporthennis (SX 43603605).

It is not possible to suggest what influence the defended enclosure on Roughtor (Fig 31) exerted at any particular time, except that it lies within the most densely settled area of the Moor and that the major block boundary system is clustered closely about it. It is possible that it was used seasonally, with the hut platforms acting as the equivalent of tent pitches. It is more likely to be associated with the main settlement phases, and perhaps replaced the Louden long cairn as a focus. We do not know what remains, if any, can be related to Neolithic activity. It is conceivable that some of the huts and fields still visible in this area and elsewhere are of this date.

The rest of the Moor

Most of the elements identified above can be found elsewhere on the Moor, but nowhere else so clearly. Curvilinear fields are found in profusion as separate farms or agglomerations of farms. The Leskernick and Craddock Moor systems are well developed with trackways to control the stock and with accreted

fields for cultivation. Almost invariably the ratio of huts to enclosed area is high, suggesting that pastoralism rather than cultivation would have been the mainstay. A clear distinction between the earlier and later cultivation as seen in the Roughtor area is not readily apparent elsewhere; differences in the extent of cultivation, as on Roughtor, may vary from settlement to settlement according to local conditions or local preference.

Larger-scale boundary development is found in a variety of forms. As in the north–western part of the Moor, it is a somewhat later phase: for example, boundaries at Treswallock Downs and East Moor (Brisbane and Clews 1979) cut across curvilinear fields. However, the boundaries may also represent a purely local reorganisation, perhaps for more intensive grazing, rather than a widespread change in land use, so that similar settlements may have been in use both before and during the boundary phase; this may be seen at Lady Down (Fig 41 no 3), where a typical irregular field system with a scatter of huts is dependent on a long boundary, perhaps an extension of the Treswallock system. In layout this settlement contrasts with the extensive coaxial systems fringing the eastern part of the Moor, their well-planned fields complete with trackways to the settlements. Functionally they may have been similar, the settlements in both cases having a small area of immediately associated enclosures likely to be for cultivation, together with a much larger area enclosed probably for controlled grazing (at East Moor this area is divided into large fields which might also have been cultivated), and perhaps a further area of grazing beyond the enclosing boundary.

There may be other coaxial systems at Carne Downs, Treswallock Downs (stretching from Harpurs Downs in the north to Lady Down in the south), and perhaps the area of Smallacoombe and Little Siblyback, but some of these are obscured in part by later cultivation. The Bearah Tor / Sharptor / Langstone Downs system is typical of the variability that can be expected. At Sharptor (Fig 44) the system is associated with coaxial boundaries and rectilinear lynchetted fields, but further into the Moor, at Higher Langstone Downs, a substantial boundary, apparently part of the same system, partly encloses a settlement of huts and enclosures, comparable to a settlement at Carburrow enclosed by a similar boundary.

Although this boundary phase is likely to have been contemporary with the Dartmoor reave systems, it is very different in character, showing much less cohesion and a wider variety of associated settlement. Even the East Moor system, superficially very reave-like, is the product of a series of accretions rather than a single layout (Brisbane and Clews 1979).

At different dates in different areas permanent settlement was abandoned, and the Moor became a seasonal grazing area, perhaps for more than two millennia. Archaeologically this may be represented by sites such as Louden (SX 137898), the southern settlement at Fernacre (SX 149799), the uphill settle-

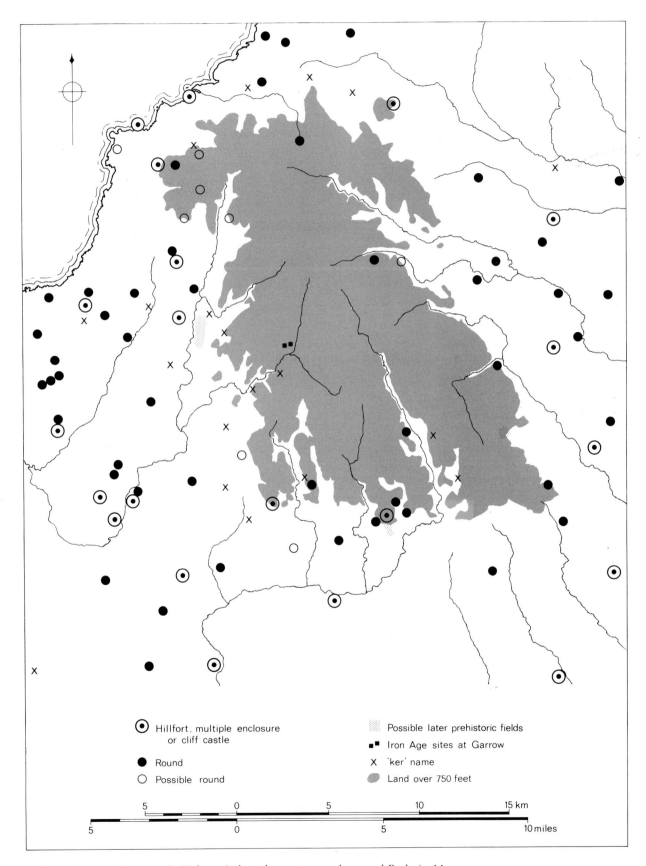

Fig 50 *Iron Age and Romano-British period settlement on and around Bodmin Moor*

ment at Brown Gelly (SX 201727: Fig 38 no 5), and the eastern one at Carburrow (SX 15557060), where the huts are mostly very small and laid out like strings of beads, in part defining an area into which they look. These are likely to be transhumance settlements but need not all belong to this late phase. Other settlements show evidence of the reuse of huts to make smaller structures, also possibly representing a phase of later seasonal activity.

The characteristic permanent settlements of the Iron Age and Romano-British period, the defended enclosures, have a distribution which largely avoids both the Moor and the ground above 230m; this includes a large area of high ground north of the granite Moor (Fig 50). The pattern is generally compatible with the distribution of the Cornish place-name element *ker* ('fort', a 'round') which may be expected to relate to settlements of this period, although in some cases the name may simply refer to settlements rather than defended settlements (Padel 1985). The complementary distribution of defended settlements and *ker* names to the west of the Moor may suggest that the settlement types need not always be equated. *Ker* names in the De Lank valley and the Fowey valley, where there is also the

enclosed site at Higher Langdon (Figs 33, 76) may suggest continued settlement of some areas of the Moor through later prehistory. This picture is reinforced by the Iron Age settlements found well up the De Lank at Garrow (Fig 50). Lynchetted fields around the fringes of the Moor at Carwether, Sharptor (Fig 44), and Berry Down may also have been in use at this period (Fig 50). In broad outline the pattern of settlement, and perhaps its economic base, may have been similar at the end of the first millennium BC and a thousand years later (p 77–9), although comparison of Figures 50 and 51 suggests a process of colonisation of the higher ground in the Davidstow area in the first millennium AD.

Finally, it seems inconceivable, with the growing evidence for prehistoric tin exploitation, that tin did not play a significant role either as a supplement to the farming 'income', or as an activity independent of farming. The dependence of medieval and post-medieval farmers on part-time tinning as an additional financial resource is well understood. In some senses the tin industry has underwritten the farming economy for centuries in those areas of the county where farming has always been hard, and this may have had a very long ancestry.

5 The historic landscape

by Peter Rose

1 Introduction

Documentary evidence, supplemented by later carto-graphic sources, provides a context for archaeological remains of the medieval period and after, and thus obviates the need for some of the basic questions that arise in examining the prehistoric evidence. Abandoned settlements and other remains can be seen in the context of manor and parish and can be related to the present pattern of settlement which is directly descended from the organisation of the land-scape in the medieval period. In addition Bodmin Moor, as one of the tin-producing districts of Corn-wall, came within the administrative and jurisdictive orbit of stannary law; it fell within the 'stannary of Foweymore' (G R Lewis 1908, 89).

The more immediate elements of this context for the medieval (and later) remains can be seen in Map 2, which, with the important exception of the indus-trial archaeology, attempts to show a totality of the evidence to *c* 1800. The discussion and description in this chapter follows Map 2 in considering the period up to *c* 1800, but concentrates on the medieval rather than the post-medieval developments. The choice of 1800 was determined by two considerations. First, the Ordnance Survey First Edition map of 1808 2″ (manuscript version), and 1″ map of 1813 (published version), provides the earliest detailed cartographic representation of the Moor. Second, there was con-siderable change during the nineteenth century, par-ticularly with extensive areas of new enclosures, whereas changes in the two centuries before 1800 did little to obscure the earlier pattern, making the period to 1800 something of a unity, as is apparent from comparison of the Ordnance Survey 1″ map of 1813 with the Tithe Maps for the area (*c* 1840) and with the Ordnance Survey 6″ map of 1881. (Map 2 has been compiled from three main sources: carto-graphic, archaeological, and documentary evidence. A detailed explanation of the use of this material and the conventions employed in the map is given on p xiv.)

2 Context and colonisation

As already mentioned, the medieval use of the sur-vey area can be seen in the context of a range of land units and settlement hierarchies which extend beyond the Moor itself. The Moor cannot be seen in isolation: it is very much a component of this wider area. This is clearly seen in the organisation of the parishes (Fig 51). The Moor is divided among 13 parishes (see p 1), within each of which, with the exception of Temple and St Breward, the bulk of medieval and modern settlement is located below 180–212m above OD, and off the Moor itself. It is also reflected in the location of the parish churches, all of which, except Temple and Warleggan, lie outside the survey area. The moorland parishioners had a long walk to church and even further to market. No towns developed within these parishes; instead they are found in a wider ring around the Moor – Bodmin, Camelford, Launceston, Callington, Liskeard (Shep-pard 1980).

The manors recorded in Domesday Book almost all have their centres on the lower ground (Fig 51 no 1, based on Thorn and Thorn 1979). Only Hamatethy, Halvana, and Draynes are on the granite. Some of these manors have huge areas of pasture recorded: seven leagues by four at Fawton (St Neot, SX 169682); five leagues by two at Hamatethy (St Breward, SX 096782); three leagues by two at Helstone (Lanteglos, SX 088813), Rosecraddock (St Cleer, SX 267678), and Trezance (Cardinham, SX 125693). This presumably refers to extensive rough grazing on the moorlands (Ravenhill 1967, 330–3, 342–3). (The exact length of the Domesday league in this area is not certain. In the context of these manors, a length of between 1.3 and 1.5 km is possible.) It is clear from later surveys of bounds that the larger manors extended into the Moor in the same way as the parishes, although not necessarily sharing their boundaries (for example Blisland Manor: Maclean 1873, 94).

Domesday settlements by themselves cannot be assumed to present a true picture of the pre-Conquest pattern of settlement, but the selective use of place-name evidence fills out and confirms the pattern which they suggest (Fig 51 no 1, based on information from O Padel). The Cornish place-name elements *tre* ('estate, farmstead'), **bod* ('dwelling'), and **hendre* ('winter homestead, home farm') (Padel 1985, 223, 129, 23) are all unlikely to have been used to coin new place-names later than *c* 1100 (Padel 1985, 24, 224), and because they are habitative names we can be confident that they refer to settlements. Figure 51 no 1 does not present the full picture of the pre-Conquest settlement pattern, as there are likely to have been many other early settlements, with non-habitative names, for which there is no compa-rable evidence for a pre-Conquest date. Nevertheless *tre*, **hendre*, and **bod* can be used to give a general representation of the areas of pre-Conquest settle-ment because they are *known* settlements. (The sym-bol * preceding a place-name element denotes a conjectural early form.)

Together with the Domesday manors, these names form a clear ring around the periphery of the Moor, avoiding the higher ground and the granite. (This is even more striking when seen against the county-wide distribution of *tre*: Padel 1985, 352 map). There are three apparent gaps in this ring, in the west at St Breward and in the south-west and south-east in Cardinham and Linkinhorne. Each is significant. In the first example the ring of *tre* names does continue, but on lower ground to the west of St Breward in the parish of St Tudy. St Breward parish is very largely

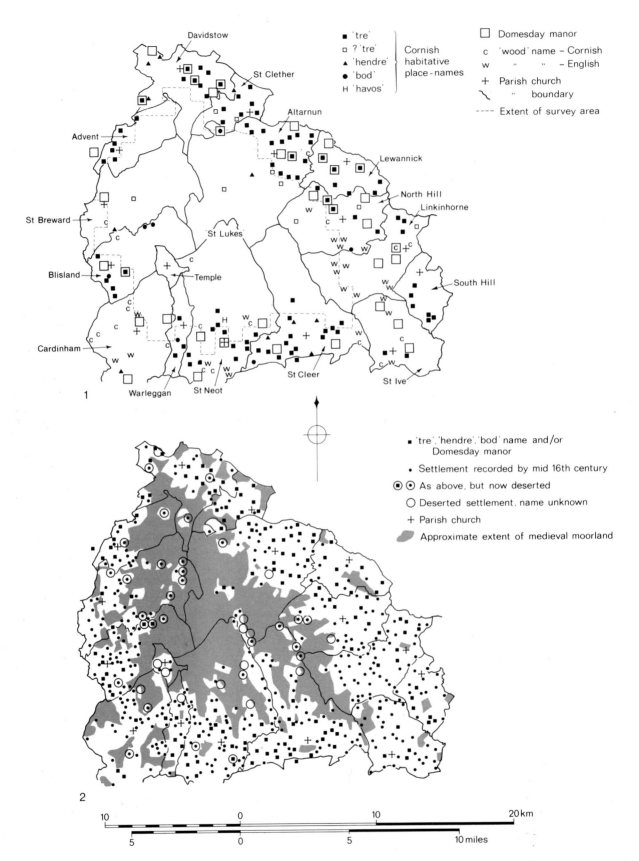

Fig 51 Medieval settlement: context and colonisation. 1, Selected aspects of early settlement, with parish boundaries; 2, the pattern of medieval settlement

above 210m OD, and does not include the large areas of lower ground found in most of the moorland parishes. The manor of Hamatethy in St Breward gives a further insight into the early character and development of the parish. Its name includes the Cornish element *havos* ('shieling'), a compound of *haf*, 'summer', and *bod* (Padel 1985, 127). This element is also found at Hammett in St Neot (SX 188697). In both Cornwall and Wales, *havos* has been paired with *hendre* to suggest two components in a system of transhumance, the summer and winter homestead (Pounds 1942; Padel 1985, 129, 127; Lloyd 1927–9; E Davies 1979). Padel notes that the largest number of *hendre* names is clustered around Bodmin Moor, 'and presumably these were settlements that used the moor for their summer shielings' (1985, 129). The apparent development of Hamatethy from a seasonal settlement to a manor by 1066 suggests an intensification of land use on this higher ground at some date before the Norman Conquest (Padel 1985, 127). For these reasons it is therefore likely that the bulk of settlement in St Breward, much of which was in the manor of Hamatethy, represents a process of medieval expansion or colonisation.

At Linkinhorne, and to some extent in North Hill, the situation is different. Here the *tre* names and Domesday manors form a ring a short distance from the edge of the Moor. This gap is filled by a large number of English place-names with elements suggesting a wooded environment (Old English forms *wudu*, *bearu*, *lēah* and *stocc*: Smith 1956). These names, together with the contrast between a predominance of Cornish names in the east of the parish and invariably English in the west, suggest a process of clearance and settlement in what may have been an extensive area of woodland around the more sheltered south-east edge of the Moor. The Domesday figures for woodland in this area are not remarkable (Ravenhill 1967, 327, fig 74), perhaps implying a relatively early date for this clearance (ie between the ninth and eleventh centuries: Padel, pers comm).

The apparently low density of pre-Conquest settlements in the Cardinham area may also be partly due to its wooded character, although in this case the 'wood' names are mostly Cornish rather than English (including *cos*, 'wood', and *kelli*, 'grove, small wood' (Padel 1985, 66, 47); in this area Cornish-speaking continued to perhaps as late as the thirteenth century (Padel, pers comm).

It is probable that the greater part of the Moor was not permanently settled until after *c* 1100, a period of extensive colonisation which created the picture seen in Figure 51 no 2 and Map 2. As well as a general movement into all the fringes of the Moor, the distribution relates closely to the river valleys, in particular the De Lank (St Breward/Blisland) and the Fowey. The bulk of the settlements are recorded by the thirteenth and fourteenth centuries, as can be seen, for example, in the settlements that extend up the De Lank (see Map 2). Settlements recorded for the first time in the sixteenth, seventeenth, and eighteenth centuries could also be much older and simply lack early documentation, but where these settlements appear together in a group it is more likely

that they genuinely represent an area of later colonisation. This may be the case in St Breward with Whiteheads, Bolatherick, Irish, Casehill, and Whitemeadow (area centred SX 1177). Elsewhere examples are more isolated and in general this period cannot be seen as one of further major expansion.

Before the thirteenth and fourteenth centuries documentation is extremely poor. Many or even most of the settlements could be earlier; only excavation and environmental work can demonstrate this. The example of Hamatethy suggests that the process is under way in the eleventh century or earlier, but the lack of *tre* and *bod* names implies that most of the expansion is likely to be eleventh-century and later. Some early settlement up the De Lank valley is suggested by Bedwithiel and Bedrawle, both containing *bod*. Also along the De Lank, Carbilly and Carkees may contain the place-name element *ker* ('fort, a round'), though it might alternatively be *carn* ('rock-pile, tor': Padel 1985, 50, 38). At Carwether, St Breward, a pre-Conquest origin is almost certain because here *ker* is qualified by a Cornish personal name (*ibid* 53, 224).

Colonisation of the Upper Fowey is likely to have taken place by the twelfth century at the latest. The chapel of St Lukes (SX 194764), equated with the 'chapel of Foweymore' referred to in 1241 (Henderson 1928b), contained a Norman font which is now at Tideford, St Germans (Sedding 1909, 152 and pl LXIX). It may have been established as a chapelry to serve an area of the Upper Fowey which in the fifteenth and sixteenth centuries evidently had parochial or semi-parochial status (*c* 1520, 'Parish of St Luke': Gover 1948, 288; Henderson 1928b). On the opposite side of the valley is Carneglos. The settlement takes its name from a topographical feature which itself probably refers to the chapel (Cornish *carn* and *eglos*, 'rock-pile, tor' + 'church': Padel 1985, 38, 91); the chapel was evidently in existence early enough to have generated a topographic name in Cornish rather than English (ie eleventh-century?). This 'parish' in the Upper Fowey would have been carved out of remote parts of Altarnun and St Neot parishes. Temple was established in a similar way, in the twelfth century (Henderson 1928, 202) probably from parts of Blisland and Cardinham.

In most parts of the Moor names are found in both English and Cornish. The many settlements with English names are likely to have been established at a time when English had replaced Cornish as the dominant language in this area, but settlements with Cornish names are not necessarily older; a Cornish name may often result from the survival of a topographical name rather than mean that a settlement was established at a time when Cornish was still spoken. In some localities the grouping of English names in relation to Cornish names can give an idea of the process of colonisation. We have already seen how in Linkinhorne the names in the east of the parish are predominantly Cornish and in the west are entirely English. Similarly, expansion into the south-east of Advent (SX 1180) is reflected by a cluster of English names there. At Cardinham all but one of a group of seven settlements 2 km south of the church (SX 1367) have English names; they appear to have been cut out of an area of moorland.

As a simple outline, four stages in the process of colonisation can be suggested (this is further refined below, p 83–7).

1   Up to the eleventh century: limited colonisation on the Moor (eg as suggested by Hamatethy).

2   Eleventh (?) to fourteenth centuries, perhaps with a concentration in the twelfth and thirteenth centuries: the main period of colonisation.

3   Fifteenth to eighteenth centuries: limited coloni-sation, also desertions.

4   Nineteenth century: major expansion and coloni-sation.

3   Summer pasture

Summer grazing

Carew tells us that 'the middle part of the shire lieth waste and open, sheweth a blackish colour, beareth heath and spiry grass, and serveth in a manner only to summer cattle' (1602). The value of summer pas-tures is nicely put in this seventeenth-century verse from the Spoure Book (manuscript from Trebartha Hall: Pounds 1947, 124, and transcript in Henderson Collection, Royal Cornwall Museum, Truro).

But our best neighbour–and he's choice and good
Is the wild moor there's the best neighbourhood
It keeps vast herds of cattle, I profess,
and flocks of sheep even almost numberless
Thus we our stock do summer on the Down,
And keep our homer grass till winter come. . .

As well as allowing a crop of hay to be taken, land may also have been freed in this way for cultivation. In the eighteenth and nineteenth centuries cattle and sheep from outlying districts were taken into pasture on the Moor by tenants of moorland edge farms from about mid-May to October at so much a head. Herdsmen were employed by these tenants to look after the flocks and to return them to their owners at the agreed time–a sort of transhumance by proxy (Brewster 1975, 226–7, 250–1, 254; Jenkin 1945, 381; Worgan 1811; Karkeet 1846; Peter 1906).

Post-medieval moorland shelters

A range of structures may relate specifically to the grazing of the Moor. Some of these are post-medieval. Some small but well-preserved structures in the open moorland are probably herdsmen's shel-ters (Fig 52 nos 1–3); other small post-medieval dwellings, though more substantial than these and with a larger floor area, may have served a similar function (Fig 63 nos 1–2). Even smaller structures (eg Roughtor South, Fig 52 no 4) are probably for ani-mals rather than people; these are normally made by enclosing a tiny area against a grounder with low drystone walling, with a small entrance, and some-times providing a 'roof' of granite slabs.

Transhumance huts

The place-name evidence for the early practice of transhumance on the Moor has been discussed above (see p 79). In the eleventh century and earlier, upwards of 200 sq km would have been available as rough grazing, and throughout the medieval period the tracts of moorland remained very considerable (Map 2). A variety of structures can perhaps be

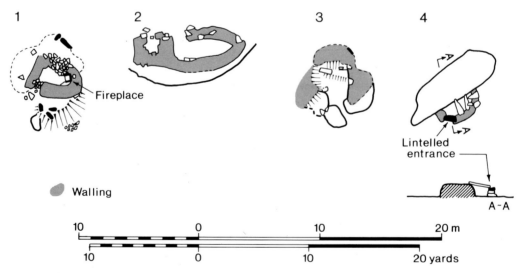

Fig 52   Post-medieval moorland shelters: all are well-preserved and constructed of roughly coursed walling surviving up to a metre high. 1, Roughtor North, SX 14088102, is built into a small cairn, and contains a tiny fireplace and flue; 2, Roughtor North, SX 14188148, is built into the west side of a large hut circle, which may then have been used as an enclosure (Fig 15); 3, Butterstor, SX 14897810, is dug into the slope behind two large grounders; it is in a low-lying position above a streamworks and may be a 'tinner's hut'; 4, Roughtor South, SX 14408044, is a small structure built against a grounder, probably an animal shelter. (No 2 after P Herring)

Table 7 Suggested transhumance huts

No	Name	NGR	Height above OD (m)	No of structures	Comments
1	Brown Willy (W)	SX 15507975	300	9	See text below
	Brown Willy (E)	SX 16027990	350	2	See text below
2	Brockabarrow (E)	SX 16127480	280	13	See text below
	Brockabarrow (W)	SX 15807486	280	7?	See p 83
3	Butterstor	SX 14897799	250	1	See p 83
4	Garrow	SX 14527798	280	1	
5	Butterstor	SX 14997740	260	1	2.5 × 2.1m (similar to Fig 53 no 5)
6	Louden	SX 13757970	270	1	5.8 × 5.1m; subrectangular, faced banks
7	Craddock Moor	SX 24347144, SX 24407158	310	2	6.0 × 2.5, 4.5 × 3.5m; rectangular; low banks
8	Roughtor South	SX 14438038	300	1	2.6 × 2.3m; subrectangular (similar to Fig 53 no 6)
9	Davidstow Moor	SX 14378558, SX 15358515	295	2	turf-walled huts (Andrew 1942)
10	Garrow	SX 14707841	270	5	typically 4.9 × 3.5m; D-shaped structures, attached to a probably prehistoric enclosure
11	Brown Gelly	SX 20027262	260	1	7.6 × 2.4m, with rounded ends

interpreted as transhumance huts established to exploit this resource. These are normally sub-rectangular structures with low stone banks, anomalous among the range of prehistoric hut circles and quite different from the permanent medieval settlements. In form and/or context parallels can be seen in the shielings of Scotland and northern England (Miller 1967, 202; MacSween and Gailey 1961, 78; Ramm 1970, 7), the Welsh *hafodau* (Crampton 1966; Allen 1979, 8–27), the Irish booley-houses (Evans 1957, 36–7), and structures at Houndtor, Devon (G Beresford 1979, 110–12). As no dialect word equivalent to the northern 'shieling' is recorded, 'transhumance hut' is perhaps the most acceptable term. Table 7 lists the most probable examples of sites of this type; further analysis may suggest more. Some hut circle settlements include markedly elongated or subrectangular structures, but these normally appear to be of similar build to the hut circles and may simply reflect variety in hut form within the group (eg Garrow, SX 14367773; Roughtor, SX 14578040). Other hut circle settlements include numbers of huts which show reuse, normally by the construction of crude subdivisions, and these may well be relevant to this discussion. The illustrated examples are described below.

Brown Willy (*SX 15507975*) *West-facing hillslope, 300m above OD (Fig 53 nos 3–7)*

by Peter Herring

In the Brown Willy West group (Herring 1986) there are nine huts scattered over 400m along the hillside. Five are small subrectangular structures with low stone banks, at most 0.4m high but generally lower, with some rough inner facing occasionally apparent (Fig 53 no 3). Their small size (floor areas 3.2 – 10.3 sq m) suggests that they sheltered single individuals and is consistent with their use by whichever sector of the community (eg teenage girls: Graham 1953–4, 75; O'Neill 1977, 84) went into the hills with the herds in the Cornish summers. Four small prehistoric hut circles were adapted, presumably by the same people, to give nine subrectangular huts in the group. A further two structures of similar type are located on the east side of Brown Willy (SX 16027990; SX 16037978). All these structures are later than the Brown Willy prehistoric hut circles and are the product of a different roofing tradition; presumably an upright at each end supported a ridge-pole. A larger hut circle had its entrance blocked and walls heightened for use as a pen, perhaps for night-folding (Allen 1979, 55), milking, or weaning (Miller 1967, 203).

One of the subrectangular huts (Fig 53 no 4; SX 15467960) predates one of a series of banks which define narrow irregular strip fields, themselves earlier than the main medieval field system (see p 107). The bank is attached to the hut in such a way as to leave its entrance open, suggesting that these few strips are contemporary with the huts. (For other examples of cultivation at transhumance sites see Gelling 1962–3, 170; Miller 1967, 194). It is suggested elsewhere that these strips are essentially experimental, to see if crops could be harvested on Brown Willy, and that they directly preceded the permanent medieval settlement (Herring 1986; see also Gaffney 1959). The Brown Willy West transhumance hut group has thus been tentatively dated to the early medieval period.

Brockabarrow (*SX 16127480*) *East slope, 280m above OD (Fig 53)*

Thirteen buildings occur in a north–south band about 300m long and 100m wide, running along the contour on a gentle slope. Most are single-cell structures of squarish or rectangular form, with rounded corners and occasionally one curved side or end. Internal measurements range from 3.8–6m long by 2.4–3.9m wide (floor areas 10–22 sq m). Three structures are larger and markedly elongated (Fig 53, 8–10), measuring internally 11.3 × 3m, 9.2 × 2.8m, and 8 × 3.2m. Two of these (8, 10) have more than one room, in 10 by the addition of an annexe to a small hut. All the elongated buildings lie along the contour. Throughout the group entrance gaps are usually on the lower side and most are centrally

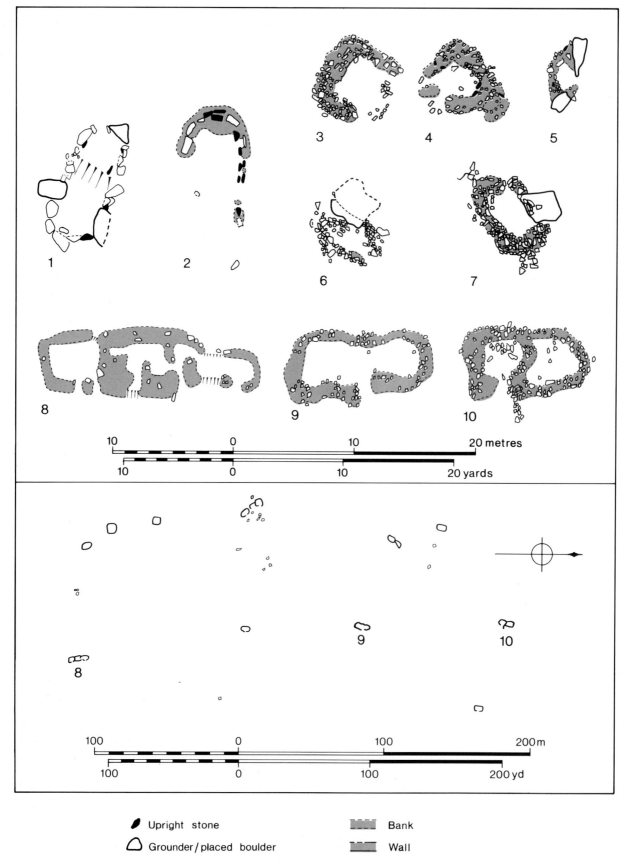

Fig 53   *Transhumance huts: probable (Brown Willy and Brockabarrow) and possible (Butterstor and Garrow); the slope runs down the page. Upper: 1, Butterstor, SX 14897799; 2, Garrow, SX 14527798 (Fig 16E; Fig 61F); 3–7, Brown Willy, SX 14527798; 8–10 Brockabarrow, SX 16127489. (Nos 3–7, 9, and 10 after P Herring). Lower: layout of huts at Brockabarrow*

placed. The structures are defined by low banks of small stones, typically 0.2–0.3m high, with no visible wall facing; timber may have been the main structural item. There is some semblance of order within their distribution: four of the huts, including 8, 9, and 10, are set out along a contour at 80–100m intervals. The small structures are, with one exception, at least 60m from the larger and mostly uphill to the west; they appear to form groups associated with the larger structures (RCHME SX 17SE1, N V Quinnell; description largely verbatim). Seven more huts of the smaller type occur 1 km to the west, within the Brockabarrow Common hut circle settlement (SX 157746). The settlement could have a context both in the pre-colonisation phase and later. It is in a remote moorland location, the nearest medieval settlements being a little over 1 km to the south-west, but 3 or 4 km to the north and east. If the site belongs to the pre-colonisation phase, the nearest settlements to the south and west may have been 5 km away.

Butterstor, St Breward (*SX 14897799*) *West slope, 250m above OD (Fig 53 no 1)*

An isolated structure in a low-lying location, this is elongated with somewhat rounded ends and defined by large grounders and single upright stones 0.3–0.6m high. There is a probable entrance gap in the south side, a little east of centre, and internal subdivision is suggested by a change in slope towards the uphill end. Unlike the Brockabarrow examples it is set across the contour, although a little obliquely, and is therefore closer to the longhouse tradition; but it is much smaller than known longhouses, has no associated cultivation, and the build is also unusual. The form bears a resemblance to House Y at Crane Godrevy, Gwithian, interpreted as an early twelfth-century house (5 × 2.4m: A C Thomas 1969, 86), and to the final house of Gwithian site 1, dated to the tenth and eleventh centuries (4.8 × 2.4m: A C Thomas 1958, 22, fig 19).

Garrow (*SX 14527798*) *East slope, 260m above OD (Fig 53 no 2)*

This robbed structure is in the centre of the deserted medieval hamlet of Garrow, almost opposite the previous site on Butterstor. It is elongated, at least 9m long, with a well-rounded uphill end, and is defined mostly by a narrow double-slab wall, 0.2–0.6m high, with little infilling surviving. In form and build it differs from the longhouses, although like them it is set across the contour and is of similar width. It is also different in form from the nearby hut circles, though some are of similar wall type. The robbing and the unusual form suggest that the structure belongs to an early phase of the medieval settlement or is even earlier. The floor area, at least as large as a hut circle, 7m in diameter and three times the size of the Brown Willy huts, suggests that this could have been a permanent dwelling. An eleventh- or twelfth-century date is perhaps likely, but alternative parallels for this structure and the one at Butterstor (above) might possibly be seen in Romano-British houses excavated elsewhere in the county (p 53).

Two features excavated by Croft Andrew on Davidstow Moor (Table 7 no 9) proved to be small turf-walled huts, probably of the sixteenth century (Christie and Rose 1987). Before excavation one structure resembled a small barrow 6m in diameter and 0.6m high. A mound at Garrow (SX 14167789) may be comparable.

The degree of variety displayed from site to site in the examples listed suggests that they cannot necessarily be regarded as a unity. For example, there is a contrast between the group of nine small structures at Brown Willy and the single larger structure at Butterstor (Table 7, no 3); and between the small structure at Butterstor (no 5) and the relatively substantial structure at Garrow (no 4). This could suggest a chronological depth and some range of function in this series of sites, but may still allow them to fit into a broadly similar post-prehistoric context. Two other resources in addition to the pastures may account for some structures of this type. First, there is the tin industry; the larger structure at Butterstor (no 3) is close to an area of streamworks. Secondly, in the pre-colonisation phase the Moor may well have been used for hunting; might one expect to find huntsmen's shelters?

4 Deserted medieval settlements

Some 37 deserted medieval settlements are known on the Moor, but only about half the desertions occurred during the medieval period: the remainder of the sites saw continued use or reuse at some level into later centuries. This is indicated in Table 8, which categorises the sites according to the degree to which the medieval layout has been affected by subsequent use, and indicates broadly the form which each site takes in the field. In Class 1 (medieval desertions) the settlement remains are intact. In Classes 2A and 2B much or most of the medieval settlement survives; in the larger sites such as Carwether and Garrow, post-medieval and probably later medieval occupation continued at a reduced level within groupings of abandoned medieval longhouses and their associated features. In the smaller settlements such as Menadue the longhouse form survives, but later use is apparent from changes to the structure and from documentary evidence (see below). The two Class C sites have continued in use to the present day. At both a single longhouse survives as an earthwork on the periphery of the settlement (Fernacre, Fig 54 no 3), but the medieval layout has otherwise disappeared. The medieval origin of the Class 3 sites is apparent from documentary evidence or from their association with surviving fields of medieval type (eg Colvannick). At Tresellern and West Colliford the remains take the form of earthworks and building platforms but the extent of any medieval survival is not clear. The other settlements are post-medieval in form.

Distribution, aspect, altitude

The deserted sites mark the high tide of medieval

Table 8 Deserted medieval settlements[1]

NGR (all SX)	Name	No of longhouses	No of corndryers	Total no of structures	Survival of fields[2]	Extent cultivated (acres)[3]	Total area associated (acres)	Height above OD (m)	Aspect
1 Medieval desertions									
11517931	East Rowden	1	–	1	B	41	100	244	NW
13207612	Bedrawle	1	–	3	C	41	120?	243	W
14057638	Carkees	1	–	1	A	18	49 or 81?	265	E/NE
13897331	(Temple)	1	–	1	C	–	–	244	SE
24057300	(Lambadla)	1	–	7	C	48?	–	274	SW
25687332	(Sharptor)	1?	–	2	C	15?	–	310	SE
11907821	(Candra)	1?	–	3	C	18?	35?	260	E
13858028	Louden	2	–	3	A	16	183	297	E
20127283	Brown Gelly	2	–	5	A	25	47?	251	E
22887847	'Fox Tor'	1–2	–	3	A	40?	?	288	SE
20577057	'Redhill'	2	–	7	C	?	107	236	SW
19967665	(Carneglos)	2	–	3	B	50	188	251	SW
18317190	(Bunning's Park)	2	–	6	A	42	252?	250	W
14367279	(Temple)	2	–	3	C	?	45?	221	SE
20307317	(Higher Langdon)	3	–	4	B	–	–	251	S
22687609	'Smallacoombe' (Trewortha Marsh)	4	2	8	B	57	139?	244	E
18298194	'Little Bowithick' (Bray Down)	4	–	8	A	96?	139?	260	W
18418179	near the above	1	–	1	–	–	–	278	SW
18688187	near the above	1	–	1	–	–	–	320	W
15908342	Lamlavery	5	–	10	A	343?	356	297	NW
14318410	Goosehill	–	–	–	–	–	–	280	SW
2 Post-medieval desertions, with medieval elements surviving									
A	**With the medieval pattern little obscured**								
12547636	Menadue	2	–	3	C	39	39	231	SE
12707599	Bedwithiel	2	1	5	C	40	114?	242	N
20447477	Goodaver	2	1	9	B	49?	82?	228	SW
20127580	(Tresibbet)	4–5	1	14	C	33	78?	229–67	SW
10187969	Carwether	5	1	14	B	103?	132?	227	NE
15317937	Brown Willy	5–6?	2	18	A	134	673	274	SW
B	**With the medieval pattern more considerably obscured**								
22727941	(Tregune)	1?	–	4	C	?	?	250	NE
14577800	Garrow	3–6?	1	6–10	A	98	436	280	E
C	**With the medieval pattern almost completely obscured**								
15607058	Tor House	1	–	1	–	–	–	259	SE
15067979	Fernacre	1	–	1	B	84	164	282	SE
3 Post-medieval desertions, with little or nothing apparent of the medieval layout									
12557136	(Colvannick)				B	45	?	200	SW
23907674	Tresellern				C	53	129	244	E
24437654	Bastreet				–	–	–	240	S
21647982	(Spettigue)				–	–	–	240	E
15347970	Higher Brown Willy				(A)	–	–	290	W
15388027	Slades				(A)	–	–	300	W
23867480	(Smallacoombe Parks)				B	38	?	270	E
24147106	'Newhall' (Little Siblyback)				B	43	?	290	E
17937085	West Colliford				C	49	163?	235	NE

[1] Conventions used for settlement names

Brackets: the bracketed name gives the location only, eg nearby hill or settlement, as the medieval name is unknown
Quotation marks: denote a possible or conjectural medieval name
Other: documented medieval name

[2] Survival of medieval fields:

A Complete or almost complete survival, either with no reuse or with reuse or destruction so limited that it is still possible to reconstruct the medieval pattern completely or almost completely
B Substantial survival: considerable reuse, but the medieval pattern is still largely apparent, eg many of the medieval elements have been fossilised and there is considerable survival of unaltered medieval features
C Partial survival: almost complete reuse, but retaining elements of the medieval layout

[3] 1 acre = 0.404678 ha

Fig 54 (Opposite) Longhouses; the slope runs down the page. 1, Garrow, SX·14557799 (Fig 16F; Fig 55; excavated, Dudley and Minter 1963); 2, Higher Langdon, SX 20307320; 3, Fernacre, SX 15067979; 4, Garrow, SX 14527796 (Fig 16J; Fig 61A); 5, Torhouse, SX 15607058; 6, Bedrawle, SX 13207612; 7, Garrow, SX 14577800 (Fig 16G; Fig 61C); 8, Brown Willy, SX 15397935 (Fig 61, top left, 3); 9, Brown Willy, SX 15387942 (Fig 61 no 1); 10, Louden, SX 13858028 (Fig 59A); 11, diagrammatic representation of the components of south-western longhouses. (Nos 2, 3, 5, 6, 8–11 after P Herring)

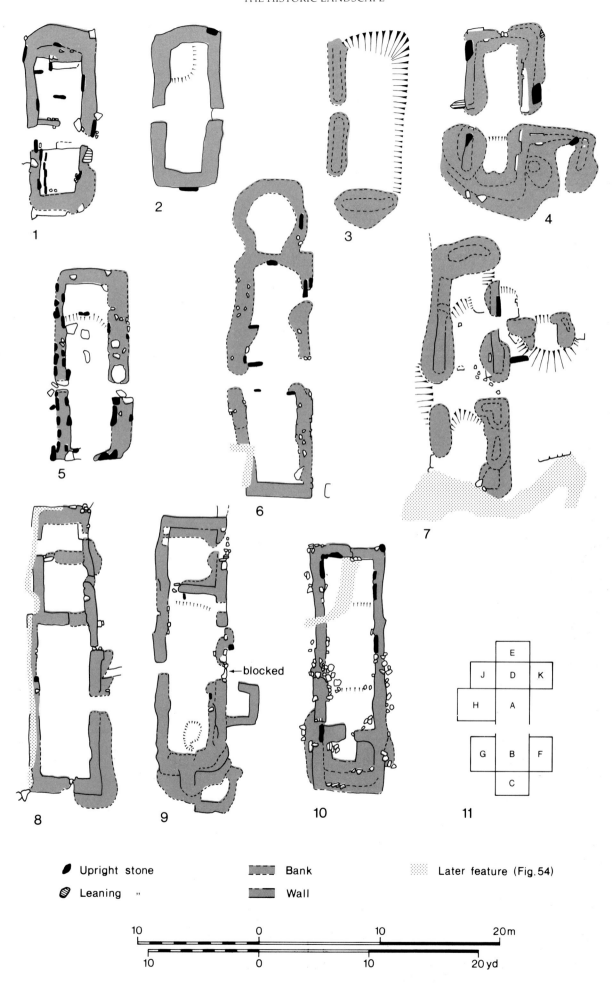

1

2

3

4

5

6

7

blocked

8

9

10

11

	E	
J	D	K
H	A	

G	B	F
	C	

🖤 Upright stone   ▨▨ Bank   ⣿ Later feature (Fig.54)

◧ Leaning ,,   ▥▥ Wall

10   0   10   20m

10   0   10   20 yd

colonisation of the Moor. Most are in the upper parts of the valleys that penetrate deep into the Moor–the De Lank, the Fowey, and the Witheybrook–or in remote moorland locations such as Lamlavery on Davidstow Moor. Most or perhaps all of the sites are likely to have been established in the eleventh- to early fourteenth-century phase of colonisation. Some may be earlier, in particular Bedwithiel, Bedrawle, Carkees, Carwether, and Tresellern (see above). The deserted sites are invariably on hillslopes, of which 6 (16%) have a northerly aspect, 12 (32%) face west or south-west, and 17 sites (45%) face east or south-east. Perhaps a slight preference is seen for a location sheltered from the prevailing westerlies, but clearly these figures will need to be compared with data from all medieval settlements on the Moor.

With the exception of Colvannick, all the sites are in the range 220–310m above OD; half are between 240m and 270m above OD. There is no clear correlation between size of settlement and altitude, no tendency, for example, for the smaller deserted settlements to be found on the higher ground. If anything, the reverse may be true: four of the larger settlements are above 260m. The character of the local topography was perhaps a more important factor in determining the relative sizes of settlements. Classes 1 to 3 in Table 8 each occur at all altitudes; there is no apparent tendency for the early desertions to be at greater altitudes than the later ones.

(Further survey and research will almost certainly locate deserted settlements in the more low-lying area around the Moor which has not been included in the present survey. The absence of these sites from Fig 51 no 2 may give somewhat overdue emphasis to the moorland distribution.)

Hamlets and farms

The relative sizes of settlements are shown in Table 9 in terms of the number of longhouses, these being the principal dwellings (see below). Only Classes 1 and 2A from Table 8 have been used. Sharptor and Candra are uncertain longhouses and have been omitted. Bray Down has been counted as three settlements, one settlement of four longhouses and two detached single longhouses. Tresibbet has been included as one settlement of five longhouses, but has two distinct nuclei and should perhaps

regarded as two settlements of two and three long-houses respectively.

In Table 9 the settlements on Bodmin Moor are compared with documentary evidence from the Duchy Manors of Helstone-in-Trigg, Tybeste, and Trematon (M W Beresford 1964; Ravenhill 1969). Helstone includes the moorland parish of Advent; the rest are more low-lying. The records are sufficiently detailed for each of the Duchy tenants to be assigned to a named settlement; in the sample above there are 203 messuages and 57 places. For the moment it is assumed that the settlements are nucleated and that the capital dwelling of a messuage can be equated with a longhouse. The similarities will be considered first.

In both samples the commonest number of 'houses' in a settlement is two and the second commonest is one. However, single houses account for only a small percentage of the total houses: on Bodmin Moor the bulk of the longhouses (88%), and presumably the bulk of the population, are in settlements of two or more longhouses; for the Duchy manors the figure is 95%. Overall the sites are not large; none of the Bodmin Moor settlements has more than six longhouses, and 88% of the Duchy settlements have under six messuages.

The main dissimilarity is in the general size of settlements, the sites on Bodmin Moor tending to be smaller. Here settlements of only one or two long-houses account for 71% of the sites (but only 46% of longhouses); for the Duchy the figure is 47%. The largest settlement on Bodmin Moor has six long-houses; 12% of the Duchy sites have seven or more messuages recorded.

If this distinction is truly representative of the pattern of settlement, it may well reflect the generally lower levels of population that the uplands were capable of supporting. As an extreme example, if a hill the size of Louden were located at 50m above OD rather than at 297m, its 74 hectares could be expected to support a rather larger settlement than the two longhouses that are in fact found there.

Part of the difference may also be due to the character of the two sources of information. In documents the single longhouses at Bray Down, for example, and perhaps initially sites like East Rowden, would probably have been grouped under the main settlement. This element of dispersal may not always be apparent in the Duchy records; the disparity of

Table 9   Comparison between medieval settlement sizes: deserted sites on Bodmin Moor and documented sites on Duchy Manors

1	Bodmin Moor: size of deserted medieval settlements (24 sites, 59 longhouses)											
	Number of longhouses	*1*	*2*	*3*	*4*	*5*	*6*					
	Number of sites	7	10	1	2	3	1					
	Percentage of sites	29	42	4	8	13	4					
	Percentage of longhouses	12	34	5	14	25	10					

2	Duchy Manors: size of medieval settlements (Beresford 1964) (57 sites, 203 messuages)											
	Number of messuages	*1*	*2*	*3*	*4*	*5*	*6*	*7*	*8*	*9*	*10*	*over 10*
	Number of sites	11	16	8	9	6	0	1	2	1	0	3
	Percentage of sites	19	28	14	16	11	0	2	3	2	0	5
	Percentage of messuages	5	16	12	18	15	–	4	8	5	–	16

single farms in each sample may therefore be less than is suggested in Table 9.

The most economic explanation for the general similarity between the two samples is that they represent a similar pattern and form of settlement both on and off the Moor. As is the case elsewhere in the South-West (eg H S A Fox 1983), in the context of manor or parish the settlement pattern is dispersed, but at the level of individual settlements, at this date the dispersal is mostly into hamlets of two or more farms rather than as single farms. Particularly large settlements (villages?) are rare in the Duchy records and not known on the Moor. What is striking about the deserted sites is the frequency of settlements of just two longhouses, accounting for 42% of the sites. This may be due to a combination of two factors: on the one hand the generally lower levels of population which the Moor was capable of supporting, and on the other a need or preference for nucleation, perhaps reflecting a cooperative element in the farming routine and possibly even some principle such as partible inheritance.

Settlement components

The deserted settlements (Table 8, Classes 1, 2A, and 2B) contain a number of elements that recur from site to site: longhouses; ancillary buildings (including further dwellings); small enclosures (gardens, paddocks, mowhays?); areas of shared access (farmyards or 'town places'); trackways. The sites are invariably longhouse settlements; the other components are usual but are not always present. The buildings normally survive as turf-covered banks of stone, 0.4–1m high and usually with some inner and outer facing of rough coursing and upright slabs still visible to suggest the original nature of the walls. The buildings at Lamlavery may be an exception, comprising turf-covered banks of earth 2–3m wide, 0.6m high, with no facing and very little stone apparent. However, this is probably due to the collapse of a predominantly earthen core and the use of small stones for the facing (the site is off the granite), rather than because of any fundamental difference in build.

The sites, as described below, do not display so great a variety in form as to suggest that they occupy widely different tiers in the social and settlement hierarchy, nor is this suggested by documentary evidence. On the contrary, the medieval and Domesday manors are found off the Moor or at its edge; this is also true of castles in the area, a motte and bailey at Cardinham (SX 12616804), and a small ringwork, perhaps a defended manor house, at Upton (SX 24547897).

Longhouses

by Peter Herring

Only three medieval longhouses have been fully excavated on Bodmin Moor, at Trewortha Marsh (Baring-Gould 1891; 1892), Garrow (Dudley and Minter 1962–3), and Bunning's Park (Austin *et al* 1989). A very small excavation was undertaken at a fourth site, Goosehill, by C K Croft Andrew in 1942 (Christie and Rose 1987). Consequently much of the detailed interpretation of the construction, chronology, and function of the longhouses on Bodmin Moor is derived from reports of excavations elsewhere in Cornwall and, more importantly, on Dartmoor (most recently listed in Austin 1985, 74 and Herring 1986).

Field identification, layout, and function

The longhouses listed in Table 8 were identified on the basis of criteria recognisable on the surface, whereas most published definitions of longhouses have been based either on extant or recently abandoned examples (eg Meirion-Jones 1982, 191–2), or produced through the analysis of excavated features (eg G Beresford 1979, 124). The definition of a longhouse for use in fieldwork therefore had to incorpo-

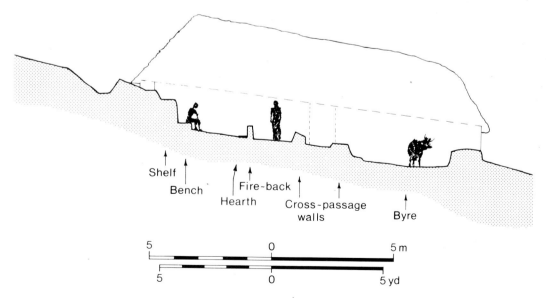

Shelf
Bench
Fire-back
Hearth
Cross-passage walls
Byre

5   0   5 m

5   0   5 yd

Fig 55   Garrow: profile through excavated longhouse (Fig 54 no 1). The outline reconstruction assumes a wall height of 1.8m and a roof pitch of 45°.

rate the key architectural and functional elements known from more comprehensive sources, and had also to be simple enough to be applied with confidence to superficial remains that were often altered by later reuse or mutilated.

At its simplest a longhouse is a long rectangular structure which housed both humans and animals (usually cattle) sharing a common entrance (Alcock 1969, 83; G Beresford 1979, 124). In medieval south-west England two opposed entrances, placed roughly centrally in the side walls of the houses, defined the boundary between the domestic area and the shippon, as the cow house or byre is usually known in East Cornwall. Almost invariably the buildings are levelled into the hillslope, their long axes aligned across the contour, with the animals (for obvious drainage reasons) occupying the downhill end. The Garrow longhouse, excavated in the 1950s, well illustrates these basic features (Fig 54 no 1; Fig 55; Dudley and Minter 1962–3, 274, fig 88). Stone mangers identify the shippon, or byre, and are normal on Cornish longhouse sites (eg Baring-Gould 1891, 61 pl. II); at Bunning's Park, however, stone mangers succeeded wooden ones (Austin et al 1989), and the Dartmoor sites invariably have wooden mangers and stalls (eg Austin 1978, figs 5, 7, 9; G Beresford 1979, 129). Other sites may also have central, stone-lined drains in the byre. The dwelling-room at Garrow has a central hearth with a vertical fireback, others have cooking pits and occasionally stakeholes for fixed furniture. The two rooms at Garrow are separated by a stone-walled cross-passage. Relatively few surviving long-houses show field evidence for walled cross-passages (Herring 1986).

Not all Bodmin Moor longhouses are as simple as the Garrow house; only 20 of the 55 with recoverable plans have just two rooms (Garrow, Higher Langdon, and Fernacre examples are illustrated, Fig 54 nos 1–3). The others all have more rooms, either beneath the main roof line or to the sides, as penthouses. With the main dwelling-room designated A and the shippon B, Figure 54 no 11 demonstrates the range of rooms additional to the simple A–B plan found in south-western longhouses (discussed further by Herring 1986). By far the most common is room D, normally entered from the dwelling-room A (eg Fig 54 nos 5, 7–10). Over half the Bodmin Moor longhouses had such a room, which would probably have been either a parental bedroom or a store for important domestic goods (eg at Dinna Clerks: G Beresford 1979, 136; such functions are also known in recent Irish and Scottish examples: O'Neill 1977, 21; Laing 1969, 77). A number of houses had second inner rooms, in positions E or J (Fig 54, 11), again with only internal access. Such a room (J) at Houndtor (Dartmoor) was interpreted as accommodation for a dependent relative (G Beresford 1979, 133). Additional rooms at the domestic end, with external entry only, may be provisionally interpreted as outhouses, perhaps dairies, kennels, stores, etc. At Meldon such a room was heated and presumably, therefore, at some stage inhabited (Austin 1978, 214). Extra rooms at the lower end, below the cross-passage, were probably to do with animals, serving as fodder

stores, calf sheds, pig sheds etc. Room C is, indeed, sometimes reached only via the shippon (eg Louden Hill, Fig 54 no 10; Trewortha Marsh: Baring-Gould 1891, 61, pl II; and Bunning's Park: Austin et al 1989). In general, however, it is difficult to ascribe functions to such rooms; excavated examples reveal no features other than occasional drains (eg G Beresford 1979, figs 16, 19, 20, 21).

The two common rooms, A and B, formed the nucleus of the house and farmstead, where the principal domestic and agricultural activities took place. Other rooms and outhouses, attached or detached, were essentially peripheral bedrooms, stores, and animal sheds. It is tempting to equate variations in size and complexity of individual houses and farmsteads with differences in the wealth or social and tenurial status of their occupants (G Beresford 1979, 133; but note Austin 1985, 73). Although some diversity of form was no doubt due to these factors, such equations should be made with caution as differences in the livestock/arable balance of particular farms could also lead to differing building requirements.

Fabric and construction

The walls had two roughly coursed faces with a core of smaller stones; occasionally larger flatter stones were used as binders (eg Dudley and Minter 1962–3, 275). Vertical slabs were often incorporated into the faces (eg Louden Hill, Fig 54 no 10) and at many sites these are the only stones visible, poking through the grassed-over banks of tumbled rubble (eg Torhouse, Fig 54 no 5). The walls were generally between 0.8m and 1.1m wide, and excavators of Dartmoor long-houses have estimated original heights of 2m from the quantity of rubble found (Austin 1978, 202; G Beresford 1979, 127; Milne 1979, 69). Most excavated longhouses lack postholes to take ridge beams and it seems, therefore, that roofs were supported by trusses laid directly on the side walls. One might presume either a collar, or a tie beam and struts, to give the truss strength and help relieve the walls of outward thrust. The wall heights thus suggest that the longhouses lacked full first floors, but the form of the roof timbers could have allowed lofts beneath the rafters. These would, however, be confined to the areas above the shippon, for hay, and above the inner rooms (D and E), for extra sleeping quarters.

The central open hearths would require roof openings, probably louvred, to allow smoke to escape, and the main dwelling-room (A) would thus be open to the roof. It is probable that the roofs were hipped (Alcock 1977, 85; G Beresford 1979, 128) and covered with an organic material, either thatch or turf (Alcock 1969, 85; Minter 1965, 44; G Beresford 1979, 128).

Windows, if they existed at all (Fairhurst 1968, 145), would have been unglazed and high up in the walls (G Beresford 1979, 128), and natural light would have been mainly obtained from the doorways. The doors were wood-framed (eg Dudley and Minter 1966, 46), and were probably halved (Jenkin 1934, 27). The interiors of the houses were almost certainly poorly lit and many domestic chores would have been undertaken outside, weather permitting.

The arrangement of opposed entrances is a functional, not merely a stylistic, feature. It defined the cross-passage which divided the longhouse into two major parts (see Austin 1985, 76). Milking cattle could enter, from a yard, through one door and exit directly by the other. The opposed entrances provided a draught useful for winnowing: this could be manipulated, by adjusting the doors, to expel smoke (Evans 1939, 216). Today the evidence for such an arrangement of doors in a ruined building is a powerful indicator that the building was originally a working longhouse.

Dating

On Bodmin Moor too few longhouses have been excavated for conclusive proof of their date range. From excavations on the north coast at Mawgan Porth (Bruce-Mitford 1956 and forthcoming), it is clear that the south-western longhouse tradition goes back at least to the tenth or eleventh centuries, but no excavated south-western longhouse in the uplands has produced material evidence to suggest a date before the (later?) twelfth century (Jope and Threlfall 1958, 116). The rural pottery of the region is undiagnostic and difficult to date precisely (Austin *et al* 1980, 46). It has indeed been suggested that the upland longhouse sites are typical of the wider regional settlement pattern in that they appear to reflect a short period of more intensive moorland settlement between the twelfth and fourteenth centuries when climatic, demographic, and economic factors encouraged lords to allow tenants, both free and unfree, to settle and enclose the more marginal land (Austin 1985, 73–5).

None of the material from the Garrow longhouse need be earlier than the thirteenth century, though what are probably twelfth-century sherds have been found elsewhere on the hill (Dudley and Minter 1962–3, 291); pottery from Bunning's Park has a thirteenth- to fourteenth-century date range (Austin *et al* 1989); that from Trewortha Marsh may include twelfth-century sherds (Jope and Threlfall 1958, 136). Excavation at Garrow and Trewortha Marsh was too restricted to preclude the possibility of an earlier date. The argument that turf buildings preceded the stone ones on a number of sites (Minter 1965, 208–10; Dudley and Minter 1966, 39–43; G Beresford 1979, 112–24) has been convincingly challenged (Austin 1985, 71–3), and such structures have yet to be identified on Bodmin Moor either by excavation or as earthworks, with the possible exception of turf-built shelters (see above). With or without a succession of turf houses, a pre-twelfth-century date remains likely for some, perhaps many, settlements.

The length of occupation of the longhouses is equally uncertain. Presumably many were abandoned in the medieval period. Of the three excavated examples, Bunning's Park was probably abandoned in the fourteenth century (Gerrard pers comm), but the house at Garrow was probably in use to the sixteenth century (Dudley and Minter 1962–3, 287; and compared to Allan, 1984) – although other houses in this settlement may well have been abandoned earlier. At other settlements the longhouses were occupied into much later periods. Those at Menadue and Carwether were still inhabited in the mid-seventeenth century (Maclean 1873, 93, 364–5; Herring 1986) the latter perhaps as late as the early nineteenth century (Ordnance Survey 1″ Map, 1813). On both these sites longhouses had been modified by blocking one of the opposed doors. Other longhouses had been similarly adapted, eg one at Brown Willy (Fig 54 no 9); and at Bedwithiel and Tresibbett fireplaces were inserted and more doors blocked. Although originally true longhouses, these modified examples almost certainly no longer functioned as such. The blocking of doors and the insertion of fireplaces in the shippons indicate that people were no longer sharing the buildings with cattle. They were being modified at the same time that houses solely for human habitation were being built by people of comparable status (Chesher and Chesher 1968, 26–38; Pearce 1981, 228). There is no evidence that longhouses were being newly built on Bodmin Moor after the fourteenth and fifteenth centuries.

Ancillary buildings

by Peter Herring

Roofed working-space additional to that within the longhouses was provided by the detached outbuildings found on many south-western sites (see Austin 1985, 74, table 7.1, and 76). Several have been excavated, including one at Garrow (Fig 56 no 7) and two at Bunning's Park, but they tend to be internally featureless, except in some instances for a stone-covered drain (Austin 1978, figs 5, 6, 8, 10; G Beresford 1979, Figs 17, 18, 20, 21). Some were no doubt animal sheds (A Fox 1958; Austin 1978, 205, 207; G Beresford 1979, figs 17, 18, 20, 21), others barns and stores for grain, straw, tools, and equipment, and yet others may have housed labourers or dependent relatives – hearths are found in some buildings (eg G Beresford 1979, 133). These structures are distinguished in the field from longhouses by their generally smaller size (compare Figs 54 and 56, and see also Austin 1985, fig 7.2) and, in most cases, single entrances. Like longhouses, their long axes generally lie across the contour, but there are several exceptions (eg Brown Willy, Fig 56 no 4). Because they are usually freestanding it is difficult to decide whether these ancillary structures were built at the same time as the longhouses or later as the farm expanded, or as the longhouses were modified to exclude animals.

The corn-drying barn is an instantly recognisable type of ancillary building and one of particular importance in the economy of a settlement. A number have been recorded on Bodmin Moor (Herring 1986) since Beresford's publication of Mrs Minter's East Dartmoor excavations (G Beresford 1979, 140–2 and fig 24). Two structures at Trewortha Marsh (Baring-Gould 1891, 59, 65, and pl III; 1892, 289 and pl XIII) can now be recognised as corn-drying barns (one was built into an already abandoned longhouse), and others are at Brown Willy (eg Fig 56 no 2), Garrow (Fig 56 no 3), Carwether, and Goodaver. A

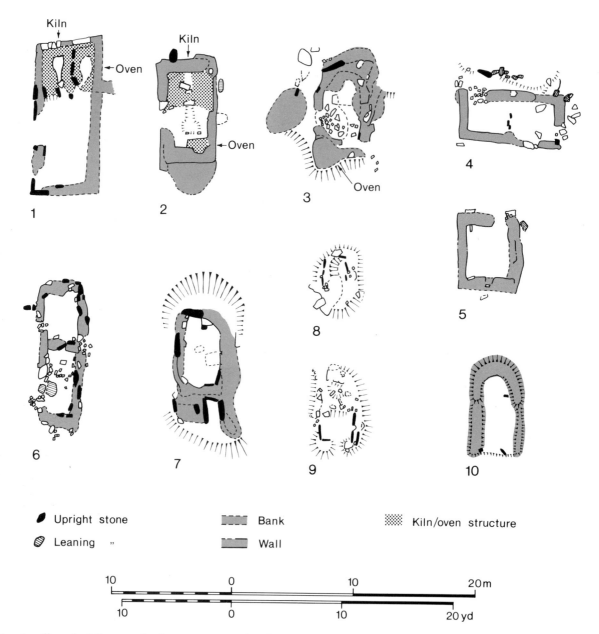

Fig 56   *Ancillary buildings and other structures; the slope runs down the page. 1–3, corn-drying barns: 1, Bedwithiel,*
SX 12727598 (Fig 59); 2, Brown Willy, SX 15427943 (Fig 61 no 7); 3, Garrow, SX 14537800 (Figs 16H; 61). 4–7,
barns: 4, Brown Willy, SX 15407939 (Fig 61 no 9); 5, Brown Willy, SX 15387943 (Fig 61 no 8); 6, Louden, SX
13848028 (Fig 59); 7, Garrow, SX 14547794 (Figs 16K; 61D); 8–10, structures beyond settlements: 8, Garrow,
SX 14667866; 9, Garrow, SX 14227808; 10, Bray Down, SX 18618237. (Nos 1, 2, 4–6 after P Herring)

well-preserved example at Bedwithiel (Fig 56 no 1) is
associated with the early post-medieval reuse of a
longhouse (p 89); and their general association with
settlements in use in the post-medieval period rather
than with medieval desertions (Table 8) suggests a
predominantly late date for them on Bodmin Moor.

The ears of corn brought in from the fields, either
wet or unripe, were placed on beds above hot-air
flues, and dried before threshing (Scott 1951, 196; G
Beresford 1979, 140). The threshed grain was further
dried in corbelled ovens, to remove remaining mois-
ture, and was then ground, by hand, in small querns
such as that found at Trewortha Marsh (Baring-
Gould 1892, pl XIII; many pestles were found on the
East Dartmoor sites: G Beresford 1979, 150).

Ancillary buildings which probably functioned as
field barns and stores are sometimes found at a
distance from the settlements, for example at Louden
(Fig 59) or at Garrow (SX 14117862), where an open-
ended building is associated with fields on the far
side of the hill from the settlement. Other small
structures occasionally found in this context may
have had similar functions, for example the small
building within an area of cultivation at Bray Down
(Fig 56 no 10), or two very small structures at Garrow
(Fig 56 nos 8, 9). The latter are of unusual form, small
with double-slab walls and covered by rubble, one at
the northern extent of the medieval fields (Fig 56 no
8), the other beyond the fields on top of the hill. If not
stores, these might have been little shelters.

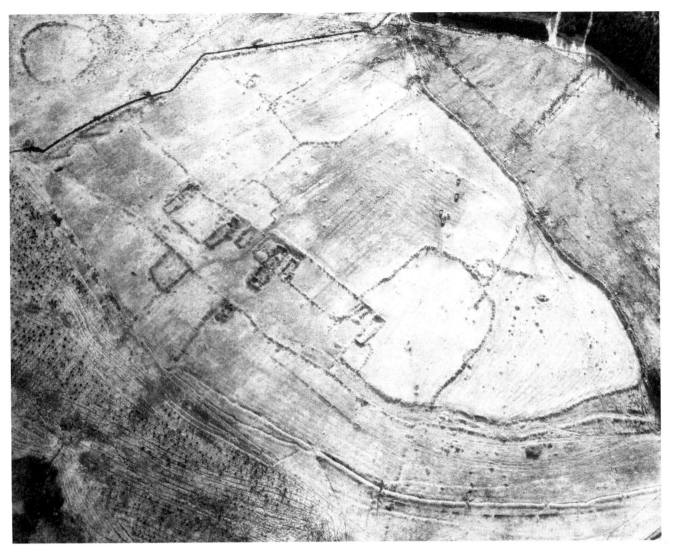

Fig 57   Trewortha Marsh, SX 226760, looking west and uphill: the medieval settlement of Smallacoombe, with part of its associated field system (which contains some hut circles); see also Fig 58. (Photo NMR SX 2276/7/88, 28 February 1979; Crown Copyright Reserved)

Settlement layout

The relationship between the longhouses, ancillary buildings, and other components can be seen in Figures 58, 59 and 61. These are interpretative plans that doubtless disguise some, perhaps much, of the complexity and chronological depth that will be revealed only by further fieldwork and, above all, by excavation. Within the settlements the individual farm units are usually clearly defined, that is each longhouse with its associated enclosures and ancillary buildings, and most settlements show a degree of order in the layout of these units; even Carwether is somewhat more organised than it at first appears, being essentially a linear arrangement of farms spaced out along the contour. However, by comparison with many English deserted medieval villages (eg Wharram Percy, Hurst 1985) where the longhouses are marshalled into a more rigid layout of tofts and crofts, the Bodmin Moor settlements may appear as rather informal clusterings. The settlements are relatively compact, rather than sprawling, perhaps for social reasons as well as for the more

obvious need to avoid encroachment on the fields. Even so, the longhouses are generally well spaced out, typically 20m to 30m apart but sometimes closer, as at Carwether (15m to 20m). This contrasts with the greater irregularity at Houndtor, where some of the houses are as close together as 5m (G Beresford 1979, 103, fig 2).

The layout of larger settlements *(Figs 57, 58, 74)*

The relationship between the individual farmsteads of a settlement and access to it tends to contribute an element of regularity to its layout. At Carwether (Fig 58) access was from a banked trackway leading through the associated fields into the moorland (Map 2); a kink in the track where it joined the settlement may suggest that the track was inserted into pre-existing fields. Trewortha Marsh (Figs 57, 58) lay along and within a trackway widening from 7m to 22m; entrance to the north end of the settlement was probably controlled by a gate. Bray Down (Fig 58) may have been similar, perhaps with an unenclosed track approaching it along the lower valley side. At Lamlavery (Fig 58) a trackway running south to the

Moor from the off-moor farms opened out to give access to the settlement. At each site the buildings sat within or around an area of shared access (or communal farmyard?) formed almost as an opening-out or broadening of the approach to the site. On the nineteenth-century tithe maps such an area would be called a townplace. Each longhouse opens directly on to this area. At Bray Down and Carwether this appears to have been completely enclosed, but at Lamlavery and Trewortha Marsh the townplace is open at one end.

Access to a water supply is also important. At Carwether 'a second banked trackway leads from the northern extremity to a copious spring' (RCHME SX 17NW18, N V Quinnell). Trewortha Marsh is set just above the valley bottom with a narrow track leading

to the marsh, and Bray Down is at the foot of a slope, almost immediately above a stream. At Lamlavery the arrangement is less clear; two widely spaced parallel banks may have extended the hamlet's thoroughfare down to a water supply in the marsh.

At Bray Down (Fig 58) building A, though probably a longhouse – it has opposed entrances – is smaller than the other longhouses in the hamlet. Both it and longhouse B open on to an enclosure between them, suggesting some relationship between the inhabitants of the two houses. House A, being the smaller, may have been in some way dependent on or subsidiary to B. House A also appears to have its own little enclosure, detached and to the south of it. Another building, C, is larger than other ancillary buildings in the settlement and

Fig 58   Larger longhouse settlements; the slope runs down the page. (See Table 8 for grid references)

has an associated enclosure; it might therefore be a dwelling, perhaps for a labourer or dependent relative. Similarly, building D at Lamlavery, set at the edge of the settlement, and building A at Carwether, both with enclosures, might also be dwellings (see also Garrow, below and Fig 61).

A degree of chronological depth can be seen at some of the sites. At Carwether there is a possibility that the site has been extended to the north. In addition, houses here continued in use to the beginning of the nineteenth century. At Trewortha Marsh the northern unit is conceivably an extension of the hamlet. Lamlavery has a large and roughly rectangular shared yard, but the houses are not regularly arranged around it; house B seems to have been set in the middle of it. Another odd feature is the very slight boundary bank and ditch which divides this area, suggesting the possibility that there were two distinct elements to the hamlet, or that there has been an expansion to the north-west from an original nucleus of A, B, and perhaps C. Expansion can also be seen at Brown Willy (see below).

Almost all the longhouses have one or more associated enclosures. At Bray Down they are defined by turf-covered banks (0.3m high, 1.0m wide) or by scarps on the lower side, perhaps once a base for fencing or a quickset hedge (RCHME SX 18SE25, N V Quinnell). In most cases the enclosures are not entered direct from the longhouse; where there is such access it may suggest a use for penning livestock. Otherwise, the enclosures can most reasonably be interpreted as gardens, as suggested at Houndtor (G Beresford 1979), some perhaps doubling as mowhays. At Lamlavery all but one of the longhouses have more than one enclosure, one having four – perhaps because the enclosures could serve different functions which here have been physically separated.

The layout of smaller settlements

The smaller sites (Fig 59) generally display the elements seen at the larger settlements. Examples are the shared yards or townplaces at Redhill, Brown Gelly, and Louden. At Louden a gate at the east end of the yard is reached by a trackway defined on either side by banks with ditches on the track side, presumably dug there to assist in controlling the movements of stock. The banks are fairly slight (0.25m high, 1m wide) and the ditches shallow (0.1m deep, 1m wide). It is difficult to see how they could have provided much of an obstacle to stock unless completed with a hedge. The two small enclosures attached to longhouse A are both defined by stone banks with outer facing (0.4m high), suggesting that they were intended to keep animals out rather than in; similarly at Redhill the enclosures are slight banks with outer ditches. At Louden a boggy area uphill from longhouse B, the product of a feeble spring, may have been the source of the site's water supply.

Direct controlled access to the sites is not always apparent (Brown Gelly, Redhill, Carkees). Access is normally to and from the Moor (Menadue, Goodaver, Bedwithiel). The settlement at Fox Tor is next to a trackway, defined by low parallel banks and scarps, which would have given access to the houses but may have been primarily for the benefit of the hamlets of Altarnun, providing them with access through the fields of Fox Tor so that they could enjoy their grazing rights on East Moor (see below).

A set of unusual earthworks at Carneglos may have been building platforms. Three large sub-oval platforms are levelled into the hillslope with scarps averaging 0.9m high.

Menadue, Goodaver, and Bedwithiel (Fig 59) all continued into or were reused in the post-medieval period, but were all deserted by 1808. At Menadue both structures appear to have been longhouses, though unusually close together. At Bedwithiel (Fig 60) three of the four or five buildings are grouped around a small yard. The turf-covered walling of longhouse A (Fig 59) survives only to the height of 0.2–0.5m. House B, probably a longhouse originally, has walling up to 1.7m high where a possible fireplace lintel projects from the northern end wall. The adjacent corn-drying barn (Fig 56 no 1) is also very well preserved. Probably contemporary with this later phase is the refurbishment of elements in the medieval field pattern as substantial 'Cornish hedges' (typically 1m wide, 1.4m high). A walled track leads south to the Moor.

Medieval and post-medieval settlements at Brown Willy and Garrow (Fig 61, 62: discussion of Brown Willy by Peter Herring)

At both Garrow and Brown Willy there is a considerable element of post-medieval use or reuse. At Brown Willy (Herring 1986) it was felt possible to distinguish six discrete clusters of medieval buildings, arranged around a central herding area. Each cluster or farmstead comprised a dwelling-house (four were longhouses) with outbuildings; and the total roofed area of each cluster was directly comparable. Farmsteads were carefully laid out with domestic/private space placed away from the communal/public space. Two corn-drying barns, presumably shared (Herring 1986; Batt 1980, 24), are located at either extreme of the settlement and serve to emphasise the communal basis of the economy of the hamlet. Two farmsteads, 5 and 6 (Fig 61), postdate the original layout of the north-west field, a primary element in the medieval field system (see p 107); it is probable that the medieval settlement originally consisted of all, or at least some, of the other four farmsteads. Later in the medieval period, probably after the nucleated settlement had either shrunk or dispersed, the longhouse in farmstead 1 was adapted for use solely as a domestic structure by the blocking of one of its doors (see p 89, and Fig 54 no 9).

In the post-medieval, or more precisely the post-nucleation, phase there were no more than two farmsteads at any one time on the site, known later as Lower Brown Willy (St Breward Tithe Apportionment Map 1840). The two dwelling-houses now standing ruined each have round-buttress chimneys (Weaver 1967; 1969) and probably date to the eighteenth century (Herring 1986). One reuses a plain

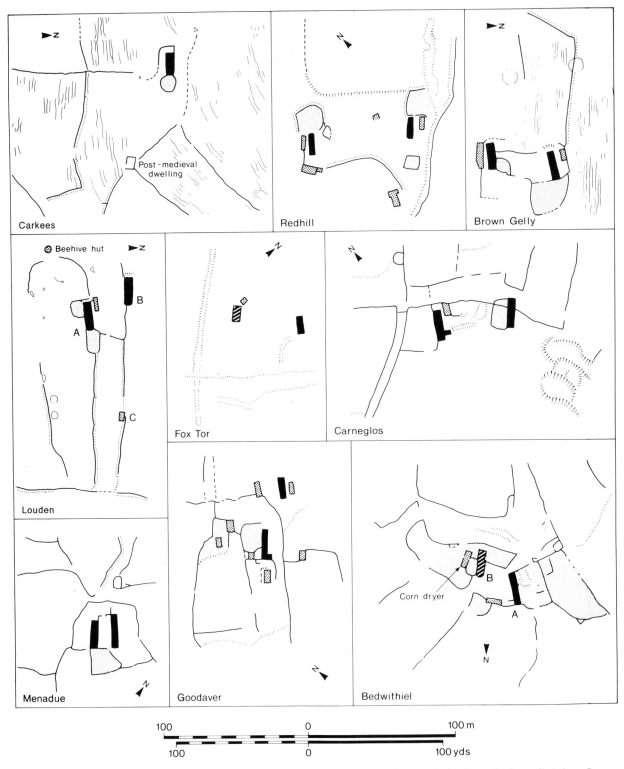

Fig 59   Smaller longhouse settlements; the slope runs down the page. Some of the boundaries adjoining Carneglos, Menadue, Goodaver, and Bedwithiel show post-medieval refurbishment, but most are probably medieval in origin. (See Table 8 for grid references)

chamfered jamb-stone of the previous century (Chesher and Chesher 1968, 131; S R Jones 1971, 14–15), presumably derived from an earlier post-medieval house on the site. Lower Brown Willy was certainly abandoned by 1840 and probably by the end of the eighteenth century (St Breward Tithe Apportionment Map 1840, O S 1″ Map 1813).

Garrow, comprising two farms at the beginning of

the nineteenth century, had only one by 1840, through the abandoning of Higher Garrow. The original character of Higher Garrow farmhouse is difficult to establish from the remains. It is set in an enclosure added to the north end of the settlement where a series of small ruined structures is probably associated with it. Garrow farmhouse (still roofed) is essentially a small seventeenth-century farmhouse,

Fig 60   Bedwithiel, SX 126759, looking southwest and uphill: a medieval and post-medieval settlement. Many of the medieval boundaries have been refurbished. At A, there is post-medieval cultivation in 'lands'; see Fig 59. (Photo NMR SX 1276/3/334, 28 February 1979; Crown Copyright Reserved)

though considerably altered in the late nineteenth century, particularly by the raising of the walls and the replacement of windows. Its date is apparent from the chamfered door jambs, the form of the chimney, the survival of a two-light mullioned window, and a kneeler stone projecting south from the east gable end showing the original height of the roof. It was probably a one-and-a-half- rather than a two-storeyed building, with two rooms upstairs and two downstairs, probably a hall and a service room, as one was unheated (see Chesher and Chesher 1968, 54–6). Like Higher Garrow, it could conceivably be on the site of a longhouse; traces of a rectangular

structure extend 5m uphill to the west on the same alignment as the building. The associated remains visible today are largely those of a nineteenth-century farm. Seven small enclosures, defined by substantial stone-faced walls, lie south of the farmhouse. The three nearest, with access controlled by gates, are yards integrated with the track through the settlement and all are associated with ancillary structures. In the eastern yard, a late nineteenth-century farm building, comprising cow shed, stable, and privy, probably replaced the now ruined scatter of small structures which include a fine 'beehive hut' described in 1873 as 'modern', ie not an antiquity

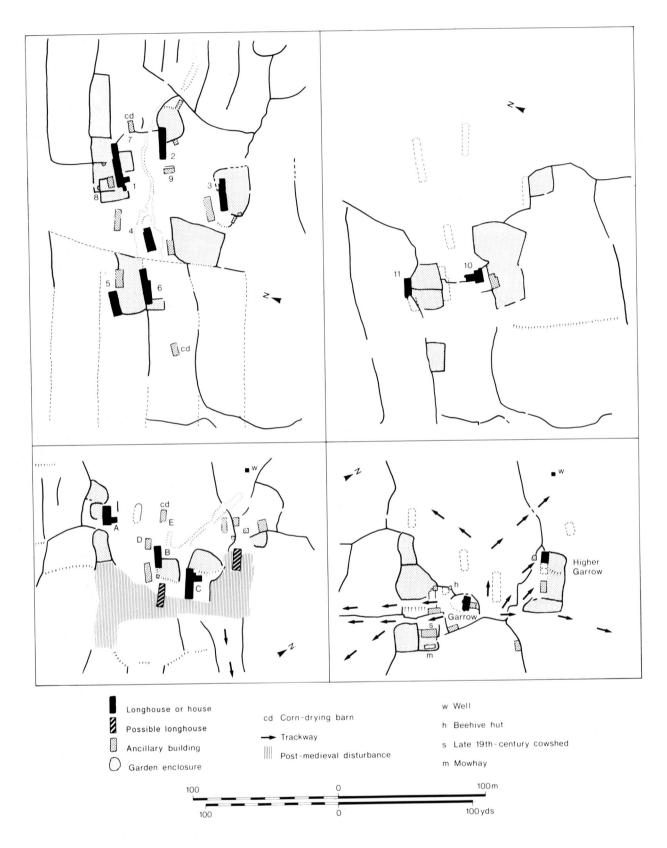

Longhouse or house

Possible longhouse

Ancillary building

Garden enclosure

cd Corn-drying barn

Trackway

Post-medieval disturbance

w Well

h Beehive hut

s Late 19th-century cowshed

m Mowhay

100   0   100m

100   0   100yds

Fig 61   Medieval and post-medieval phases of settlement at Brown Willy (top, after P Herring) and Garrow (bottom).
Left, medieval; right, post-medieval; the slope runs down the page. For detailed plans of individual structures:
Brown Willy 1 and 6, see Fig 54, nos 9, 8; 7, 8, 9, see Fig 56 nos 2, 5, 4; 10 and 11, see Fig 55 nos 3, 4; Garrow A,
B, C, see Fig 54 nos 4, 1, 7; D and E, see Fig 56 nos 7, 3; F, see Fig 53, no 2 (see also Fig 16 and Table 8 for grid
references)

Fig 62   Brown Willy, SX 153793, looking east and uphill: a medieval and post-medieval settlement. At A (top, right of centre) a late boundary cuts across the medieval fields; at B (a little left of, and below centre) a number of medieval strip boundaries have been refurbished and fossilised, others have been abandoned or effaced. A hut circle is visible centre left (see Figs 61, 70). (Photo NMR SX 1579/22/199, 28 February 1979; Crown Copyright Reserved)

(Maclean 1873). The yards were primarily for the control of stock. The three southernmost enclosures are gardens or cultivation plots; the western plot is markedly lynchetted and probably medieval in origin. The seventh enclosure, below the cow shed, is described as 'Mowhay' on the 1840 Tithe Apportionment Map and still contains a rick stand. A small eighth enclosure gave the farmhouse privacy from its farmyard.

The medieval layout was probably partly destroyed by the post-medieval phase. Three long-

houses with their associated structures and enclosures survive, and there may have been others. Longhouse A and barn B were excavated (Dudley and Minter 1962–3). An area of burning at the west end of Barn B (ibid, 277–8) and a structure like a fireplace in the same place, suggest that the building might have been a small house. The longhouse was probably in use as late as the sixteenth century, and conceivably late enough to have been directly replaced by the surviving farmhouse. At the northern extremity of the settlement a small structure with a little garden was perhaps another dwelling. A series of hollow-ways lead through the settlement, the best-defined to a well, essentially a stone-lined pit capped with drill-split granite, nineteenth-century in its present form but presumably medieval in origin.

5   Post-medieval buildings and settlements (to c 1800)

by Peter Herring and Jacqueline Nowakowski

Buildings and settlements

There are two particular respects in which the Moor is important for the study of vernacular architecture. First, it is possible to trace and date the structural changes of the longhouse into its late medieval and post-medieval successors, as discussed above. (Presumably the same change was occurring in lowland Cornwall; study of this phase of development has increased the likelihood that some extant structures originated as longhouses.) Second, a range of post-medieval structures survives here (as ruins) that may once have existed off the Moor but are now difficult to find, ie the humble single-storey dwellings.

The settlements deserted in the post-medieval period, whether of medieval or later origin, normally consist of one, at most two, dwellings. Deserted settlements at Casehill (SX 12397824), White Meadow (SX 11547857), and Irish (centred SX 11207732) are all

single farms, possibly ranging from the sixteenth to the eighteenth century. At Irish five separate farms are scattered within a block of fields which, had it been carved from the Moor in the twelfth century, would probably have served a single hamlet.

In many cases these later structures are little, if at all, better preserved, than the longhouses, but are distinguishable in several ways: they are not of longhouse form, normally having a single entrance; some are set along the contour (eg Colvannick, SX 12557136; Temple, SX 13817324); frequently there is a fireplace, sometimes with a round-buttress chimney. Some of the buildings are tiny. At Bowda (SX 26277527), a building shown as a ruin on the North Hill Tithe Map is 7 × 4.8m internally and has a subdivision; a small enclosure adjoining is presumably a garden. At Codda, an isolated structure, probably a herdsman's hut (Fig 63 no 1, SX 18017906) 4.6 × 3m internally, has a fireplace at one end, with a round-buttress chimney (Herring 1986). There are similar small structures in the open Moor at Brown Willy (Fig 63 no 1, SX 15877841) and at Carkees (Fig 59, SX 14087636). Some of these smaller buildings were possibly herdsmen's huts; that at the south end of Brown Willy is more likely to have been a tinner's hut, being adjacent to a streamworks (that is, an area where alluvial deposits have been dug over for redeposited tin ore). Other single-roomed heated huts are apparently associated with mining, at Roughtor East (SX 15248117), Shallow-water Common (SX 15337626), and Barbers Hill (SX 16307837). These small houses were perhaps the homes of bachelor tinners.

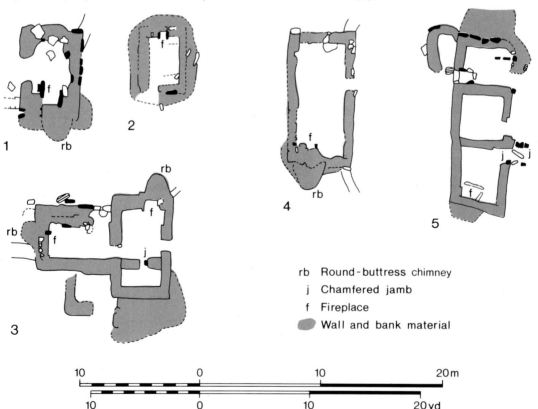

rb   Round-buttress chimney
j   Chamfered jamb
f   Fireplace
⬤   Wall and bank material

10   0   10   20m

10   0   10   20yd

Fig 63   Post-medieval dwellings; the slope runs down the page. 1, Codda, SX 18017906, and 2, Brown Willy, SX 15877841: small isolated dwellings, perhaps for single occupants; 3 and 4, Lower Brown Willy, SX 15337936, SX 15317940 (see also Fig 61); 5, Higher Brown Willy, SX 15337970. (After P Herring)

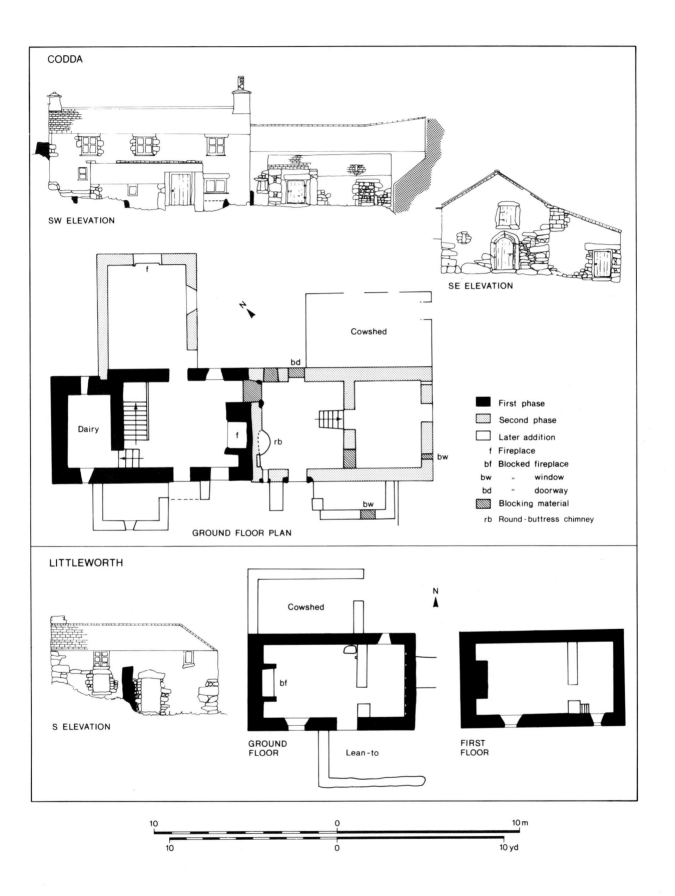

Fig 64   Post-medieval farmhouses at Codda, SX 180784, and Littleworth, SX 196757. (After J Nowakowski)

There is much variety in the plan and function of post-medieval houses on Bodmin Moor; this contrasts with the uniformity of the medieval longhouse tradition. The variety is well illustrated by the five post-medieval houses on Brown Willy (Herring 1986). Two, Higher Brown Willy (Fig 63 no 5) and the 'House in Catteshole' (SX 16357946), have shippons and dwelling-rooms under the same main roof-line, but unlike longhouses they have separate entrances with no intercommunication. These two are primitive forms of a house type common on central Bodmin Moor in the nineteenth century (see Nowakowski 1982). The 'House in Catteshole' was referred to in the 1613 boundary confirmation of St Breward parish (Royal Cornwall Museum [formerly Royal Institution of Cornwall], Henderson MS, East Cornwall Book, 60). Higher Brown Willy is of essentially eighteenth-century date, although the west wall, with the collapsed open fireplace, belongs to an earlier house, the main axis of which was on a slightly different orientation, as is clear from the angles at the western corners (Herring 1986).

Both Lower Brown Willy houses (Fig 63 nos 3, 4) were dwellings proper, although single-storeyed. Round-buttress chimneys in gable walls are unusual so far east in Cornwall, although two others have now been recognised at Codda, one in the surviving dwelling-house and the other in the herdsman's hut previously mentioned. Walls stand to about 1.5m high in places, but no window openings were found in either house. Originally, Fig 63 no 3 comprised a single room, but it now has three rooms, the northern probably secondary and the south-western made by the insertion of a stone partition. The use of wooden partitions should not, however, be ruled out (cf Christie et al 1979, 110).

Slades farmhouse (SX 15408026) is a late nineteenth-/early twentieth-century dwelling of simple two-up, two-down type. It incorporates a fine seventeenth-century window and fireplace; the latter, with well-cut plain-chamfered jambs and lintel, seems somewhat out of place in such a remote and small farmhouse. Other chamfered stones have also been reused at Lower Brown Willy and Higher Brown Willy as well as at Butterstor, Fernacre, and Garrow, all in the same Upper De Lank area (Herring 1986; Nowakowski 1982).

Eric Mercer's comment that no pre-1800 farmhouses are to be found on Bodmin Moor (1975, 33) reflects the immediate impression gained of its surviving vernacular architecture. The bulk of the inhabited houses are indeed of the nineteenth century, but a number of seventeenth- and eighteenth-century houses do survive. The Cheshers have already noted those at Leaze, Ivey, Casehill, Durfold, Trehudreth Mill, and, most impressively, Mennabroom (Chesher and Chesher 1968). Garrow is described above. To these can be added the sadly neglected ruins at Bedrawle, Littleworth, and in the farmyard at Fernacre; the first a fine small seventeenth-century farmhouse with chamfered and mullioned windows, the other two probably of eighteenth-century date. Littleworth (Fig 64) might in fact be seventeenth-century, as its layout is strikingly similar to that at Higher Spargo, Mabe (Chesher and Chesher 1968, 56), having a single chamber reached via a ladder from a dairy/larder separated from the main ground floor room (Nowakowski 1982). Other occupied houses built before 1800 include Dryworks (eighteenth-century?) and Codda, both in the Fowey valley. Codda is an amalgam of styles (Fig 64); much of it may be dated to the seventeenth century, especially the chamfered stonework, arched doors etc, but it may incorporate the remains of a longhouse. The northern half has opposed entrances and walls suspiciously thick in places (1m across, whereas those of most post-medieval houses are 0.6–0.7m). An east wing was added in the eighteenth or nineteenth century.

Beehive huts

Beehive huts form an individual class of moorland building found largely in the north-western part of the Moor. The distinctive features of these small, granite-built structures can be illustrated by the well-preserved example at Fernacre (Fig 65 no 1). The walls are of uncut stone built with vertical internal faces to support a corbelled roof, capped with turf. Turf was also used to seal any gaps in the walls. The huts have been listed and discussed by Nowakowski and Herring (1985). They are found in two specific settings: on farmsteads (13), or on the open Moor (3 at Brown Willy; 1 at Louden – Fig 65 no 4). The example at Fernacre (SX 15137972) is an exception, being neither on a farmstead nor on the open Moor proper.

Dating is indirect. At Brown Willy the evidence of wall relationships suggest that there the moorland huts are likely to be of medieval date (Herring 1986). At Louden (SX 13808025) the hut is very ruined and lies 50m from the abandoned longhouse settlement with which it need not be contemporary. The 13 huts found on farmsteads are later in date, and documentary work makes it possible to date them securely to the eighteenth and nineteenth centuries. Their differing settings within the farmsteads suggest a variety of functions, for example as roosting houses, animal houses, tool sheds, or cold stores for vegetables and/or dairy products.

The huts on open moorland are in positions offering impressive panoramic views of pasture, and those at Brown Willy can be regarded as relics of medieval stock herding (Herring 1986). Distance from any surface evidence of tin working discounts any theory that they may have been tinners' shelters (cf Greeves 1981, 168, who notes a number of beehive huts on Dartmoor close to streamworks).

6   Fields, cultivation, and the organisation of the landscape

Here it is possible only to give some indication of the wealth of archaeological evidence that demonstrates how the Moor was used during the medieval period and later. The value of field and boundary systems is greatest where they survive complete with their

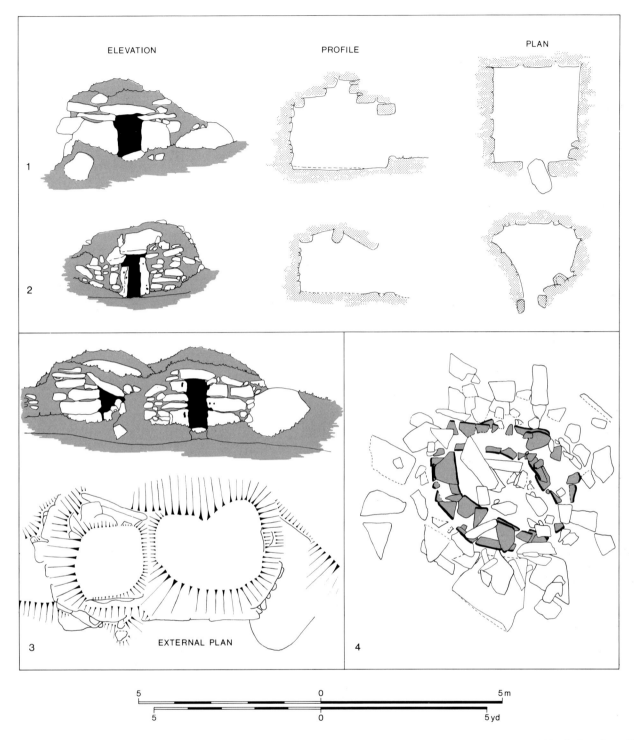

ELEVATION PROFILE PLAN

EXTERNAL PLAN

5   0   5 m

5   0   5 yd

Fig 65   Beehive huts: 1, Fernacre, SX 15137972; 2, Leaze, SX 13287686; 3, Butterstor, SX 15667832; 4, Louden, SX 13808025   (1–3 after Nowakowski and Herring 1985)

associated settlements. In Table 8 the extent of survival of each associated field system is categorised
according to its survival as a whole. The table covers
almost all the more complete survivals, but there are
also examples where only limited parts of field systems survive intact, normally as the remains of
medieval or post-medieval outfield to surviving settlements (eg Craddock Moor, SX 241722; Trehudreth
Downs, SX 122726).

Enclosures and trackways: the organisation of the landscape

In many cases the form of the boundaries makes it
possible to identify the areas associated with each
settlement. Commonly a relatively large area is
enclosed around each settlement, of which a smaller
acreage, but sometimes the whole area, is cultivated.
This can be seen in the Upper Fowey (Carneglos,

Fig 66 Organisation of the medieval landscape in north-west Bodmin Moor (Enclosures at Casehill and in the northern part of Leaze may be post-medieval)

Goodaver etc, Map 2) and in the De Lank valleys. Here there is a clear succession of holdings enclosed from the Moor. Bedwithiel (SX 127760) appears to postdate Carbilly, and Carbilly postdates fields to the south. Many of the enclosing boundaries have been maintained to the present day and are now substantial stone-faced walls, normally with outer ditches (eg Stannon); but their early origin is usually clear. Boundaries in their early form normally survive as banks, sometimes with an outer face, and usually with an outer ditch (eg Garrow).

The most extensive survival of the medieval landscape is in the north-west part of the Moor. Many features occur regularly, as shown in Figure 66, and may be illustrated with reference to the layout at Louden. The areas associated with individual settlements frequently are, or appear to be, the product of topography: those at Louden, Garrow, and Brown Willy all encompass hills. At Louden there are two enclosing boundaries, one enclosing the hill (41ha), the other enclosing 33ha of lower ground, defined on three sides by bog. Somewhat similar localities are enclosed north-west of Garrow and to the north and north-east of Casehill, the latter areas associated, perhaps, with Candra and Casehill respectively. In all these cases the boundaries are defined by banks with outer ditches. As well as enclosing large areas of grazing land they may have helped to define tracks and routeways; certainly this is so at Louden, where the boundary forms one side of a track or droveway. A subdivision, defined by a slight bank and ditch, divides the western part of the main enclosure at Louden in two, perhaps for the control of grazing stock, though it would have needed the addition of a fence or hedge to make it an effective barrier. Subdivisions of the enclosed pasture have also been noted at Garrow and Brown Willy.

At Louden the character of the main enclosure boundary is variable. In the north it is generally a stone-faced bank, rarely more than 0.3m high on the outside, often with a build-up of soil on the inside, and with a shallow ditch on the outside. In the south it is generally a low stone bank, often no more than a single line of small stones, set 'bookshelf' fashion (see Fig 12). Originally this part of the boundary could have had no function in stock control and in its initial stage could have done no more than define the extent of the Louden holding, perhaps a necessary requirement in a litigious society. Interestingly, the only documentation for Louden reflects the need for careful definition of grazing rights. In 1288 'Henry Cauvel took out a writ of new disseizin against Hugh Peverell and David Wof of common pasture in Hamatethy, which he claimed as pertaining to his free tenement in Lauedon. Henry did not appear, and judgement was given for Hugh and David in default' (Maclean 1873, 355). Henry may have been claiming grazing rights on Roughtor. In Altarnun parish in 1840 (Tithe Apportionment) and presumably earlier, most of the settlements on lower ground had common rights on either East Moor or West Moor, according to their location in the parish; but many of the moorland settlements, for example Codda and Carneglos, lacked such rights. There are

perhaps two reasons for this: first, that farms like Codda already possessed adequate enclosed pasture, and second, that when new settlements were established in the moorland they were allocated no share in the common pastures to avoid depleting the resources of the existing farms. This seems to have been the case at Louden.

The importance of common rights, particularly of pasture and turbary but also of pannage, estovers, piscary, and common in the soil (Brewster 1975, 224–5) is reflected in the provision of access. At Louden it is apparent that when the boundaries were set out broad trackways or droveways were defined on either side of the hill. This would have allowed the uninterrupted movement of stock to and from areas of common grazing, and also the passage of longer-distance traffic across the Moor. Such features occur repeatedly (see Map 2), and their provision for the controlled movement of people and stock shows that the landscape is an organised one. The intensity of this movement becomes evident only where the routes traverse steeper ground. Then there are 'swarms' of hollow-ways as at Stannon, where they form two bands, each 200m long and spread over 80m and 200m respectively (SX 12797970 and SX 12358000).

As on Dartmoor, some routes are marked by stone crosses to guide the traveller across the Moor. There are at least seven in the survey area. Four mark the main east–west track across the Moor, now followed by the A30; the Longstone at Minions (SX 25557056) is on a track which skirts the south-east edge of the Moor; and two in the north-west, Middle Moor Cross (SX 12507930) and one near King Arthur's Hall (SX 12817764), are set in the centre of droveways and may have been placed to signpost exits from the Moor.

Cultivation

Evidence for tillage is visible in the form of clearance, cultivation ridges, and lynchetting.

Clearance

In stony areas clearance is a necessary accompaniment to cultivation. It normally takes the form of small stones heaped on to grounders, varying from a few stones to mounds up to 3m across and 0.5m high, all but engulfing the grounder below. Mounds with no evident grounder are less common (whereas this appears to be the normal form for prehistoric clearance). Occasionally clearance is in the form of rough lines or short lengths of clearance banks, normally along the grain of the cultivation, but sometimes across it on lines of grounders or stony areas.

Cultivation ridges

Cultivation ridges vary in date and type. Most of the ridging with a medieval context is narrow, typically 2.2–2.7m wide, at most 0.2m high and generally much less. Often it is visible only in very favourable conditions of light. The character of this ridging can be seen in Fig 67 (Roughtor South, SX 147804). Frequently sinuous and irregular, it almost always lies across the contour, often a little obliquely. Differences in the clarity of definition (compare fields A and B) may reflect differences in the intensity of use. Ridging may have been developed partly to make a reasonable seed bed in an area of thin stony soils and partly for drainage, factors which may help to account for the narrow width. Drainage would also be assisted by cultivating across the contour; and if a plough were involved its use would be made easier by working up and down the slope rather than along it (Twidale 1972).

The ridges are sometimes irregular within a single field. In C they range somewhat haphazardly from 1.8m to 3.5m across, apparently according to how they can best fit in with the rest. At A the ridges are much broader on the west side of the field than on the east, perhaps the product of two phases of cultivation or of two cultivators. Note also how an extra ridge has been introduced halfway up the west side of field C.

It is rarely clear how much is spade-dug and how much ploughed. The ridges, and clearance cairns without apparent ridges, are frequently found in very stony areas, as in parts of Garrow where some patches of cultivation may be no more than 5m to 10m long. At Roughtor South ridges in the stonier northern parts, visible on the ground but not on Fig 67 (except at F), may be spade-dug, but many of the

remainder have the appearance of ploughing: at the bottom of some of the fields the ridges curve slightly to the right onto a 'headland' or 'head' (see Fig 68), also very much a feature of the cultivation on Garrow. Sometimes there is a slight dip along the uphill side of the headland, seen on Fig 67 as a darker line. Although the presence of a headland suggests ploughing, almost invariably the 'furrows' continue over the headland to the very crest of the lynchet. It is difficult to see how this could have been achieved by a plough team; perhaps the ridges were completed by hand. Similarly a very short ridge inserted in the south-east corner of field C, to fill a gap caused by the curve of the ridges, is likely to have been spade-dug. A mixture of plough and spade cultivation may, therefore, be expected. Even in moderately stony areas the plough may have been lifted over smaller boulders, easier on the descent than the ascent! In all, the nature and adaptability of the ridges reflects the difficulty of the terrain and suggests that any plough team must have been small and manoeuvrable.

Lynchets

Headlands are relatively uncommon; more often the ridges just end (or fade) at the bottom of the field. Usually there is some lynchetting; at Garrow heights of 0.6m to 1m are common. Occasionally there is

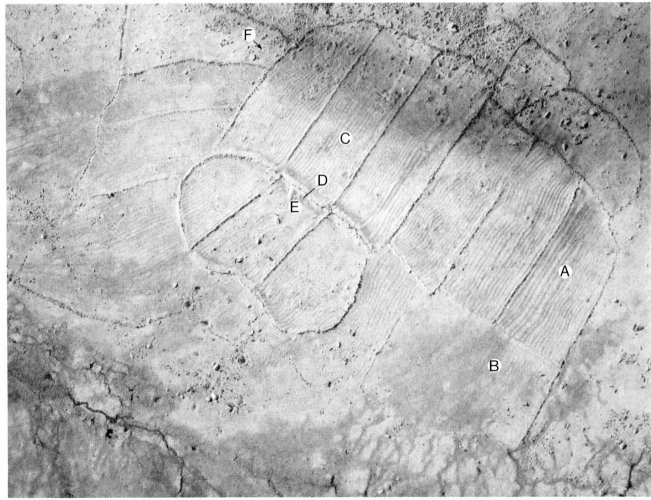

Fig 67   Roughtor South, SX 147804; a group of medieval fields; north and uphill is top right. Points A–F are described in the text above; for profile E–D see Fig 68. (Photo NMR SX 1480/28/232, 28 February 1979; Crown Copyright Reserved)

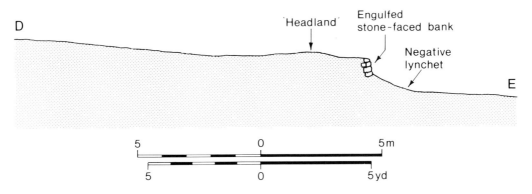

Fig 68   Profile through headland at Roughtor South (E–D on Fig 67)

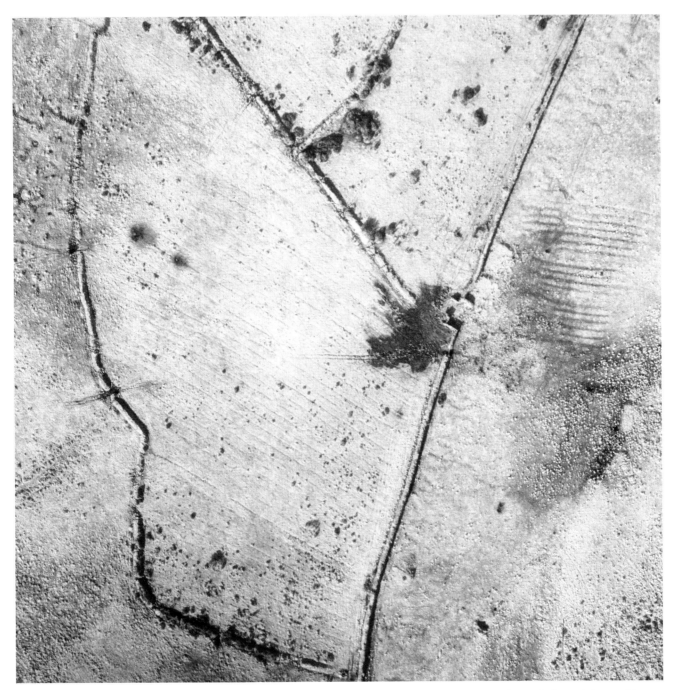

Fig 69   Druglets, SX 139760, post-medieval cultivation, probably in 'lands': north top right, uphill top left; see Fig 75.
(Photo NMR SX 1376/3/300, 28 February 1979; Crown Copyright Reserved)

evidence of considerable soil movement over very short distances, as at SX 14417768 (Garrow), where a lynchet 1.1m high has formed at the bottom of an area of cultivation which extends 30m up the slope above it. (Ridges curve on to a headland here, suggesting plough cultivation.) Does the often considerable lynchetting reflect a long period of successful cultivation or a short and perhaps disastrous episode of soil loss and hillwash? Excavation of an area of cultivation adjoining the longhouse at Bunning's Park showed that the exceedingly stony subsoil was covered by the present turf line and little else; soil loss here, and at other sites, may have been a major contributory factor to desertion (Austin *et al* 1989). Lynchets are not, however, ubiquitous and they vary considerably in size and frequency from one field system to another in a way that cannot be accounted for by differences in local topography alone (eg the steepness of the natural slope). Coupled with evidence for the development of some field patterns over several phases, this suggests that some lynchets at least can be the product of a long period of cultivation, which at Garrow has given the east side of the hill an almost sculpted appearance.

Later cultivation

Broader ridging (3.5m is typical) normally has a post-medieval context, as in refurbished fields at Brown Willy and in a nineteenth-century field at Butterstor (SX 15557790). Narrow ridges can also be post-medieval, for example in fields at Casehill (SX 125783) and at Leaze (SX 136776). Such ridging is generally regular and often extensive, as at Casehill where 29ha appear to be associated with a single farm. As sometimes happened elsewhere on the Moor in the present century (Brewster 1975, 262), perhaps when the land was reclaimed, a crop was taken for a year or two before the fields were put down to grass.

A further form of cultivation, generally of post-medieval date but recurring in a medieval context at Lamlavery, is characterised not by a ridge but more by a sharp channel or furrow, evidently the double furrow resulting from ploughing in lands. The narrow, plough-formed (as opposed to spade-formed) ridges of medieval date were presumably also made by ploughing in lands, but the end product is quite different. These lands are broader than the ridge cultivation, 3.5–6m at Druglets (SX 13957603, Fig 69), 4–7m at Bedwithiel (SX 12607595, Fig 60) where it is presumably associated with the post-medieval use of the settlement, abandoned before the nineteenth century. It is also found at Lamlavery (Figs 73, 74) where from the form of the deserted settlement one would expect a medieval date for the surrounding cultivation. Here the lands are mostly 120–270m long but can be as much as 340m; most are 7–11m wide, a few 15–19m. Some lands have subdivisions, defined by similar furrows, as narrow as 2m or less (Fig 74A); for example, a land 9m wide might be divided into four by three furrows. Does this reflect slightly different cultivation types, or deliberate subdivision of lands? Ridges (2m wide) are found only in the small field immediately adjoining the north side of the hamlet (Fig 74B). The general lack of ridging could be deliberate and reflect the cultivation technique, but might be due to limited cultivation which has not led to the formation of ridges (and see p 111).

Boundary types

The function served by the various types of boundary depends on the original form, which is not always clear from the surviving evidence. This can be seen today with unmaintained 'Cornish hedges'. Over the years, as the stone face falls away, the earth core sinks back into the ground to leave just a broad earth and stone bank.

Boundaries enclosing areas of grazing normally have a form that suggests a function for stock control, typically a bank with an outer ditch. The bank may also have an outer face (see also Fleming and Ralph 1982). The banks are not always substantial and may have been finished with a hedge to make a stock-proof barrier. In terms of the expected requirements of stock control the form of some boundaries is surprising. For example, at Brown Willy the outer boundaries of the subdivided fields are of the same character as the subdivisions, that is, low stone banks, suggesting that the surrounding area would not have been grazed when the fields were in cultivation unless a herdsman kept watch or some temporary fencing was erected around the field.

Within field systems the commonest boundaries are stony banks and lynchets which from their present form do not seem to have been intended for stock control. Some are no more than trickles of stone, the product of clearance or subdivision; others are more substantial, as at Garrow, where a common form is a neat stone bank (perhaps 0.5m high), sometimes with a face on one side, projecting through the middle of an earth bank and suggesting two structural phases. Such boundaries also tend to change in character according to the material available: higher up the slopes they are single-stone walls, commonly of slabs on edge, but at the bottom they are broad banks of earth with little stone apparent.

The lower ends of fields are sometimes defined by stone-faced banks, as at Garrow and Roughtor South (Fig 68). These may become so engulfed by accumulation of soil that the face of the bank now appears halfway down the lynchet, as at Garrow. Some lynchets are revetted, perhaps to stop the boundary moving downhill or to prevent cattle from eroding it.

Field patterns

Field patterns on the Moor show greater variety and complexity than the settlements they sustained; it is premature to attempt a classification. In many cases cultivation ridges are found in a large number of relatively small fields, often in a strip-like pattern suggesting some form of subdivided arable cultivation. There are also instances where the cultivated land is divided among a small number of large fields with little or no subdivision apparent. Where settlements of more than one longhouse are associated with the second type (eg Lamlavery, Fox Tor, Redhill, and perhaps Louden) it is possible that the fields were ploughed and harvested in common and without subdivision; but it is, of course, possible that subdivisions existed but were not marked in such a way as to be apparent today. In 1602 Carew wrote of the Cornish husbandmen: 'These in times not past the remembrance of some yet living, rubbed forth their estate in the poorest plight, their grounds lay all in common, or only divided by stitchmeal' (ie in separate strips). The apparently undivided fields on Bodmin Moor may have been the sort that 'lay all in common'. Some of the different types will be more apparent from descriptions given below.

The relation of prehistoric and medieval field patterns

Medieval settlements and fields are very often found adjacent to or including groups of hut circles and their associated fields (Fig 76). The reuse of prehistoric field systems may take two forms. In some instances, the impact is relatively slight, leaving the prehistoric layout very largely unaffected, as with the outfield cultivation on Craddock Moor (SX 244723); elsewhere the prehistoric layout, while still apparent, is more completely incorporated in the medieval pattern, as has happened to a small area of curvilinear fields at Garrow (SX 14957780) or, most strikingly, at Little Siblyback (SX 240740, Fig 40). At Bowhayland (SX 240773) the medieval farmers incorporated the boundaries of the coaxial system on East Moor; these are now fossilised in the modern landscape. The situation may be similar at Rowden (SX 128793, Fig 9) and conceivably at Trewortha Marsh (SX 229755), though in these instances it is less clear how much of the layout is prehistoric.

Quite distinct from the incorporation of prehistoric boundaries through reuse is the survival into the medieval period of elements of prehistoric field systems through continuity of use. At present this cannot be demonstrated on the Moor, but at Carwether (SX 098795) parts of the field system are reminiscent of some of the prehistoric-based modern field patterns surviving in parts of West Penwith (CAU, various surveys). The place-name also allows an early origin for the settlement, as it contains the Cornish element *ker (a fort or round; Padel 1985, 50–4).

Most of the medieval field patterns appear little affected by earlier arrangements.

Field patterns associated with larger settlements

Brown Willy (Fig 70; Map 3) by Peter Herring

The earliest elements of the main Brown Willy strip field system (Herring 1986), apart from the strips associated with the transhumance huts (p 81), are the north-west field and the south field. They are in the most suitable part of Brown Willy for cultivation and both were subdivided into regular strips of carefully measured widths of 108ft, ie 6 Cornish rods (18ft): 11 strips in the north-west field and 6 in the south field.

Other measured divisions, but of 4 Cornish rods, occur at Bray Down. (For discussions of the conventional 18ft rod in Devon and Cornwall see also

Finberg 1951, 30; Hull 1971, 1ix; Fleming and Ralph 1982, 113.) They were so positioned in relation to each other as to suggest that the nucleated settlement with which they were associated was that of the four medieval farmsteads (1–4, see p 93). The five southernmost strips of the north-west field were discovered only after a carefully measured survey revealed otherwise anomalous features in the area of the post-medieval settlement. Strip boundaries were confirmed by removing the turf with strategically placed trenches (Herring 1986).

A secondary phase involved the extension of the south field southwards and the creation of the north-east field. Both were subdivided, but their strips were of irregular widths with more sinuous boundaries; no comparable commitment to equality of area is discernible. That strips incorporate uncultivable clitter suggests they were designed for ease of allotment rather than ploughing.

The three main fields (north-west, north-east, and south) formed the equivalent of the 'infield' (see Dodgson 1980, 83–103 for a more detailed discussion); they were probably employed in a crude rotation, perhaps based on a short-ley system (described by Hatcher 1970, 3; Jewell 1981, 95–7). When the fields were under grass stock could roam freely through them as the boundaries of the strips were only 'mearings' or stony balks; similar strip boundaries are well known in subdivided field systems in western and upland Britain (described for example by McCourt 1953, 72; 1954–5, 372–3; M Davies 1956, 94; G R J Jones 1973, 437–73; Whittington 1973, 537; Taylor 1975, 86). Beyond these infields were small bundles comprising three, four, or five outfield strips, no doubt reflecting the number of farmers involved in the intake. To the north of the field system the bundles were contained by successive perimeter walls which faced onto the open summer pastures.

Although the outfields represent an expansion of the arable land of the settlement, they do not necessarily mean that arable output also increased. Particular outfields were probably only cultivated once or twice every generation or so; for most of the time they would be, as today, rough pasture. Similarly at Colliford evidence from excavated ridges has been interpreted as suggesting only episodic cultivation (Griffith 1984, 90). The increased area of cleared land, however, gave the settlement greater arable potential and allowed greater economic and social flexibility. If it so wished, the community could produce for an attractive market, and it would also be better able to cope with a rise in its subsistence requirements caused by any population increase. Towards the end of the medieval period modifications of the strip field system indicate that its allotment principles were no longer so strictly observed. Farmsteads 5 and 6 at Brown Willy were built over the three southernmost strips of the north-west field and the refurbishing of strip boundaries in the outfields was unsystematic. These farmsteads were most probably built before the 1273–6 reference to six different householders (P R O, Assize Rolls J1/1/1224, m.7). In the later medieval period the nucleated settlement

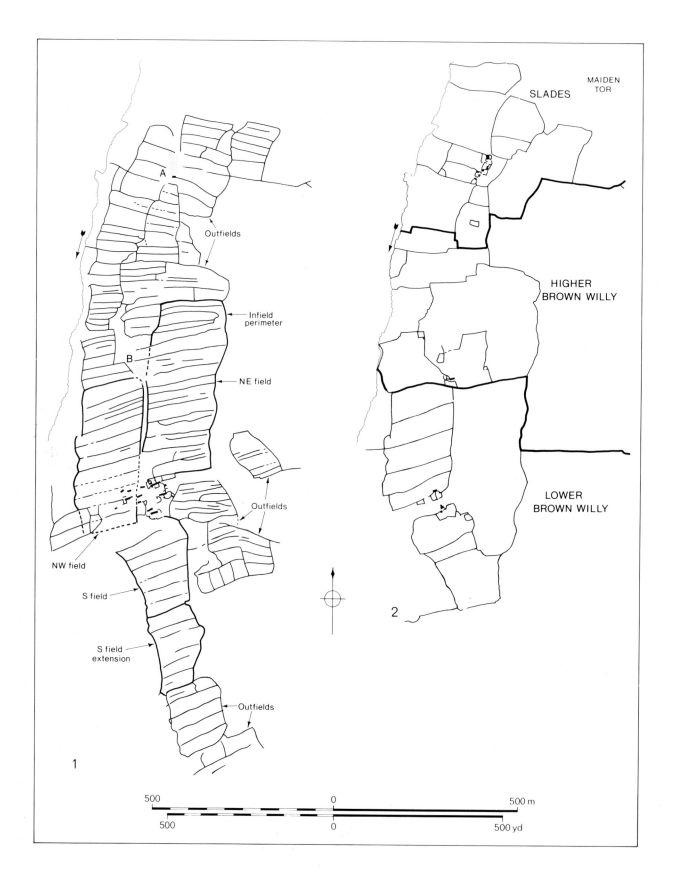

Fig 70 Medieval and post-medieval field patterns at Brown Willy, SX 153793 (after P Herring): 1, medieval: settlements at A (Slades) and B (Higher Brown Willy) were probably established in the fields of Brown Willy as early as the late 14th century; 2, c 1800

split into three separate farmsteads; Slades, Lower, and Higher Brown Willy; Slades is first mentioned in 1362 ('Sladland': Rowe 1914, 382).

The three farmsteads operated intermittently until the late eighteenth/early nineteenth century when both Lower and Higher Brown Willy were finally abandoned; only Slades survived into the present century. Their fields, by then in severalty, no longer needed strip divisions. Some groups of strips were thrown together and enclosed and walls were built over others as an irregular layout of fields gradually evolved. The situation at *c* 1800 is illustrated in Figure 70 no 2. Remnants of the regular strips of the north-west field are visible at Lower Brown Willy, but the former existence of the strips would hardly be suspected at Slades and Higher Brown Willy.

Garrow (Map 3; Fig 71)

As at Brown Willy, the layout at Garrow is strip-like. The strips are mostly about 30m wide, except in the south-west block where they are only 15m to 19m. A regular pattern throughout was impracticable because of areas of extreme stoniness, existing prehistoric fields, and sharp changes in slope.

On the east side of the hill almost all the available land was cultivated, though some of it is incredibly stony. As at Brown Willy there is a process of accretion. The fields on either side of the settlement were presumably the first to be laid out, but the next blocks were at the extreme north-east and extreme south; the areas in between are stonier and at first were avoided. From the north-east block (SX 14707870) the system expanded south in a series of

Fig 71   Medieval fields east of Garrow Tor, SX 147783 (viewed from east). Enclosures A and B have been refurbished (probably in the medieval period), but contain numerous hut circles and are probably prehistoric in origin. Small structures attached to the outside of enclosure B are of unknown date. On the north, the uphill limit of cultivation has shrunk to C because of stoniness above. Lynchets are well developed, notably in a line from D to E. (Photo NMR SX 1478/1/359, 8 April 1976; Crown Copyright Reserved)

eight or nine stages. Three further isolated groups of fields were established on the north-west side of the hill. The system appears well used and well developed throughout, with no distinction apparent between an infield and an outfield on the east side of the hill. Large lynchets are general, and many of the field boundaries are rather more substantial than low stone banks or trickles of stone (p 106). The exception is in the north-west (centred SX 140786), where patches of clearance and short lengths of slight banks and lines of stone suggest very limited outfield cultivation. It is not clear whether such cultivation is early or late, but it is possible that other parts of the hill saw similar use before they were more regularly subdivided. There is a hint of this in the south-west block, where the boundaries follow the topography so closely as to suggest that the strips were laid out over an area already in cultivation. This contrasts with the north-east block which was laid out apparently without regard for the stoniness of the upper part of the area; at some stage the upper edge of cultivation retreated and was redefined further down the slope.

At Garrow moderately intensive post-medieval use or reuse was restricted to a small area immediately south of the farm, where some of the boundaries were refurbished to make a few rectilinear closes. On the hilltop an enclosure (SX 14307805; Fig 37) with a high (1.3m) drystone wall and a small funnel-mouthed pen in one corner was probably used for sheep.

Fernacre (Map 3)

At Fernacre post-medieval use has been more extensive, but elements of the medieval layout survive in the system; and beyond the area of reuse groups of strips survive intact (Fig 72). Perhaps because of its topographical setting, Fernacre differs from Brown Willy and Garrow in that the series of intakes or accretions so evident here were taken from the open Moor rather than from within a large enclosed area already associated with the settlement (Fig 66). This can be seen elsewhere on the Moor, for example on Craddock Moor (SX 240715 and SX 241722). Fernacre is a good example of how the enclosed area expanded without blocking the through trackways. The final area of intake at the north-west is defined by a very slight bank with outer ditch which incorporates the Fernacre stone circle in its line, thus explaining a short stretch of bank identified by Barnatt as anomalous to the circle (1982, 170). This boundary is either unfinished or would have required a planted hedge to make it stockproof.

The detached block of fields at Roughtor South (Fig 67) is also likely to belong to Fernacre. At the centre is what is probably a prehistoric enclosure divided into three, with subsequent additions also

Fig 72 Medieval and post-medieval fields at Fernacre, SX 149794, looking west, upslope. To the left medieval strips incorporate ridging and numerous clearance heaps on large boulders. To the right, where the fields have been thoroughly cleared of boulders, some of the strip boundaries are fossilised in the modern field pattern. (Photo NMR SX 1579/19/249, 28 February 1973; Crown Copyright Reserved)

in blocks of three, suggesting that the work was shared and the fields allotted among three families.

Lamlavery (Figs 73, 74)

The settlement is associated with some 8–10 fields defined by earth banks 2m wide and 0.5m high, some with slight outer ditches. The system expanded with the addition of the south-west field and the detached block south-east of the settlement, the latter block leaving access for traffic to and from the Moor. A series of tracks and hollow-ways, contemporary with and later than the fields, converge on David-stow Moor from the rest of the parish and lead south, forking to Roughtor and High Moor. Most of the cultivation is in two large undivided fields, south-west and north-west of the hamlet, 18ha and 45ha respectively. In the north-west field the lands (p 00) form seven or eight blocks (furlongs?), largely reflecting the topography. The size and character of the fields suggest that co-aration was practised. What is not clear is the way in which land was allotted. It is likely that the 'land' acted as the unit of subdivision. Strips of similar widths but defined by slight stone banks are found elsewhere, for example Treskilling Downs, Luxulyan (SX 035577). Alternatively the lands may be a product of cultivation technique in fields that 'lay all in common' (p 107).

Lamlavery differs from the other moorland field systems, partly because of its very bleak and exposed setting, but probably also because of its location just off the granite. Here there is little surface stone to damage the plough, there are no clearance cairns, and the banks are largely of earth with occasional stone uprights, probably for setting out the fields. The layout is possibly more typical of lowland Cornwall than of the granite moors. Lamlavery also has a larger cultivated acreage than the other moorland settlements, possibly reflecting a greater emphasis on arable here, but more probably infrequent use of extensive but unproductive land.

Field patterns associated with smaller settlements

These also show considerable variation; a few examples are given.

Fields with little subdivision

At Louden (Map 3) the two longhouses are associated with only 6.5ha of cultivation. The area south of the settlement is not ridged but looks cleared and has an upper limit of cultivation defined by a rough negative lynchet to which boulders and smaller stones have been added by clearance. The area north of the settlement is ridged and scattered with clearance cairns. No provision was made for a permanent barrier to divide the cultivated from the uncultivated land. Three slight stone banks, generally discontinuous and often no more than trickles of stones, seem to form two strip fields (14m to 19m wide) within part of this area, and are possibly the first steps of some form of strip layout, perhaps present throughout this small area but otherwise unmarked; their fragmentary nature, however, suggests that they may be no more than the product of linear clearance.

The limited extent of cultivation at Louden and its undeveloped appearance may be due to a greater emphasis on stock rearing, although the weakness of the main enclosure boundary does not suggest this (p 103). Perhaps the occupation of Louden was of only limited duration.

At Fox Tor (SX 228784) the cultivation is more extensive, but as at Louden there is little evidence for subdivision. If there are, indeed, two longhouses here rather than one, this may again suggest either that the land was cultivated and cropped entirely in common or that subdivisions existed but were not marked. This may also be the case at Redhill (SX 205706), where the two longhouses are associated with three large fields apparently without subdivisions.

Smaller settlements with strip fields

There are several examples of strip fields or strip-like fields associated with the paired longhouse settlements so common on the Moor, for example in the Fowey valley at Goodaver, at Higher Langdon (Fig 76), and at Brown Gelly. At Brown Gelly (Fig 75) cultivation occurs in four fields but in only one is there a clear indication of subdivision. The field is bounded on three sides by a stone bank 1.5m wide, 0.4m high, with an outer ditch 0.4m deep, and on the downhill side by an eluvial tin streamworks. It has been divided into twelve strips defined by slight stone banks and lynchets. The strips are 17m to 21m wide, up to 290m long, and typically 0.5ha in extent. Unusually, they cross the contour obliquely. At Colvannick (SX 125713) a fine set of strips is perhaps unique on the Moor in following the contour.

Cultivation not of strip type

Cultivation like that at Brown Gelly is of unmistakable strip form and can only be the result of land allotment in a system of subdivided arable. Other systems are also strip-like, for example a series of broader rectilinear fields at Carneglos (SX 19857672); but it is uncertain whether or not these form part of a system of allotment. It is relatively easy to see, from subdivision and strip-like fields, where some form of shared or allotted cultivation is likely. It is less easy to see where it is not. At Carkees there can be no doubt; here the fields are associated with a single longhouse (Fig 75). The eight or nine ridged fields are rectilinear, 35m to 90m wide, and cover 7.5ha. They are bounded by low banks, some with orthostats, and some have slight ditches. There is no substantial lynchetting. The pattern hardly suggests a single planned act, rather it has probably developed through the accretion of indivual fields. Other examples of irregular fields occur at Little Siblyback ('Newhall', SX 239738) and in the De Lank valley at Bedwithiel, Bedrawle, Leaze etc. In these last instances, however, there is no substantial survival of the medieval layout and some of the irregularity, for example at Leaze, could be due to the removal of many of the boundaries; there is even a slight hint of former strips at SX 13287698.

Relict strips

In some cases where field systems have continued in

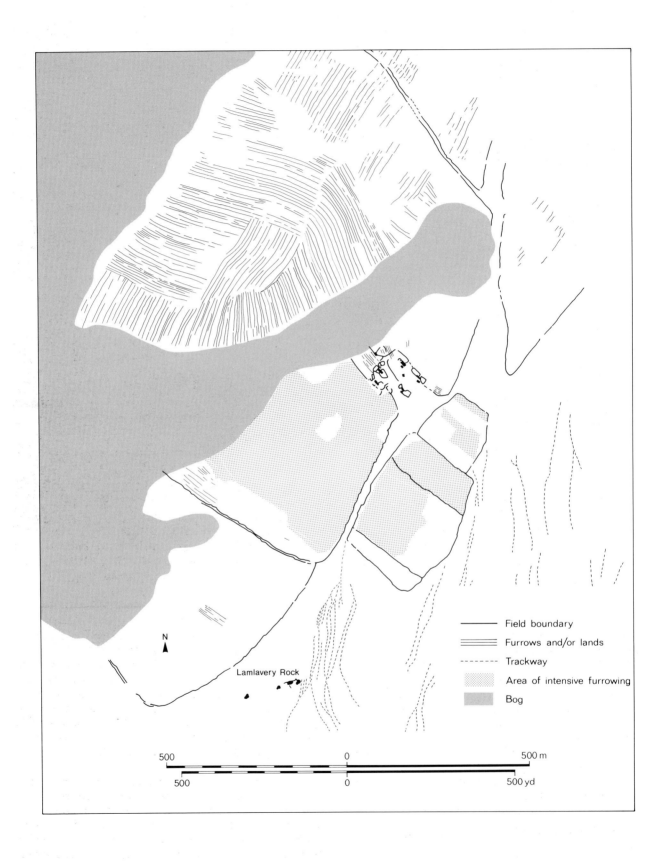

Field boundary

Furrows and/or lands

Trackway

Area of intensive furrowing

Bog

N

Lamlavery Rock

500   0   500 m

500   0   500 yd

Fig 73   Medieval fields at Lamlavery, Davidstow Moor, SX 159834. (See also Figs 58, 74 and p111)

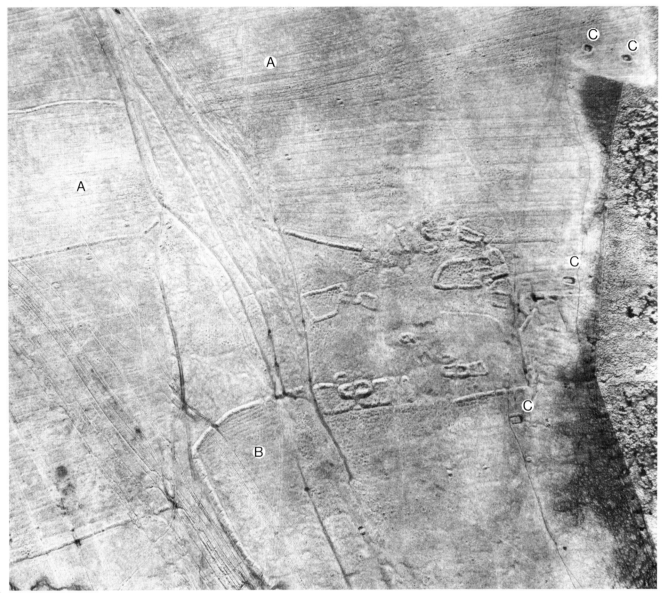

Fig 74   The medieval settlement of Lamlavery, Davidstow Moor, SX 159833, looking south-west. A, cultivation in lands, with 'subdivisions'; B, cultivation ridges more typical of Bodmin Moor; C, peat-drying platforms. (See also Figs 58, 73.) (Photo NMR SX 1583/3/167, 28 February 1979; Crown Copyright Reserved)

use fossilised elements of the strip layout are still apparent in the modern field pattern, as at Tresellern (SX 237764) and Fernacre. This can also be seen in many examples surrounding the Moor, as at Trecollas, Trenhorne, Kingswood, and Tregenna (SX 208832, SX 275786, SX 106665, SX 092738). Elsewhere a probable strip pattern has disappeared. In the Fowey valley there is little to indicate a former strip layout on the farms neighbouring Goodaver, Brown Gelly, and Higher Langdon, although there is little reason to suppose its absence. At Brown Willy (p 109) we have already seen the process by which a strip system might completely disappear.

'Open field' cultivation in Cornwall and on Bodmin Moor

There is now considerable evidence that some form of open-field cultivation was general throughout Cornwall (Rowse 1941, 32–6; Pounds 1947, 113–15, 1945; Ravenhill 1969, 106–9; Flatrès 1957). By the time that Carew was writing (1602) the practice was evidently becoming unusual, but survivals can be found on the 1696 Lanhydrock Atlas (Pounds 1945), on several nineteenth-century Tithe Maps (Flatrès 1957; Chesher 1974) and in one instance, the Forrabury Stitches (Wood 1963), at the present day.

It is suggested that a high proportion of the larger hamlets on the Moor, perhaps all of them, practised some system of common or subdivided arable cultivation, at least in the thirteenth and fourteenth centuries. The picture is less clear for the smaller hamlets of just two farmsteads, but subdivided arable did occur, and may have been the norm.

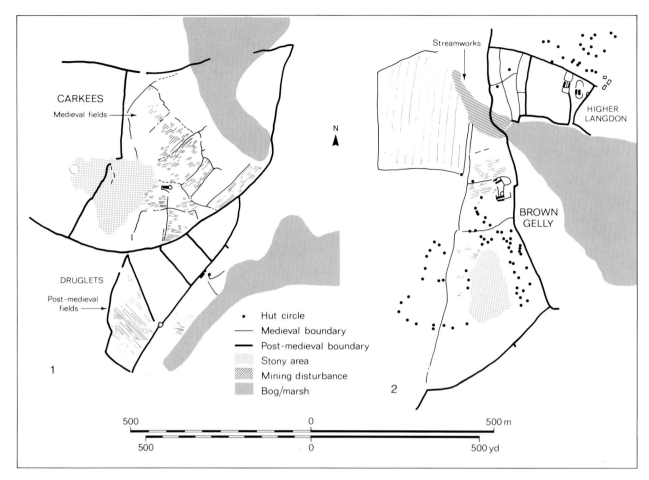

Fig 75   Medieval fields at Carkees, SX 140763, and at Brown Gelly, SX 201728   (See also Figs 59, 76, 38 no 5; also 69 for ridging at Druglets)   Ridging simplified at Carkees and Brown Gelly

7   Chronological summary of the main developments

Before c 1100

For a long period up to the eleventh century the area was an extensive tract of rough grazing without permanent settlement and acting as the upland component of a wider area around the Moor. Transhumance was probably practised. There are indications of some early colonisation, as at Hamatethy and along the De Lank; indeed some areas in the De Lank and Fowey valleys may have been settled continuously from the Iron Age or earlier.

The late eleventh or twelfth to the early fourteenth centuries

This appears to have been a period of colonisation, represented mostly by hamlets of two or more farmsteads practising some form of subdivided arable cultivation, probably a reflection of contemporary practices off the Moor. This development may have been due in part to the relaxing of rigid controls which deliberately maintained the Moor as an area or areas of common grazing. It may also have been

related to the general expansion of population and of the economy in Britain at this time (Postan 1972; Platt 1978, 42–4). The other elements of Cornwall's diverse economy – tin-streaming, fishing, shipping, shipbuilding, textile manufacturing, and quarrying – though probably competing with agriculture in the labour market, will also have provided it with a powerful stimulus by creating a market for agricultural produce (Hatcher 1970, 29). Large areas were cultivated, probably largely for oats (Hatcher 1970, 15; G Beresford 1979, 143) and blocks of pasture were also enclosed for grazing, but expanses of moorland remained available as summer pastures and common grazing for settlements off the Moor or along its edge.

The late fourteenth to the eighteenth centuries

During this period the dominant form of settlement changed from hamlet to single farm. This change can be paralleled in a non-moorland context elsewhere in the South-West, for example Hartland, Devon (H S A Fox 1983). Some sites like Bunnings Park may have been deserted in the fourteenth century. At others, such as Garrow and Carwether, the period of shrink-

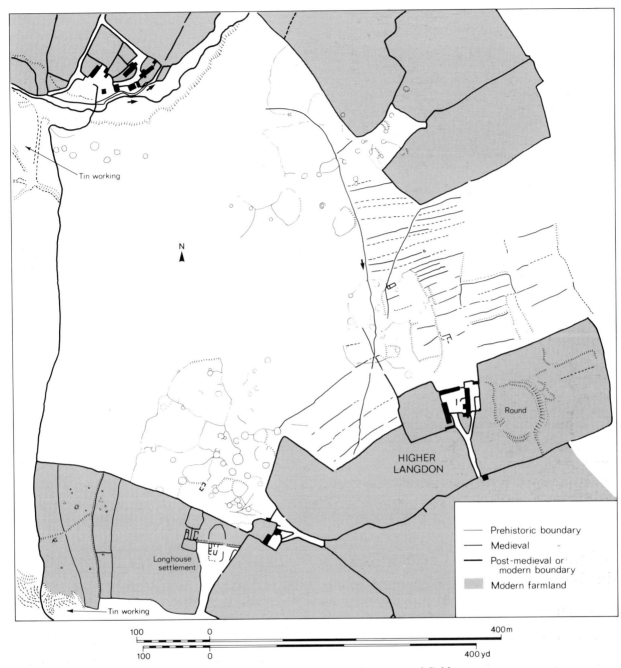

Fig 76   Higher Langdon, SX 203731, prehistoric and medieval settlements and fields

age of the settlement remains unknown. Change at this period is often seen in the context of upheaval caused by the Black Death and of the need to adapt to a worsening climate (G Beresford 1979, 143–5); but two centuries of relatively intensive cultivation may also have taken their toll on the poor moorland soils. The period is a complex one and in some ways the least understood. As well as a retreat from the moors, with many settlements abandoned permanently or temporarily, others were newly established. Very localised factors may be involved.

The nineteenth century

Much of the nineteenth-century expansion of settlement on and around Bodmin Moor was linked to the great burst of industrial activity that produced mining and quarrying villages such as Minions, Henwood, and Upton Cross in the south-east corner of the area (Brewster 1975, 279). In addition a large number of farmsteads were established with their characteristic rectangular, straight-sided fields. Most were hard-won holdings in remote and exposed locations. Many now stand deserted, the optimism of their builders betrayed by changing times and the uncompromising character of the Moor.

6   The future – scheduling, management, and presentation

by the late R W Smith (with minor revisions interpolated)

1   Introduction

The survey reported here is one of a number of such stocktaking exercises initiated and funded by English Heritage (formerly DoE) throughout England since 1979 with the active participation of RCHME, certain local authorities, and local archaeological interests. Their common aim has been to assess and to map the archaeological resource so that priorities for preservation can be established. In south-western England efforts have been largely concentrated on important upland areas such as West Penwith, Bodmin Moor, Dartmoor, and Exmoor.

The Bodmin Moor project has a special significance within this work. It was the first to be started and was therefore additionally used as a methodological testing ground for air and ground survey techniques. Also, in terms of the area covered and the level of detail sought, it was unquestionably the most ambitious such project of its time. The opportunity was taken to review the archaeology of the upland area and to determine priorities from within that landscape.

The survey not only revealed an archaeological landscape richer even than most optimists would have suspected, but also signposted many exciting prospects for future research into early man's exploitation of the uplands. However, if this landscape is to remain intact for future generations to study and enjoy, positive steps to preserve and manage the resource need to be taken.

The purpose of this concluding chapter is to outline how English Heritage is approaching the task. The review moves from basic analysis of the field data, through a discussion of how preservation priorities are initially established, to an explanation of the strategy for preserving, managing and presenting the heritage of Bodmin Moor.

2   Analysis

Many of the questions asked of the survey data seem to have little relevance to academic research but are nevertheless vital to a proper assessment of preservation priorities. Apart from identification and assessment of importance one must ask; Who owns this monument? How does he or she now use the land upon which it stands and what changes are planned? What is the owner's attitude to conservation? Does the site lie within a Site of Special Scientific Interest (SSSI) or any other similarly designated area where special constraints apply?

Clearly, it is far easier to gather this type of information at the time of survey than in any subsequent and separate operation. Similarly, there is no substitute for local knowledge when it comes to interpretation of results and the inevitable untangling of ownership details (always complex in

upland areas where common rights are so prevalent). For these reasons English Heritage often opted for the basic analyses to be carried out by the local survey team through the medium of the County Sites and Monuments Record. In the particular context of Bodmin Moor it is doubly fortunate that the work was carried out by original surveyors from the Cornwall Archaeological Unit using English Heritage-approved software in their machine-based sites and monuments record at Truro.

3   Approaches to preservation

Until comparatively recently the only recourse open to those who wished to see a site or monument formally preserved was to propose to the Secretary of State for the Environment that it should be added to the Schedule of Monuments, which is restricted to those considered to be of national importance. For much of this century such a system has worked tolerably well. But, against a background of rising landscape destruction and significant increases in our awareness of all that the heritage entails, its limitations have become obvious.

Improvements have materialised in three ways. First, much of the subjectivity of selecting monuments to be scheduled has been eliminated by the publication (PPG 16, Annex 4) of scheduling criteria. Second, because of the wealth of new comparative data emerging from other survey projects and the existing archives of the National Monuments Record and County Sites and Monuments Records, the task of identifying the true relative merit (or current scarcity) of a monument is now much easier than it was. Finally, thanks to the foresight and persistence of the Cornwall Archaeological Unit, a framework exists within local plans which recognises and provides for the preservation of monuments for which scheduling may not be appropriate or which may not be deemed of national importance, but are nevertheless vital elements of the regional and county heritage. As in some other counties, the Cornwall County Structure Plan identifies a class of County-grade monuments where the presumption will normally be in favour of preventing damage by modern development. This philosophy is carried through to the detailed designation of sites within the local plans that cover Bodmin Moor. The approach towards preservation priorities, therefore, can now be made with greater objectivity, accuracy, and sensitivity than hitherto.

4   Scheduling

After the phase of analysis by the Cornwall Archaeological Unit some semblance of pattern and priority emerged within the complex picture revealed by the survey. The data have been ordered into a series of interpretative period-type overlay maps keyed by a unique number sequence to an accompanying set of data sheets summarising all that is known about any given feature or group of features. Subsequently English Heritage staff have begun to apply the scheduling criteria to the selection process. Some of the monuments under consideration will clearly be of schedulable quality, but there will be numerous instances where rigorous application of the criteria is necessary before a final decision can be reached.

Current scheduling practice places rather more emphasis on such factors as 'group value' and 'potential' than was previously the case. On Bodmin Moor, where survey identified, for example, not just a Bronze Age settlement but also its fields and funerary area, all three elements would normally now be recognised as worthy of preservation. Furthermore, should there be a polleniferous peat deposit close to the complex, then that too would be identified as important because of the considerable information it could yield on past land use and environment.

When monuments thought to be of schedulable quality have been identified, they are visited by a representative from English Heritage. This may be an Inspector or a Fieldworker from the English Heritage Monuments Protection Programme, a project designed to bring the Schedule of protected monuments up-to-date with current knowledge. Apart from a final check on such things as descriptive accuracy, this site visit is also the moment when owners are consulted about the intent to schedule and about their plans for future use of the land. The notification meeting is frequently a delicate affair where it is important to explain properly all that is involved and if possible to enlist the sympathy of the owner, for the success of scheduling ultimately depends to a considerable extent on his or her goodwill.

In the aftermath of the final inspections, scheduling documentation is completed and passed with the recommendation of English Heritage to the Secretary of State for legal acceptance. In due course new schedulings are formally notified to owners and occupiers, local authorities, etc, and the monument's new status is registered as a land charge.

5 Management

Preservation simply does not work without an active and regular management input by the owner. In moorland areas this usually takes the form of keeping bracken, bramble, and gorse out of sensitive stone-built structures and associated archaeological layers below ground; left unchecked, their roots and rhizomes can cause considerable damage. Other recurrent problems include damage caused by animals rubbing against or sheltering within monuments, and in areas of high public accessibility, littering, and even some vandalism.

English Heritage has a small team of Field Monument Wardens who work from the management statement drawn up at the time of scheduling. They make regular visits to all monuments and owners in their area to assess whether the condition of the monument is stable or deteriorating. Monuments known to be at risk are monitored more frequently than others. Where the Field Monument Warden's report identifies an actual or potential problem, headquarters staff assess the appropriate remedial action and contact the owner.

The most common form of assistance given to owners is the rendering of advice; and a site meeting with the Inspector for the region is frequently all that is needed to resolve the problem. In some situations it is clear, however, that to get the monument into satisfactory condition or to keep it that way an owner finds it necessary to undertake more work than could reasonably be expected within the framework of his or her normal activities. When dealing with, for example, a badly overgrown monument, English Heritage may offer a grant to the owner to encourage the undertaking of works such as clearance, returfing, fencing etc. Then, having got the monument into good condition, the owner might be invited to enter into a management agreement which will reimburse him or her for undertaking agreed regular maintenance work. Such agreements can be renegotiated on an annual basis, but most are taken out over periods of between five and ten years. At the outset the owner receives a tax-free lump sum based on the size of the monument, the length of the agreement, and the amount of work required. This approach has proved to be popular with owners, effective in conservation terms and seems likely to be the right mechanism for Bodmin Moor.

Unfortunately management is not always as straightforward as this. In a working landscape, preservation of archaeological remains often finds itself in competition with other equally valid claims on the land. Those who build our new roads and reservoirs, or those who endeavour to bring modern services to people living in outlying areas, or even those who seek to develop land for new houses or industrial estates, can all claim, with justification, that they are working for the public good. In rare instances, where conspicuously important monuments are involved, English Heritage may take the unusual step of organising and grant-aiding acquisition of land by a third party – usually the National Trust, the local authority, or a specialist conservation body operating locally.

A more usual course is to seek to resolve potential conflicts before they materialise by giving prompt advice on developmental threats at the planning stage; there is often some alternative which will leave the scheduled monuments untouched. Inevitably there are instances where no easy solution can be found, and in such cases scheduled monument consent procedures come into operation. In essence these mean that those who seek to carry out works to a monument must make a formal application to the Secretary of State for the Environment for consent to proceed. After receiving from English Heritage carefully weighed advice on the implications, the Secretary of State determines whether or not consent should be given and then notifies the applicant who, should he feel unable to accept, has the right of appeal at an informal hearing or, if necessary, at a public inquiry.

Regrettably, management must also include dealing with damage cases. Where damage is wilful or due to gross negligence there is an established prosecution procedure which, under the terms of the 1979 Ancient Monuments and Archaeological Areas Act, has been successful in the majority of the cases where it has been applied. However, the preferred course is to secure preservation of monuments by persuasion and in partnership with their owners.

6 Presentation

The Act of Parliament which created English Heritage in 1983 also charged it with promoting public understanding and appreciation of the monuments which make up the national heritage. While good progress is being made in the conventional media of education, there remains also a need to bring more monuments into the public eye. This is no easy task; there are so many factors to be weighed before taking a particular course of action. Is there existing public access? Is it adequate? Is the monument sufficiently interesting to be worthwhile for enhanced presentation? Would it be sufficiently robust to withstand the erosion associated with increased visitor numbers? What would be the effect on adjoining land; would farming be disrupted or local people aggrieved?

In an area like Bodmin Moor, where much of the land is used as commons, it becomes especially difficult to achieve total support for a new presentation initiative. It is necessary with such initiatives to consult as early as possible with commoners' associations, local landowners, local authorities and national bodies such as English Heritage and the Countryside Commission. However, the actual negotiation of these presentation schemes is best handled by local bodies.

In many ways this final phase of the project is potentially the most demanding professionally. But it is also potentially the most rewarding because it provides a major opportunity to explain and justify all that has gone before to the public who have supported the project since its inception.

7 Conclusions

It has been said many times within this report that the Bodmin Moor project served throughout its duration as a testing ground for new techniques and ideas. Perhaps the most important conclusion to have emerged from it is that success has depended throughout on strong, effective partnerships. In the survey stages these existed between the professional bodies involved. As attention began to focus on the everyday implications of the survey so new links were forged with local authorities and other conser-

vation bodies. Now, in the ultimate stage of bringing the archaeological landscape into stable management and the public eye, so landowners will form one of the most important elements in the partnership. Without their goodwill, understanding and cooperation the future of the archaeology of Bodmin Moor would look very bleak indeed.

Addendum 1994

by Rob Iles

Bob Smith wrote this chapter seven years ago following the completion of the Bodmin Moor survey. Virtually all that he wrote is still relevant today. However, there have been a number of recent developments in countryside management which are worth noting here.

The Monuments Protection Programme now has a Fieldworker, based on Bodmin Moor, who has been systematically revising the Schedule of Monuments utilising the material produced by this survey. Although this work is progressing well it will be some years before it can be completed. Important though scheduling is, English Heritage is now looking to the positive management of historic landscapes and their settings as well as of tightly defined sites.

Historic landscapes need to be managed as part of the wider rural economy, and particularly to be integrated with countryside management. In this context the future is beginning to look brighter with changes to the Common Agricultural Policy. Farmers can no longer claim grants to reclaim moorland and make other 'improvements' which were both widespread and damaging in the early to mid eighties. New grant mechanisms are beginning to emerge which encourage farmers to farm in a manner that has environmental benefits.

In his last paragraph, Bob Smith wrote about the partnerships that were starting to develop between different bodies. These are now regarded as essential to the success of integrated environmental schemes. At last archaeology and historic landscapes are no longer seen in isolation and separate from all other environmental concerns.

In this context one new initiative, a proposal to designate Bodmin Moor as an Environmentally Sensitive Area, would have been particularly beneficial to the landscape but unfortunately the Ministry of Agriculture, Fisheries and Food decided recently not to designate. However, it is hoped by many environmental groups and local farmers that Bodmin Moor will eventually be designated an Environmentally Sensitive Area. In the meantime there are other smaller-scale schemes, like the Countryside Commission's Stewardship, which are beginning to improve the management of some monuments and historic landscapes on Bodmin Moor.

Appendix 1: Chronological summary of past archaeological work

by Peter Rose

The late nineteenth century

General descriptions Thomas 1852; Maclean 1873; Brent 1886; Malan 1888
Stone circles Dymond 1879; Lukis and Borlase 1885; Malan 1889a; Tregelles 1893–4, 1906; Lewis 1895, 1896–9 (and King Arthur's Hall)
Cairn excavations and openings Smirke 1867; Brent 1886; Malan 1889b; Worth 1890; Baring-Gould 1891, 68; 1892, 290
Others Blight 1869; survey of post-medieval settlement at Smallacoombe. Baring-Gould 1891, 1892; excavation of Trewortha Marsh, medieval settlement

1900–1950

General descriptions Hencken 1932; Malim 1936
Stone circles [excavations] Gray 1909 [Stripple Stones]; Radford 1935, 1938 [The Hurlers]
Others Langdon 1907: Buttern Hill, opening of cairn, and finds from streamworks. Curwen 1927: field systems and settlements at Roughtor and Garrow. Croft Andrew 1938 (unpub): excavation of Wallagate barrow. Christie and Rose, 1987 (Croft Andrew 1942): Davidstow Moor, excavation of cairns, longhouses (Goosehill), and turf huts

1950–1975

Excavation

Prehistoric settlements Dudley 1950s (unpub) [Garrow]; Dudley 1963 [Smallacoombe]; Mercer 1970 [Stannon]
Medieval settlement Dudley and Minter 1962–3 [Garrow]
Cairns Wainwright 1965; Thomas 1975

Environmental

Conolly *et al* 1950; Dimbleby 1963

Others

Miles 1973: general account Wainwright 1960, 1961; the Mesolithic (including finds from Dozmary)

1975–1985

Excavation

Cairns King and Miles 1976; Trudgian 1977a; Brisbane and Clews 1979; Griffith 1984; Harris *et al* 1984
Medieval fields Griffith 1984
Medieval tin-stamping mills Austin *et al* 1989 [Colliford; Stuffle]
Medieval settlement Austin *et al* 1989 [Bunning's Park]

Environmental

Brown 1977; Mercer and Dimbleby 1978; Brisbane and Clews 1979; Caseldine 1980; Austin *et al* 1989

Survey

Cornwall Archaeol Soc, mid-1970s, surveys of prehistoric settlements at Roughtor and Twelve Men's Moor
Parochial checklists Sheppard 1977 [St Neot]; King and Sheppard 1979 [North Hill]
Cairns Trehair 1978; Herring 1983
Prehistoric settlement Herring 1979; Brisbane and Clews 1979; Holgate and Smith 1981; Trudgian 1977b [flint scatters]
Stone circles Barnatt 1980, 1982
Medieval settlement Herring 1986
Medieval fields Griffith 1984
Medieval tin industry Gerrard 1986
Post-medieval settlement Nowakowski 1982

General

Mesolithic Jacobi 1979
Bronze Age Johnson 1980, Barnatt 1982
First millennium (BC) settlement Silvester 1979
Environmental Caseldine 1980

Others

Hawkes 1983 [Rillaton Gold Cup]; Walker and Austin 1985 [Redhill, Mesolithic]

Appendix 2: Locations of cairns illustrated in Figs 23–26

Fig 23		County SMR No
1	SX 1427 8032	3314.2
2	SX 1347 7988	3047.3
3	SX 1569 7356	1769.5
4	SX 1255 7949	1972.2
5	SX 1436 8034	3314.4
6	SX 1465 8094	3381.6
7	SX 1466 8094	3381.5
8	SX 1441 7893	1936.1
9	SX 1411 7846	1961.5
10	SX 1345 7986	3047.2
11	SX 1516 7756	3056.2
12	SX 2523 7102	1405
13	SX 1410 8072	3286.12
14	SX 1906 8064	3513.2
15	SX 1439 7905	1936.2
16	SX 1192 8196	3388.2
17	SX 1192 8199	3388.3
18	SX 1387 7681	3007
19	SX 1401 7138	1637.4
20	SX 1417 7104	1637.5
21	SX 1906 8064	3513.2
22	SX 1291 7433	1642.1
23	SX 2463 7441	1430
24	SX 1189 8195	3388.1
25	SX 1268 8301	3366
26	SX 1962 7265	1770.4
27	SX 2552 7380	1413.1
28	SX 2696 7018	1411.8
29	SX 1181 7873	1970.5
30	SX 1722 7856	3191
31	SX 1162 7783	1970.2
32	SX 1700 7849	3160
33	SX 1931 7701	3174
34	SX 1396 7200	1644.3
35	SX 2737 7075	1409.6
36	SX 2733 7086	1409.7
37	SX 1262 7794	1924
38	SX 2036 7560	1046
39	SX 1355 7969	3047.8
40	SX 1183 7838	1970.4
41	SX 1998 6918	1581
42	SX 2311 7714	1082
43	SX 1324 7905	1982.2
44	SX 1371 8090	3359.8
45	SX 1160 7782	1970.1
46	SX 1409 8152	3286.4
47	SX 1407 7862	1961.3
48	SX 1408 8102	3286.8

Fig 24		
1	SX 1432 7806	1963
2	SX 1508 7736	3056.1
3	SX 1310 7699	1931
4	SX 1495 7810	3057.4
5	SX 1380 8025	3347.2
6	SX 1349 8099	3359.15
7	SX 1498 7793	3057.1
8	SX 1436 8034	3314.4
9	SX 1407 7843	1961.6
10	SX 1368 8075	3359.1
11	SX 1369 8097	3359.10
12	SX 1379 8028	3347.1

Fig 24 (Cont'd)		County SMR No
13	SX 1411 7846	1961.5
14	SX 1351 7968	3047.9
15	SX 1510 8043	3521
16	SX 1388 7977	3047.17
17	SX 1364 8076	3359.4
18	SX 2452 7499	1012.5
19	SX 1498 7793	3057.1
20	SX 1370 8090	3359
21	SX 1411 8069	3286.11
22	SX 1290 7987	1972.5
23	SX 1321 7902	1981.1
24	SX 1481 7771	3055.4
25	SX 1883 8219	3502.1
26	SX 1172 7816	1970.3
27	SX 1831 8034	3504
28	SX 1748 8165	3506.3
29	SX 1468 8182	3288.1
30	SX 1605 7477	1783

Fig 25		
1	SX 1725 7056	1774.2
2	SX 1720 7051	1774.1
3	SX 1156 7516	1998
4	SX 1965 7927	3146.1
5	SX 1305 7549	3043
6	SX 2236 7768	1088.2
7	SX 1335 7994	3047.13
8	SX 1153 7707	3026
9	SX 2429 7132	1234.1
10	SX 1260 7963	1972.4
11	SX 2306 7479	1265
12	SX 1776 6742	1568
13	SX 1299 7294	1634.2
14	SX 2514 7126	1408.1
15	SX 2241 7761	1088.1
16	SX 2501 7196	1404
17	SX 2255 7267	1258.3
18	SX 1232 7936	1972.2
19	SX 2600 7194	1420
20	SX 2479 7549	1013.1
21	SX 2487 7547	1013.2
22	SX 1378 7984	3047.20
23	SX 1747 8170	3506.1
24	SX 1628 8116	3515.2
25	SX 1547 8239	3546
26	SX 1746 8169	3506.5

Fig 26		
1	SX 1627 7711	3164
2	SX 2445 7169	1235.2
3	SX 1946 7281	1770.2
4	SX 1967 7927	3146.2
5	SX 2442 7167	1235.1
6	SX 1303 7302	1634.1
7	SX 1419 8154	3286.3
8	SX 1753 8160	3506.4
9	SX 1630 8115	3515
10	SX 1448 8173	3288.5
11	SX 1325 7959	3047.10
12	SX 1897 8218	3502.3
13	SX 1747 8167	3506.2
14	SX 1357 8117	3359.12

Bibliography

Abbreviations

BAR   *British Archaeological Reports*
CBA   *Council for British Archaeology*
DoE   *Department of the Environment*
OUCA *Oxford University Committee for Archaeology*

Alcock, N W, 1969 Devonshire farmhouses pt II: some Dartmoor houses, *Trans Devonshire Assoc*, **101**, 83–106
——, 1977 What is a gravelfork?, *Vernacular Archit*, **8**, 830–2
Allan, J P, 1984 *Medieval and post-medieval finds from Exeter, 1971–1980*, Exeter
Allen, D, 1979 Excavations at Hafod y Nant Criafolen, Brenig Valley, Clwyd, 1973–74, *Post-medieval Archaeol*, **13**, 1–59
Andrew, C K C (see Croft Andrew, C K)
Austin, D, 1978 Excavations in Okehampton Park, Devon, 1976–1978, *Proc Devon Archaeol Soc*, **36**, 191–239
——, 1985 Dartmoor and the upland village of the south-west of England, in *Medieval Villages* (ed D Hooke), OUCA monogr no 5, Oxford
Austin, D, Daggett, R H, and Walker, M J C, 1980 Farms and fields in Okehampton Park, Devon: the problems of studying a medieval landscape, *Landscape Hist*, **2**, 39–57
Austin, D, Gerrard, G A M and Greeves, T A P, 1989 Tin and agriculture in the middle ages and beyond: landscape archaeology in St Neot parish, Cornwall, *Cornish Archaeol* **28**, 5–251
Balaam, N D, Smith, K and Wainwright, G J, 1982 The Shaugh Moor project: fourth report – environment, context and conclusion, *Proc Prehist Soc*, **48**, 203–71
Baring-Gould, Rev S, 1891 An ancient settlement on Trewortha Marsh, *J Roy Inst Cornwall*, **11**, 57–70
——, 1892 Ancient settlement at Trewortha, *J Roy Inst Cornwall*, **11**, 289–90
Barnatt, J, 1980 Lesser known stone circles in Cornwall, *Cornish Archaeol*, **19**, 17–29
——, 1982 *Prehistoric Cornwall: the ceremonial monuments*, Wellingborough
——, 1989 *Stone circles of Britain*, BAR (British ser), **215**, Oxford
Barnatt, J, and Moir, G, 1984 Stone circles and megalithic mathematics, *Proc Prehist Soc*, **50**, 197–216
Batt, M, 1980 Lann-Gouh, Melrand, Morbihan, *Medieval Village Research Group 28th Annu Rep*, 24
Beresford, G, 1979 Three deserted medieval settlements on Dartmoor: a report on the late E Marie Minter's excavations, *Medieval Archaeol*, **23**, 98–158
Beresford, M W, 1964 Dispersed and grouped settlement in medieval Cornwall, *Agric Hist Rev*, **12.1**, 13–27
Blight, J T, 1868 Notice of enclosures at Smallacombe, Cornwall, *J Roy Inst Cornwall*, **3**, 10
Bowen, H C, and Fowler, P J, 1978 *Early land allotment*, BAR, **48**, Oxford
Bradley, R, Lobb, S, Richards, J C, and Robinson, M, 1980 Two late Bronze Age settlements on the Kennet Gravels: excavations at Aldermaston Wharf and Knight's Farm, Burghfield, Berkshire, *Proc Prehist Soc*, **46**, 217–95
Brent, F, 1886 On occurrence of flint flakes and small stone implements in Cornwall, *J Roy Inst Cornwall*, **9**, 58–61
Brewster, C, 1975 *Bodmin Moor – a synoptic study and report on a moorland area*, Institute of Cornish Studies, Camborne
Brisbane, M, and Clews, S, 1979 The East Moor systems, Altarnun and North Hill, Bodmin Moor, *Cornish Archaeol*, **18**, 33–56
Brown, A P, 1977 Late Devensian and Flandrian vegetational history of Bodmin Moor, Cornwall, *Phil Trans Roy Soc London*, **B276**, 251–320
Bruce-Mitford, R L S, 1956 A Dark Age settlement at Mawgan Porth, Cornwall, in *Recent archaeological excavations in Britain* (ed R L S Bruce-Mitford), London
——, (in preparation) *Mawgan Porth – a settlement of the late Saxon period on the north Cornish coast: excavations 1949–52, 1954, and 1974*
Burl, A, 1976 *The stone circles of the British Isles*, London
Burnside, C D, 1979 *Mapping from aerial photographs*, London
Carew, R, 1602 *The survey of Cornwall* (ed F E Halliday, 1969), New York
Caseldine, C J, 1980 Environmental change in Cornwall during the last 13,000 years, *Cornish Archaeol*, **19**, 3–16
Chesher, V M, 1974 Mullion in the mid-nineteenth century: the

anatomy of a Lizard parish, *The Lizard*, **5.2**, 19–25
Chesher, V M, and Chesher, F J, 1968 *The Cornishman's house*, Truro
Christie, P M, 1988 A barrow cemetery on Davidstow Moor, Cornwall: wartime excavations by C K Croft Andrew, *Cornish Archaeol*, **27**, 27–169
Christie, P M, Miles, T, and Goodall, I, 1979 A post-medieval cottage at Carn Euny, Sancreed, *Cornish Archaeol*, **18**, 105–23
Christie, P M and Rose, P, 1987 Davidstow Moor, Cornwall: the medieval and later sites; wartime excavations by C K Croft Andrew 1941–1942, *Cornish Archaeol*, **26**, 163–95
Coleman, A, and Maggs, K R A, 1968 *Second land utilisation survey*, London
Conolly, A P, Godwin, H, and Megaw, E M, 1950 Studies in the post-glacial history of British vegetation, 11: late-glacial deposits in Cornwall, *Phil Trans Roy Soc London*, **B234**, 397–469
Crampton, C B, 1966 Hafotai platforms on the north front of the Brecon Beacons, *Archaeol Cambrensis*, **115**, 99–107
Croft Andrew, C K, 1937–8 Two unrecorded stone circles, *J Roy Inst Cornwall*, **25**, 61–2
——, 1942 *Davidstow Moor excavations, 20th October, 1941 to 27th June, 1942: a synopsis of the results* (typescript: see also Christie, P M, 1988 and Christie, P M, and Rose, P, 1987)
Curwen, E C, 1927 Prehistoric agriculture in Britain, *Antiquity*, **1.3**, 261–98
Davies, E, 1979 Hendre and hafod in Caernarvonshire, *Trans Caernarvonshire Hist Soc*, **40**, 17–46
Davies, M, 1956 Rhosili open field and related South Wales field patterns, *Agr Hist Rev*, **4.1**, 80–96
Dimbleby, G W, 1963 Pollen analysis from three Cornish barrows, *J Roy Inst Cornwall*, new ser, **4**, 364–75
Dodgson, R A, 1980 *The origin of British field systems: an interpretation*, London
DoE, 1990 *Planning and policy guidance: archaeology and planning*, Department of the Environment, London
Dudley, D, 1957–8 The early Iron Age in Cornwall, *Proc West Cornwall Fld Club*, **2.2**, 47–54
——, 1963 Smallacombe and Trewortha Downs, *Cornish Archaeol*, **2**, 56
Dudley, D, and Minter, E M, 1962–3 The medieval village of Garrow Tor, Bodmin Moor, Cornwall, *Medieval Archaeol*, **6–7**, 272–94
——, 1966 The excavation of a medieval settlement at Treworld, Lesnewth, 1963, *Cornish Archaeol*, **5**, 34–58
Dymond, C W, 1879 The Hurlers, three stone circles near St Cleer, Cornwall, *J Brit Archaeol Assoc*, **35**, 297–307
Emmett, D D, 1979 Stone rows: the traditional view reconsidered, *Proc Devon Archaeol Soc*, **37**, 94–114
Evans, E E, 1939 Donegal survivals, *Antiquity*, **13**, 207–22
——, 1957 *Irish Folk Ways*, London
Fairhurst, H, 1968 The archaeology of rural settlement in Scotland, *Trans Glasgow Archaeol Soc*, **15.4**, 139–58
Finberg, H P R, 1951 *Tavistock Abbey: a study in the social and economic history of Devon*, Newton Abbot
Flatrès, P, 1957 *Géographie rurale de quatre contrées celtiques*, Rennes
Fleming, A, 1978 The prehistoric landscape of Dartmoor, pt 1: south Dartmoor, *Proc Prehist Soc*, **44**, 97–123
——, 1983 The prehistoric landscape of Dartmoor, pt 2: north and east Dartmoor, *Proc Prehist Soc*, **49**, 195–242
Fleming, A, and Collis, J, 1973 A late prehistoric reave system near Cholwich Town, Dartmoor, *Proc Devon Archaeol Soc*, **31**, 1–21
Fleming, A, and Ralph, N, 1982 Medieval settlement and landuse on Holne Moor, Dartmoor: the landscape evidence, *Medieval Archaeol*, **25**, 101–37
Fowler, P J, 1981 Later prehistory, in *The agrarian history of England and Wales*, **1.1**, *Prehistory* (ed S Piggott), 63–298, Cambridge
Fowler, P J, and Thomas, A C, 1962 Arable fields of the pre-Norman period at Gwithian, *Cornish Archaeol*, **1**, 61–84
Fox, A, 1958 A monastic homestead on Dean Moor, S Devon, *Medieval Archaeol*, **2**, 141–57
Fox, H S A, 1973 Outfield cultivation in Devon and Cornwall: a reinterpretation, in *Husbandry and marketing in the south west 1500–1800* (ed M Havinden), Exeter Pap Econ Hist, no 8, 19–38, Exeter
——, 1983 Contraction: desertion and dwindling of dispersed

settlement in a Devon parish, *Medieval Village Research Group, 31st Annu Rep*

Gaffney, V, 1959   Summer shealings, *Scot Hist Rev*, **38**, 20–35

Gelling, P S, 1962–3   Medieval shielings in the Isle of Man, *Medieval Archaeol*, **6–7**, 156–72

Gerrard, G A M, 1986   The early Cornish tin industry, an archaeological and historical survey, unpubl PhD thesis, Univ Wales

Gover, J E B, 1948   *The place-names of Cornwall* (typescript in the Royal Cornwall Museum, formerly the Royal Institution of Cornwall, Truro)

Graham, J M, 1953–4   Transhumance in Ireland, *Advancement Sci*, **10**, 74–9

Gray, H St George, 1908   On the stone circles of East Cornwall, *Archaeologia*, **61**, 1–43

Greeves, T A P, 1981   *The Devon tin industry 1450–1750: an archaeological and historical survey*, PhD thesis, Univ Exeter

Griffith, F, 1979   Colliford reservoir 1978, *Cornish Archaeol*, **18**, 56

——, 1984   Archaeological investigations at Colliford Reservoir, Bodmin Moor, 1977–8, *Cornish Archaeol*, **23**, 49–139

Grimes, J, and Sheppard, P A, 1978   Treninnow: a chambered tomb in Rame parish, *Cornish Archaeol*, **17**, 137

Grimes, W F, 1963   The stone circles and related monuments of Wales, in *Culture and environment: essays in honour of Sir Cyril Fox* (eds I L L Foster and L Alcock), 93–152, London

Harris, D, 1978   A cist at Trevemedar, St Eval, *Cornish Archaeol*, **17**, 137–9

Harris, D, Hooper, S, and Trudgian, P, 1984   Excavation of three cairns on Stannon Downs, *Cornish Archaeol*, **23**, 141–55

Hart, C R, 1981   *The North Derbyshire Archaeological Survey*, North Derbyshire Archaeol Trust

Hatcher, J, 1970   *Rural economy and society in the Duchy of Cornwall 1300–1500*, Cambridge

Hawkes, C F C, 1983   The Rillaton Gold Cup, *Antiquity*, **57**, 124–6

Hencken, H O'Neill, 1932   *The archaeology of Cornwall and Scilly*, London

Henderson, C, 1928a   *The Cornish church guide*, Truro

——, 1928b   The manor of Fawton and the chapel of St Luke on Fowey Moor, in Rev G H Doble, *St Neot, Patron of St Neot, Cornwall and St Neot's, Huntingdonshire*, Cornish Saints ser, no 21, 52–6, Exeter

Herring, P, 1979   *Prehistoric settlement of Bodmin Moor*, unpubl dissertation, Univ Sheffield

——, 1983   A long cairn on Catshole Tor, Altarnun, *Cornish Archaeol*, **22**, 81–4

——, 1986   *Prehistory and history of land-use and settlement North-West Bodmin Moor, Cornwall*, unpubl MPhil thesis, Univ Sheffield

Higginbotham, E A K, 1977   Excavations at Woolley Barrows, Morwenstow, *Cornish Archaeol*, **16**, 10–16

Holgate, R, and Smith, P, 1981   Landscape studies in prehistory: two examples from Western Britain, *Inst Archaeol Bull*, **18**, 171–89

Hooper, S, 1976   Excavation of a ring cairn at Castle Hill, Innis Downs, Luxulyan, *Cornish Archaeol*, **15**, 86–9

Hull, P L (ed), 1971   *The Caption of Seisin of the Duchy of Cornwall*, Devon Cornwall Rec Soc, new ser, 17, Torquay

Hurst, J G, 1985   The Wharram Research Project: problem orientation and strategy 1950–1990, in *Medieval Villages* (ed D Hooke), OUCA monogr no 5, Oxford

Jacobi, R M, 1979   Early Flandrian hunters in the south west, *Proc Devon Archaeol Soc*, **37**, 48–93

Jenkin, A K Hamilton, 1934   *Cornish Homes and Customs*, London

——, 1945   *Cornwall and its people*, London

Jewell, A, 1981   Some cultivation techniques in the south-west of England, in *Agricultural improvement: medieval and modern* (ed W Minchinton) Exeter Pap Econ Hist, no 14, Exeter

Johnson, N D, 1980   Later Bronze Age settlement in the Southwest, in *The British later Bronze Age* (eds J Barrett and R Bradley), BAR, **83**, Oxford

——, 1983   The results of air and ground survey of Bodmin Moor, Cornwall, in *The impact of aerial reconnaissance on archaeology* (ed G S Maxwell), CBA Res Rep, **49**, 5–13

——, 1985   Archaeological field survey – a Cornish perspective, in *Archaeological field survey in Britain and abroad* (eds S Macready and F H Thompson), London

Johnson, N D, and Rose, P, 1982   Defended settlement in Cornwall – an illustrated discussion, in *The Romano-British countryside*, pt i (ed D Miles), BAR, **103 (i)**, Oxford

——, and ——, 1989   Bodmin Moor, Cornwall – post survey observations, in *From Cornwall to Caithness*, (eds M Bowden, D Mackay, and P Topping), BAR, **209**, 65–9

Jones, G R J, 1973   Field systems of North Wales, in *Studies of field systems in the British Isles* (eds A R H Baker and R A Butlin), Cambridge

Jones, S R, 1971   Chamfer stops: a provisional mode of reference, *Vernacular Archit*, **2**, 12–15

Jope, E M, and Threlfall, R I, 1958   Excavation of a medieval settlement at Beere, North Tawton, Devon, *Medieval Archaeol*, **2**, 112–40

Karkeet, W F, 1846   On the farming of Cornwall, *J Roy Agr Soc England*, **6(1)**, 400–62

King, G, and Miles, H, 1976   A Bronze Age cist burial at Trebartha, North Hill, *Cornish Archaeol*, **15**, 27–30

King, G, and Sheppard, P, 1979   Hundred of East, 10: parish of North Hill, *Cornish Archaeol*, **18**, 128–32

Laing, L R, 1969   Medieval settlement archaeology in Scotland, *Scot Archaeol Forum*, **1**, 69–79

Langdon, A G, 1907   Some prehistoric and other antiquities from Buttern Hill, *Proc Soc Antiq*, **21**, 456–61

Leighton, D, 1984   Structured round cairns in West Central Wales, *Proc Prehist Soc*, **50**, 319–50

Lewis, A L, 1895   Prehistoric remains in Cornwall, Pt 1: East Cornwall, *J Roy Anthropol Inst*, **25**, 2–16

——, 1896–9   Rude stone monuments of Bodmin Moor, *J Roy Inst Cornwall*, **13**, 107–13

Lewis, G R, 1908   *The Stannaries: a study of the medieval tin miners of Cornwall and Devon*, Harvard

Lloyd, J E, 1927–9   Hendref and Hafod, *Bull Board Celtic Stud*, **4**, pt 3, 224–5

Lukis, W C, and Borlase, W C, 1885   *Prehistoric stone monuments of the British Isles*, **1**, Cornwall, London

Lynch, F, 1972   Ring-cairns and related monuments in Wales, *Scot Archaeol Forum*, **4**, 61–80

McCourt, D, 1953   Traditions of Rundale in and around the Sperrin Mountains, *Ulster J Archaeol, 3 ser*, **16**, 69–83

——, 1954–5   Infield and outfield in Ireland, *Econ Hist Rev, 2 ser*, **7**, 369–76

Maclean, J, 1873   *The parochial and family history of the Deanery of Trigg Minor*, **1**, London

MacSween, M, and Gailey, A, 1961   Some shielings in North Skye, *Scot Stud*, **5**, 77–84

Malan, A H, 1888   Notes on the neighbourhood of Brown Willy, *J Roy Inst Cornwall*, **9**, 341–52

——, 1889a   Notes and queries, no 1: Re-erection of the Nine-Stones, *J Roy Inst Cornwall*, **9**, 496

——, 1889b   Notes and queries, no 4: Opening of a cairn on Ridge Hill, *J Roy Inst Cornwall*, **9**, 498–9

Malim, J W, 1936   *The Bodmin Moors*, London

Maltby, E, 1980   Buried soil features and palaeoenvironmental reconstruction at Colliford, Bodmin Moor, in *Quaternary Research Association Field Handbook West Cornwall Meeting* (ed P C Sims), 9–11, Plymouth

Meirion-Jones, G I, 1982   *The vernacular architecture of Brittany*, Edinburgh

Mercer, E, 1975   *English vernacular houses*, London

Mercer, R J, 1970   The excavation of a Bronze Age hut-circle settlement on Stannon Down, St Breward, Cornwall, 1968, *Cornish Archaeol*, **9**, 17–46

——, 1975   Settlement, farming and environment in south-west England to c1000 BC, in *Recent work in rural archaeology* (ed P Fowler), 27–40, Bradford-on-Avon

——, 1980   *Archaeological field survey in northern Scotland 1976–79*, Univ Edinburgh, Dept Archaeol, occas pap 4

——, (ed), 1981a   *Farming practice in British prehistory*, Edinburgh

——, 1981b   Excavations at Carn Brea, Illogan, Cornwall 1970–7, *Cornish Archaeol*, **20**, 1–204

——, 1981c   *Archaeological field survey in northern Scotland 1980–81*, **2**, Univ Edinburgh, Dept Archaeol, occas pap 7.

Mercer, R J, and Dimbleby, G W, 1978   Pollen analysis and the hut circle settlement at Stannon Down, St Breward, *Cornish Archaeol*, **17**, 25–8

Miles, H, 1973   The archaeology of Bodmin Moor, *Archaeol J*, **130**, 225–8

——, 1975   Barrows on the St Austell granite, Cornwall, *Cornish Archaeol*, **14**, 5–81

Miles, H, and Miles, T, 1973   Excavations at Trethurgy, St Austell: interim report, *Cornish Archaeol*, **12**, 25–9

Miller, R, 1967   Land use by summer shielings, *Scot Stud*, **71**, 193–221

Milne, G, 1979   The peasant houses, in *Wharram, a study of settlement on the Yorkshire Wolds; 1 Domestic settlement 1: areas 10 and 6* (eds D D Andrews and G Milne) 67–73, Soc Medieval Archaeol monogr ser, no 8, London

Minter, E M, 1965 Lanyon in Madron: interim report on the Society's 1964 excavation, *Cornish Archaeol*, **4**, 44–5

Norden, J, 1584 *Speculi Britanniae Pars: a topographical and historical description of Cornwall*, London

Nowakowski, J A, 1982 *Abandoned farmsteads in an upland area: a behavioural approach*, unpubl dissertation, Univ Sheffield

Nowakowski, J A, and Herring, P C, 1985 The beehive huts of Bodmin Moor, *Cornish Archaeol*, **24**, 185–95

O'Neill, T, 1977 *Life and tradition in rural Ireland*, London

Padel, O J, 1985 *Cornish place-name elements*, English Place-Name Society, **56 and 57**, Nottingham

Pearce, S M, 1981 *The archaeology of south west England*, London

Peter, T C, 1906 *History and geography of Cornwall*, Truro

Platt, C, 1978 *Medieval England, a social history and archaeology from the Conquest to AD 1600*, London and Henley

Postan, M M, 1972 *The medieval economy and society*, London

Pounds, N J G, 1942 Note on transhumance in Cornwall, *Geography*, **27**, 34

——, 1945 The Lanhydrock atlas, *Antiquity*, **19**, 20–1

——, 1947 *The historical geography of Cornwall*, PhD thesis, Univ London

PPG 16 (see DoE, 1990)

Quinnell, N V, 1978 The Borlase 'stone altar', Tresco, Isles of Scilly, *Cornish Archaeol*, **17**, 140–1

Radford, C A R, 1935 Notes on the excavation of the Hurlers near Liskeard, Cornwall, *Proc Prehist Soc*, **1**, 134

——, 1938 Notes on the excavation of the Hurlers near Liskeard, Cornwall, *Proc Prehist Soc*, **4**, 319

Ramm, H G, 1970 Shielings, farmsteads and stackstands in the northern Border Country, in *Shielings and bastles* (eds H G Ramm, R W McDowall and E Mercer), RCHME, London

Ravenhill, W L D, 1967 Cornwall, in *The Domesday geography of south west England* (eds H C Darby and R Welldon Finn), Cambridge

——, 1969 The early settlement of south west England, in *South west England* (eds A H Shorter, W L D Ravenhill, and K J Gregory), 81–111, Cambridge

Rose, P G, and Herring, P, 1990 *Bodmin Moor, Cornwall: an evaluation for the Monuments Protection Programme*, Cornwall Archaeological Unit, Truro

Rowe, J H (ed), 1914 *Cornwall Feet of Fines*, **1**, *1195–1377*, Exeter

Rowse, A L, 1941 *Tudor Cornwall*, London

Saunders, A D, and Harris, D, 1982 Excavations at Castle Gotha, St Austell, *Cornish Archaeol*, **21**, 109–53

Saunders, C, 1972 The excavations at Grambla, Wendron 1972: interim report, *Cornish Archaeol*, **11**, 50–2

Scott, L, 1951 Corn-drying kilns, *Antiquity*, **25**, 196–208

Sedding, E, 1909 *Norman architecture in Cornwall*, London

Seymour, W A, 1972 A history of the Ordnance Survey: the overhaul of the 1:2500 County Series Plans, *Profess Pap*, new ser, no 25, Southampton

Sheppard, P, 1977 Hundred of West, 2: parish of St Neot, *Cornish Archaeol*, **16**, 143–54

——, 1980 *The historic towns of Cornwall, an archaeological survey*, Truro

Silvester, R J, 1979 The relationship of first millennium settlement to the upland areas of the south west, *Proc Devon Archaeol Soc*, **37**, 176–90

Smirke, E, 1867 Some account of the discovery of a gold cup in a barrow in Cornwall AD 1837, *Archaeol J*, **24**, 189–95 (repr *J Roy Inst Cornwall*, **3**, 1868, 34–9)

Smith, A H, 1956 *English place-name elements* (parts 1 and 2), English Place-Name Society, **25 and 26**, Cambridge

Smith, G, and Harris, D, 1982 The excavation of Mesolithic,

Neolithic and Bronze Age settlements at Poldowrian, St Keverne, 1980, *Cornish Archaeol*, **21**, 23–62

Smith, K, Copper, J, Wainwright, G J, and Beckett, S, 1981 The Shaugh Moor Project: third report – settlement and environmental investigation, *Proc Prehist Soc*, **47**, 205–73

Spratt, D A, 1981 Prehistoric boundaries on the North Yorkshire Moors, in *Prehistoric communities in northern England – essays in economic and social reconstruction* (ed G Barker), 87–104, Univ Sheffield

Stamp, L D, 1938 *The land of Britain, part 91: Cornwall*, London

Taylor, C C, 1975 *Fields in the English landscape*, London

Thomas, A C, 1958 *Gwithian: ten years' work, 1949–1958*, Camborne

——, 1969 Excavations at Crane Godrevy, Gwithian, 1969 interim report, *Cornish Archaeol*, **8**, 84–8

——, 1975 Excavation of a cist on Emblance Downs, St Breward, *Cornish Archaeol*, **14**, 82–4

——, 1985 *Exploration of a drowned landscape – archaeology and history of the Isles of Scilly*, London

Thomas, R, 1852 *Letters to the West Briton 1852* (abstracted by A Rowe, 1942; typescript in the Royal Cornwall Museum, formerly the Royal Institution of Cornwall, Truro)

Thorn, C, and Thorn, F (eds), 1979 *Domesday Book, 10, Cornwall*, from a draft translation by Oliver Padel, Chichester

Tregelles, G F, 1893–4 The stone circles of Cornwall, *Trans Penzance Nat Hist and Antiq Soc*, 1893–4, 147–70

——, 1906 The stone circles, in *Victoria County History: Cornwall*, **1**, 379–406

Trehair, J E R, 1978 A survey of cairns on Bodmin Moor, *Cornish Archaeol*, **17**, 3–24

Trudgian, P, 1977a Excavation of a cairn at Crowdy Marsh, Advent, near Camelford, *Cornish Archaeol*, **16**, 17–21

——, 1977b Mesolithic flint scatters around Crowdy Marsh, *Cornish Archaeol*, **16**, 21–4

Twidale, C R, 1962 'Lands' or relict strip fields in South Australia, *Agr Hist Rev*, **20**, 46–60

Wainwright, G J, 1960 Three microlithic industries from south-west England and their affinities, *Proc Prehist Soc*, **26**, 193–201

——, 1961 *The Mesolithic period in south and western Britain*, PhD thesis, Univ London

——, 1965 The excavation of a cairn at St Neot, Bodmin Moor, *Cornish Archaeol*, **4**, 4–9

Wainwright, G J, Fleming, A, and Smith, K, 1979 The Shaugh Moor project, first report, *Proc Prehist Soc*, **45**, 1–34

Wainwright, G J, and Smith, K, 1980 The Shaugh Moor project, second report – the enclosure, *Proc Prehist Soc*, **46**, 65–122

Walker, M C C, and Austin, D, 1985 Redhill Marsh, a site of possible Mesolithic activity on Bodmin Moor, Cornwall, *Cornish Archaeol*, **24**, 15–21

Weaver, M E, 1967 Notes on a farmhouse complex at Penrice, Kerslake Downs, *Cornish Archaeol*, **6**, 64–7

——, 1969 Current evidence for the distribution and possible origins of the round buttress chimney, *Cornish Archaeol*, **8**, 66–80

Whittington, G, 1973 Field systems of Scotland, in *Studies of field systems in the British Isles* (eds A R H Baker and R A Butlin), 530–79, Cambridge

Williams, G, 1984 A henge monument at Ffynnon Newydd, Nantgaredig, *Bull Board Celtic Stud*, **31**, 177–90

Wood, P D, 1963 Open field strips, Forrabury Common, near Boscastle, *Cornish Archaeol*, **2**, 29–33

Worgan, G B, 1811 *General view of the agriculture of the county of Cornwall*, London

Worth, R H, 1945 The Dartmoor hut circles, *Trans Devonshire Assoc*, **87**, 225–7

Worth, R N, 1890 On an ancient urn from the Cheesewring district, *Trans Plymouth Inst*, **10**, 244

Index

by Lesley Adkins and Roy Adkins

Major types of monument (such as cairns, fields, longhouses) and places have been indexed. Because of the difficulty of dating an indication of date has been given only in selected entries. **Bold** *type indicates the main entry.*

124